CHURCHILL A[

C000202258

THE GREAT

FIRST PUBLISHED IN ENGLAND BY HEADCORN INSTRUMENTATION LTD.,
HEADCORN , KENT, ENGLAND 2009

THE RIGHT OF CLIFFORD ALAIN STOSSEL TO BE IDENTIFIED
AS THE AUTHOR OF THIS WORK HAS BEEN ASSERTED BY HIM
IN ACCORDANCE WITH THE
COPYRIGHT, DESIGNS AND PATENTS ACT, 1988

ISBN   978-0-9563287-0-0

CHURCHILL AND DE GAULLE

ACKNOWLEDGEMENTS

Jasper Gerard wrote, in the Sunday Times of the 29th August, 2004, that the French had no right to celebrate the 60th anniversary of the Liberation of Paris because their contribution had been too puny. He went on to state that de Gaulle had spent the war holed up in Soho, like one of those iffy Iraqui gentlemen who sat out the Saddam years as a guest of Washington.

I knew that this was an outrageous calumny, for my mother had worked in de Gaulle's office in London during the early part of the war and my father, then a Frenchman, had reported for duty to de Gaulle and had been released, as a maitre pointeur (master aimer) to join the Middlesex Regiment of the Home Guard, serving with the anti-aircraft battery on Hampstead Heath, the highest point in London north of the river Thames.

Challenged, The Sunday Times did not retreat from Gerard's position. Don't get angry, get writing, was my determination and thus the genesis for this book.

I have been greatly helped in this task by the example and assistance of Dr. Adrian Greaves, founder and Chairman of the Anglo Zulu War Historical Society. In a long and happy friendship he has shown me methods of historical investigation which have been most useful and instructive and the example of his books, Rorke's Drift, Isandlwhana and other volumes has demonstrated for me what might be achieved.

The staff of the Imperial War Museum have provided special assistance, both for the exploration of associated texts in the Reading Room and for the provision of special illustrations from the picture library.

Above all, my special thanks are due to my wife Katie. We

worked quietly together, she on her volume Sister Janet, Nurse and Heroine of the Anglo Zulu war, while I toiled at the translation of many French texts and documents. Her kind patience and eagle eye in spotting useful books and journals among the antique fairs and second hand shops of Normandy have been of the greatest assistance, as has been her patient tolerance of the mountain of material scattered about in disorder when the writing has been much more imperative than tidiness.

Clifford Alain Stossel.

Headcorn , Kent and Gatteville Phare, Normandy. March 2009.

DE GAULLE AND CHURCHILL

THE GREATEST ALLIES

INTRODUCTION

Much has been written about the relationship between de Gaulle and Churchill. The impression is that the relationship was one of annoying hostility, and yet there is evidence that their regard and respect for each other transcends all the annoying details that forthright and brave men find blocking the path to their destinies.

The first clue came when I observed General de Gaulle returning to the airport after attending Churchill's funeral in 1965. As it happened I was going in the same direction out from London when his car drew alongside.

I had seen de Gaulle in London in 1943, addressing a great audience of the Free French at the Albert Hall. The man in the car alongside me had that terrible expression of wounded solitude which shows how the loss of a very great friend affects men who have faced the greatest trials in life.

Their close relationship began when, in the darkest days for France in 1940, Churchill passed close to de Gaulle as Churchill left a meeting with the French Prime Minister, Paul Reynaud. The eventual French separate armistice was becoming clear. De Gaulle was not party to the meeting, although he was Minister for War. Churchill said, as he passed de Gaulle 'L'homme du destin.' This was heard by Churchill's secretary, Colville, but apparently not by de Gaulle.

If, at that terrible moment for the Allies in 1940, Churchill recognised that de Gaulle was 'The man of destiny,' what did he mean and what did he expect? Churchill himself, recalled to lead Britain, always felt that he had a special destiny. He recognised a kindred spirit for the future of France. In that one moment and that simple phrase everything of their future relationship and regard was recognised. The path for them both and for their two countries would be most painful, but the outcome essential and certain. From this beginning de Gaulle had to resurrect the honour and the fighting spirit of France. When Churchill had asked General Weygand, the French commander, in French, "Where are your reserves?" and Weygand replied "There are none" the Allied defeat in France was certain and they both recognised it.

At that moment of defeat did either Churchill or de Gaulle have any idea how the combined cause of France and Britain could continue? When did this emerge and who were the driving forces behind setting up the Free French movement? Other governments of defeated countries of Europe had set up governments in exile in Britain and their forces continued the fight under British command.

This could not be the same for France, for France's legal government continued in being at Vichy, having gone first to Bordeaux. The real decision for France's government had been whether to continue the fight from an overseas territory, such as Algeria, or to seek an armistice and retain a centre of government in metropolitan France.

Any chance of continuing the struggle was lost by the dissentions in the French government. All the personal enmities and the pressures overwhelmed the central players. They fell back on the old hero of the First World War's great battle at Sedan. Only Marshal Petain could retain the authority of a central figure to settle on any arrangement with the German Army that would end the fighting. In the First World War France had lost 27 per cent of its young men in the age group 18 to 27. No country has lost more in a formal fight. The legacy of this is seen on memorials in every town and village of France. The horror of that time stood starkly in the path of the French government and overwhelmed all other thoughts; the fighting had to come to an end.

The last desperate effort of the French to continue resistance depended on the British sending further squadrons of fighters to France. Churchill had received Dowding's letter; the warning it contained was stark. Any further loss of fighter squadrons to France would make the defence of Britain impossible. It would lead to the 'final, inevitable and complete defeat' of Britain.

Churchill's refusal to send the further squadrons settled the cause of France. It was de Gaulle who sent the message to Churchill, commenting on the decision, and in English, 'You are right.' Such a message, in those simple terms, shows no hostility to the British decision. It set up the position for a future co-operation as allies. De Gaulle's message contrasted totally with the attitude of the rest of the French government. De Gaulle resigned as Minister for War and he became an independent voice for France. He left for Britain. He had no authority and no legal status to form any kind of government. He was court martialled by the Vichy government, sentenced to death and deprived of his nationality. All his goods were seized. There could be no lower base from which to start the Free French cause.

CHURCHILL AND DE GAULLE

THE GREATEST ALLIES

MILITARY MEN

Churchill and de Gaulle shared a military education, each at the premier military academy of their countries, Churchill at Sandhurst, de Gaulle at St. Cyr. Their family backgrounds were completely different, and there was a considerable age difference between them.

Winston Leonard Spencer-Churchill was born at Blenheim Palace on the 30th November 1874. The palace was the gift of a grateful nation to John Churchill, first Duke of Marlborough, in response to his great victory in the battle of Blenheim, on the 13th August, 1704. In combination with Eugene of Savoy they defeated a Franco-Bavarian army in the War of the Spanish Succession. It was the first major defeat that a French army had suffered in more than 50 years; their victory saved Vienna from conquest and forced Bavaria out of the war.

Churchill's father was Lord Randolph Churchill. He had been born in London in 1849, the second surviving son of the 7th Duke of Marlborough. In April 1874 he married Jennie Jerome, daughter of an American stockbroker, financier, and eventually proprietor of the New York Times. Lord Randolph had a distinguished political career, holding successively the posts of Secretary of State for India, Chancellor of the Exchequer and Leader of the House of Commons. He was firstly Member of Parliament for Woodstock and then for South Paddington, until his death in 1895.

Charles Andre Joseph Marie de Gaulle was born in the northern French city of Lille on the 22nd November, 1890. He was the second son of Henri de Gaulle, a teacher in a local Jesuit school. His father's lineage was from a minor aristocratic family, an ancestor having fought at the battle of Agincourt. De Gaulle's paternal grandmother had been a noted historian and novelist. De Gaulle's mother came from a family in the industrial city of Lille and it was her cousin Henri whom she married. Part of Charles' early education was at the school where his father was a member of the staff. In 1905 many Catholic schools were closed in a Government movement against religious expression and in favour of a secular state and Charles was forced to complete his education in Belgium.

Churchill's early years could not be considered happy. He doted on his parents, but they tended to be distant and pre-occupied. On those special and rare occasions when Winston gained his father's full attention he was in a world of delight. There was always some element of mischievousness in his nature. Many years later it showed itself when, during the Second World War, he observed his grandson, Winston Junior playing with a Hornby train set which had two locomotives. Winston Senior urged the young man to stage a crash between the two trains. The younger Winston did not oblige. It was a further sign of the grandfather's rebelliousness which had shown itself even at his preparatory school, where he had kicked the headmaster's straw hat to pieces.

From preparatory school Winston went on to Harrow, the major public school in North West London. The choice of Harrow, rather than his father's and the family's traditional educational establishment of Eton, resulted from Winston having had an attack of pneumonia, whereupon the heights of Harrow might provide better air than at the marshy area of Eton. He was not generally a good scholar and his Harrow entry examination paper in Latin was woeful, and, as for imparted information, totally blank. This was an exceptional example, however, for in many areas of scholarship he proved to be satisfactorily sound. Indeed, for learning one thousand two hundred lines of Macaulay's Lays of Ancient Rome, he was awarded a prize and thereafter his name in the school records was followed by the awarded letter 'p.'

Churchill's first military adventure was at Harrow School, where he joined the Rifle Corps. This provided a major enthusiasm for him and in a letter home after a Field Day at Aldershot he reports on the various types of weapons in use in considerable detail, and describes it all as 'great fun.' This enthusiasm led him to join the 'Army Class' in September, 1889. This class had been started to avoid boys of sixteen and seventeen leaving Harrow prematurely to undertake special private studies for the Army entry examinations. In November 1890 he took the Preliminary Examination for entry to Sandhurst and managed to pass just before Latin was changed from an optional to an obligatory part of the examination. He was one of twelve who passed out of twenty nine Harrovian candidates. To improve his French he stayed for Christmas 1891 with the parents of a Harrow French master, at Versailles. Just after Christmas, in the first days of 1892, Winston was invited to luncheon by some members of the French nobility.

Winston enjoyed fencing as a sport at school and became Harrow fencing champion in 1892. He was sure it would help him in the army. In the summer of 1892 Winston sat the second part of the Sandhurst entrance examination and failed. The only two subjects in which he gained over 50% of the marks were French and English Composition. He failed the examination again in 1893, but with much improved marks, Latin again being a severe failure. A further attempt in 1893 found him successful, but only just, thereby gaining a cavalry but not an infantry cadetship. Again, his Latin result was miserable.

De Gaulle studied extremely hard at the College Stanislas and thereby gained entry to the Military Academy of St. Cyr. He was typical of many of the young military aspirants: ardent, patriotic, and unsure of the political future of France but certain, after the defeat by the Prussians in 1870, that France would always need her military men. His exceptional height inspired his nicknames, 'two metre,' or 'asparagus.' At St. Cyr he became known for his fabulous memory and his rather austere attitude. His ambition for the military was demonstrated in an essay he wrote in 1905, in which he pictured himself as the Commander in Chief of the French Armies, avenging the defeat by the Prussians of 1870 and restoring Alsace and Lorraine to France. This was perfect prescience.

At St. Cyr his marks were very good, other than in English. He passed with such good marks that he had the choice of appointments, although he was only 119th in ranking in his year on entry, he passed out an excellent 13th. The most select choice would have been an appointment to the colonial army but he chose, instead, an appointment to the 33rd Infantry Regiment, based at Arras.

If Churchill was pleased to get into Sandhurst his pleasure was not shared by his father, who upbraided him severely for not gaining enough marks to get into the infantry, and for imposing the extra cost of a horse on his father, who was not financially very strong at that time. The time at Sandhurst went well, and had another student not had an advantage of 50 marks from previous military experience, Churchill would have won the Sword of Honour. In any case, he did gain a place in an infantry regiment.

Here the difference in their ages marks out separate paths for the careers of the two men. There was time for Churchill to go to India and then to Cuba, to the Sudan, and then to report on the Boer War in South Africa. There he was captured, escaped, and avoided the possibility of death on recapture for a bounty of £25. On return to England the entered politics. The fame of his capture and escape from the Boers made him a national hero and he was able to enter Parliament, hoping to emulate his father's example and reach high office.

During the First World War de Gaulle was wounded three times, captured five times, escaping and being recaptured on each occasion. He did his duty and was appropriately decorated for it. Churchill was appointed to be First Lord of the Admiralty. His skilful preparation of the fleet enabled it to win most encounters and to punish the offenders when the first battle had been lost. The loss of the Good Hope and the Monmouth at the Battle of Coronel was punished very severely by the battle cruisers Invincible and Inflexible at the Battle of the Falklands, with almost complete destruction of the German fleet.

The campaign in the Dardanelles was Churchill's undoing. Timidity in pushing the ships through when the hard part had been accomplished, and a lack of aggression in pushing forward to seize the commanding heights by the generals when the first landings were scarcely opposed, resulted in a bloody shambles, for which Churchill was blamed. He had to resign and went back to an infantry regiment on the Western Front, in France.

Both men married, Churchill to Miss Clementine Hozier, the daughter of Colonel Sir H.M. Hozier of the 3rd Dragoon Guards, on September 12th 1908. De Gaulle married Yvonne Vendroux at Calais, on the 6th April 1921. Both unions were blessed with several children.

The inter-war years found de Gaulle rising through the ranks of the army. He incurred severe displeasure by writing several books, 'Le Discord chez l'Ennemi', 'Le Fil de l'Epee' and 'L'Armee et son Metier.' They were published outside the military establishment and his senior mentor, Marshal Petain, disowned him. One of his major propositions was for armoured units which were fully mobile, with tanks as their main offensive arm. How strange a coincidence that Churchill had been virtually the inventor of the tank in the First World War. No one took de Gaulle's idea seriously in France, nor did the British take Liddell-Hart seriously when he proposed the same idea. General Guderian did, in Germany, and the result was Blitzkrieg.

Churchill held high office in the Liberal Government in the early years after the First World War, but was then out of office. He turned to writing, from economic necessity, writing an extensive history of his ancestor, the Duke of Marlborough, and other volumes. In the 1930's he was a private member of Parliament, 'but of some prominence.' When the rise of Hitler awakened him to the new danger in Europe he warned of the disaster to come, but none would listen. So when the disaster did come he was ready for new duties in high office, and when the defeat of Dunkirk cause the unseating of Neville Chamberlain Churchill was ready to take the Prime Ministerial position. He was not daunted by the task and he felt as though this was his destiny.

De Gaulle spent the first years after the First World War with the French military mission to Poland, being involved in regaining the eastern territories from the Russians, and being awarded the appropriate Polish decorations. Later, at the outbreak of the Second World War, he became involved in the development of mobile armoured warfare using tanks, and ended up leading an armoured division, but appointed so late that there were only six weeks' training available before the German onrush into France nullified his best efforts with his embryo unit.

The stage was set of the first meeting of these two men. The meetings and the consequences are the body of this story.

5

THE ROAD TO WAR

At the end of the First World War the peace treaty signed by the Allies and Germany at Versailles forced Germany to pay for the cost of the war and placed great restrictions on the ability of German industry to recover and take part in international trade. France had lost 27% of its men between the ages of 18 and 28 – the largest loss of any large nation in any major conflict.

The burden inflicted on Germany brought severe unemployment and, in 1923, hyper-inflation. The Deutschmark was restored by the German Minister of Finance Schacht as the Rentenmark, tying the currency to land, until the financial situation stabilised, but savings in banks were lost. The destruction of the savings of the middle classes undid the cohesion of German society. The depression following the Wall Street crash of 1929 brought further havoc to the life of the German people, as in most other countries.

The despair this brought about left a void of hopelessness in the life of Germany. As Churchill put it 'Into the life of the German people-after a pause-strode a maniac of ferocious genius-Adolf Hitler.' The German people were put back to work and were organised. The German army was rebuilt, to a level in breach of the conditions of the treaty of Versailles. When the German army entered and re-occupied the Rhineland in 1935 there was no active opposition from France and Britain. The annexation of Austria in 1938 was achieved by a form of democratic vote. Britain and France regarded it as only the natural union of German speaking peoples.

There was no stomach for military preparedness amongst the allies who had won the First World War. Appeasement was the road to peace in Europe and it was only when Hitler demanded the Sudetenland from Czechoslovakia in 1938 that the warning bells really sounded. Already it was too late and Czechoslovakia was dismembered in return for a piece of paper promising 'Peace in our time.' The penalty which would be paid for this supine attitude would be immense. Of the tanks which took part in the

Blitzkrieg of 1940 one third were Czechoslovakian in origin and they were the main quantity of high quality battle tanks which were used by the Germans.

French defences against any future attack by Germany had been based on the principle of very strong fortresses along the border-the Maginot line, named after the French Minister of Defence. These would keep the garrisons safe and prevent any huge losses of men. It was understood that between these fortresses the ground would have to be held by the infantry supported by artillery and they would be protected by the covering fire from the fortresses. There seemed no need for such expensive fortifications along the friendly Belgian border. Indeed, the Belgians had some fortresses of their own.

The wooded country of the Ardennes on the Franco-Belgian border was known to be impenetrable by any large military force and, in any case, it was guarded by strong artillery formations. There were also large mobile reserves to bring into play to support these areas. France had the largest army in Europe.

The French army was commanded by generals who had been victorious in the First World War, but there were some changes. In 1935 General Weygand retired as Commander in Chief, at the appropriate age. He was a man of considerable academic strength and was elected a member of the highest French cultural elite, the French Academy. He wrote well and his book on triumphal arches, culminating with the story of the Arc de Triomphe, is a treatise of classical virtue.

After German seizure of the Sudetenland France and Britain started to understand the dangers and began to re-arm. It was clear that Poland was under severe threat, and France and Britain gave solemn guarantees to Poland about the security of her borders. When Germany invaded Poland on the 1st September 1939 Britain and France demanded immediate German withdrawal, but Hitler ignored these demands and so, at 11.00a.m. London time on the 3rd September, Britain and also France declared war on Germany.

On that day, the 3rd September 1939, Churchill was brought into the war cabinet as First Lord of the Admiralty. He had been forced to resign from the same post in 1915, after the failed assault on the Turkish Dardanelles, with its severe Allied losses. He was known for his strong warnings about Hitler's rise to power and his return to some major government post was expected. The signal sent to the Navy that evening was simple and certain- 'Winston is back.'

At the start of the Second World War de Gaulle was a colonel in command of a tank regiment. He had written a treatise about mobile tank warfare, but he had stepped outside normal protocol by publishing it outside the army, and had made enemies of those who could prefer him for promotion – in particular Marshal Petain.

COLLAPSE IN THE WEST

De Gaulle entered the French government on the night of the 5th to the 6th June 1940 as Under Secretary of State for National Defence, in the government of Prime Minister Paul Reynaud. De Gaulle was given the news in the morning by General Delestraint, Inspector of Tanks, who had heard it on the radio. Several minutes later de Gaulle received a telegram confirming the news, which was a complete surprise to him. He had to take hurried leave of his division and set off at once for Paris. He arrived at the Rue Saint-Dominique and saw the Prime Minister Paul Reynaud, officially President of the Council, who was, as expected, assured, forceful, ready to listen, and quick in decision making.

He explained why, several days earlier, he had started preparing a cabinet to work under the leadership of Marshal Petain. The purpose was to prepare for the signing of an armistice. Paul Reynaud explained that it was better to have Marshal Petain inside the cabinet than outside it.

De Gaulle told him that with events changing so quickly there was a danger that an air of defeatism was overtaking them. There was certainly an imbalance between the Allied and the German forces. The preponderance of armour in the German vanguard, with its firepower and mobility, was an irresistible advantage. Short of a miracle there was little chance of defeating the Germans in metropolitan France, even if, with a change of command, some major stroke of surprise could overturn events. Reynaud explained the air of resignation which was overtaking the government. Those who, with Marshal Petain, wanted an armistice were likely to get their way. Meanwhile, if the war in 1940 were lost, there would later be another. Delaying stopping the fighting in Europe for as long as possible was essential to allow time to prepare to continue the struggle from the empire, by evacuating troops and the Government.

To do this would require a strong political will and it would need the setting up of the means to continue the struggle from North Africa. Commanders would have to be chosen and they also would have to combine well with the English and arrange for a combination of ideas. De Gaulle intended to set up this arrangement immediately.

Reynaud agreed, and asked de Gaulle to go to London as soon as possible to explore these possibilities with the British. De Gaulle went to London on the 26th and again on the 31st May. He warned the British Government that the question of an armistice was not now totally out of the question. He tried to convince the British that there were still forces at work that would not agree to any armistice and there were preparations being made to continue the struggle from the French empire, based in North Africa. Reynaud had told de Gaulle to explain that there were divisions in the French cabinet, but that de Gaulle's duties as the messenger were to be taken as a sign of Reynaud's determination to continue the struggle.

De Gaulle's other purpose in going to London was to ensure that there would be no withdrawal of British air support in France. In particular the French government wanted more support from fighter aircraft. Churchill could not agree to any more fighters being sent because he had received information from the chief of Fighter Command, Air Chief Marshall Dowding, in the form of the stern and definite warning that if any more were sent to France Fighter Command would not be able to defend Great Britain. The message was put in clear terms: any further depletion would lead to the complete and final defeat of Great Britain. So Churchill had no choice but to refuse to send further fighters. In any case, the request for fighters was a strategic mistake, because the German armoured thrusts had been supported by dive bombers. The Allied fighters were supposed to prevent these dive bombing raids. The essential point had been missed. Such Allied dive bombing raids as did take place were often severely delayed due to poor communications. By the time they took place the Germans had brought up batteries of anti-aircraft guns and the Allied dive bombers suffered 75% losses in many of their attacks. The opportunity to defend against German assaults across the rivers at their most vulnerable time had been irretrievably lost. If the concentration had been on these in the earliest stages, to destroy the German bridgeheads, the outcome could have been different.

De Gaulle expressed to the British the hope that some of the units which had been retrieved from Dunkirk could be quickly reassembled, re-armed, and returned to southern France to continue the struggle. This was a vain hope, for all their equipment had been lost at Dunkirk, and there were no further supplies.

While negotiations were going on concerning the provision of further re-enforcements from Britain to France, de Gaulle returned to France and on the 8th June met General Weygand, who had been restored as Commander in Chief. He found Weygand calm and fully in control of himself, but after a short conversation it was clear that Weygand was resigned to defeat and had decided to seek an armistice.

Weygand told de Gaulle that he had not been mistaken in judging that the Germans would attack along the Somme on the 6th June. The attack was under way and they had crossed the river and there was now no means of stopping them. De Gaulle asked what the next stage of the battle would be. Weygand replied that they would then cross the Seine and the Marne – nothing could stop them. De Gaulle pressed on with his questioning. What would then follow? The reply – "After? But it is finished." De Gaulle pressed on with the questioning. How would it be finished? What about the world, and the Empire? Weygand replied with a shout of desperation. "The Empire – it is in its infancy. When we are beaten here England will not last eight days before suing for peace with the Reich!" Weygand then expressed the hope that the Germans would leave him enough forces to maintain order.

Further discussion with him was in vain. De Gaulle told Weygand that his view was not that of the government. He should not abandon the struggle, even if the outcome was likely to be decidedly unhappy. Weygand made no more attempts to convince de Gaulle, who left.

Before returning to Paris de Gaulle had discussions with other members of the high command. There was a general view that there was no longer any hope, or any reason to continue the struggle. All believed that the battle for France was lost. If there were to be any hope of restoring spirits to continue the battle the

Government would have to act at once. Returning to Paul Reynaud he told of General Weygand's acceptance of defeat. Reynaud saw no possibility of restoring the situation. De Gaulle raised the question of a change of the Commander in Chief. The proposed candidate was General Huntziger, then commander of the 4th Army Group. He might be able to construct a plan for making the struggle a world wide one. Reynaud agreed to explore the plan, but he himself was not prepared to do this.

De Gaulle then wanted to explore the possibility of removing as much of the mechanism of government, and as many of the armed forces as possible, to North Africa to continue the struggle. The heads of the army, navy and air force were already making plans to take their commands to North Africa. Two groups of reservists, in the west and in the Midi region of France, could be moved, making a total of 500,000 men who were trained to a good standard. Of the troops in the north of France, large groups, including some armoured units, could be embarked and added to the force which could be evacuated. The remainder of the bomber squadrons, fighter squadrons, and the air base personnel could be evacuated. The whole fleet could also escape. The merchant ships to take the troops amounted to 500,000 tons of shipping and the fleet to do this could assemble in England.

Early on the 9th June de Gaulle flew to London, with high-ranking cabinet civil servants. It was a Sunday. De Gaulle found that in London there was an air of calm, almost of indifference. The parks and streets were full of people going about their peaceful pleasures. There were long queues outside the cinemas and the streets were full of traffic. The numbers of people gathered at the clubs and hotels gave no indication that this was a country at war. The newspapers were full of trivial stories and, as in Paris, were full of false optimism. There was no sign of the approaching danger and the population showed no sign of realising the very serious state of events in France. You could see that as far as the English were concerned, the Channel was still wide.

De Gaulle was received by Churchill at Downing Street. It was the first time they had been in contact. The first impression was that Great Britain, for her part in the struggle, would never give in.

Churchill appeared most direct and most impressive. The certainty of his judgement, his cultural excellence, his enormous grasp of such a wide variety of subjects, whether of countries or of men and above all his passion for all aspects of the war, were all focussed on the war effort. Above all, by his character, he was prepared to be active, take risks, lead the cause, with eagerness and without reserve. In brief de Gaulle summed him up as the leader firmly in place and in full command. Those were his first impressions. Suddenly, for the first time, he met someone who had the same passion to see the cause through to victory, whatever the setbacks, whatever the difficulties, whatever the cost.

De Gaulle found that his first impression was confirmed. Churchill's eloquence was a unique and impressive talent which found its expression at the microphone, the lectern, the cabinet table, or behind his desk. His ability to be original, poetic, emotional, gave him an unequalled ability to rise to the heights of dramatic emphasis about the state of the world. Proved right in his political judgement, he could play the angelic or the diabolical role in explaining England's position in dealing with the hopes of foreigners. He was not without humour, which he expressed with extravagant gestures, and in a manner, which he used with such effect that it was difficult to know exactly where his thoughts would turn next.

Their characters were different, as would be expected, coming from such different backgrounds. The straightjacket of a military upbringing for de Gaulle contrasted completely with Churchill's flamboyant and expressive parliamentary style. Churchill did not seem to show to de Gaulle sufficient care for the state of France's wounds. This was upsetting to de Gaulle, but it did not alter de Gaulle's opinion, that Winston Churchill, shorn of the drama, was the great leader in a great enterprise and a man of truly historic proportions.

With this judgement, that here was the overall leader, de Gaulle exposed to the British Prime Minister that it was the wish of the French premier to continue the struggle, even if it had to be from the Empire. Churchill was pleased with this attitude, but would this course be put into effect? He let de Gaulle know that he was not entirely convinced. He certainly did not think that there was a possibility of re-establishing military control in metropolitan France and he absolutely refused to send any more air force squadrons.

Since the re-embarkation of the British army at Dunkirk the Royal Air Force had only intermittently been engaged in the battle. The struggle to defend the army on the beaches was over. Besides, apart from a small group of fighters that were still in the battle alongside the French air force, the Royal Air Force squadrons, with their bases in Great Britain, were unable to help in a battle where the front had rolled far to the south and beyond the range of aircraft operating from British bases. De Gaulle pressed Churchill to send some of these squadrons to bases south of the river Loire, so that at least a part of the air force's co-operation could be effective. Churchill's reply to this suggestion was firmly negative. He would send a Canadian division, which had just arrived, to join the 51st Highland division, which was still fighting in Normandy. He would also re-enforce some of the mechanised units that were still fighting alongside the French but he was in no position to give any definite information about when the units of the British Expeditionary Force, which had been recovered from Belgium but without their arms, might again be ready to be put back into the battle.

So it was that the strategic alliance between London and Paris was virtually broken: no integrated co-operation was possible. The defeat in France meant that all available reserves had to be retained for the defence of Great Britain. The German plan to divide Britain and France had been successful. The plan, which had been devised by von Schlieffen in the 1914-18 war had, even after his death, finally come to fruition. Such an attitude would have a most serious effect on the French tendency to defeatism.

On this visit de Gaulle also met with Anthony Eden and General Alexander, and other British war leaders, and with French officials. It became clear that if, in London, there was an air of calm, totally opposite to the anxiety and panic which was setting the scene in French government circles, there would be no chance of raising French spirits. In the evening de Gaulle returned to Paris, where a bombardment was already taking place.

During the night of the 9th/10th June de Gaulle was called to Reynaud's residence. There was grave news. The Germans had reached the Seine near Paris. At any moment a decisive German armoured attack was expected in the Champagne region and Paris was threatened from the West, North and the East. The French Foreign Minister was expecting to receive, at any moment, a declaration of war by the Italian government.

De Gaulle suggested immediately that the government should move to North Africa. Algeria was legally a part of Metropolitan France. During that night, spent mostly at the Prime Minister's residence, de Gaulle became convinced that there was no other action which could be taken. Events were moving too fast for any half-way house measures to be adopted. Everything else was taking on an air of unreality. One recalled the precedents of the 1914-18 war. It was no use thinking that there was still a defendable front line, or an effective command structure, or a people ready to make the necessary sacrifices. To believe so would be just dreams and memories. What had happened was that the nation had been beaten and dumbfounded, behind an army that was without hope, and where the government machine which might have turned things around was in irremediable confusion.

De Gaulle did the rounds of all the political departments. They seemed to have an air of calm and dignity, but it was clear that behind this facade there was no activity. In the midst of the hurricane of events there were fatuous public statements and all the characters were acting as dumb figureheads. There was no policy, other than capitulation. Events had overwhelmed them and De Gaulle saw that only major changes could save the situation and that these were not going to happen. The defensive line would have to move from the Marne to the Mediterranean.

The 10th of June was a day of agony. The government was preparing to leave Paris in the evening because the collapse of the front was accelerating: Italy had declared war. Above all, the collapse had destroyed their hopes, but at the highest levels of the State the tragedy which was being played out was like a dream. At times it seemed like a terrible joke that the collapse of France was rolling from the heights of history into the depths of the abyss of hopelessness.

In the morning the Italian ambassador came on a strange visit. He saw Mr. Baudouin, a high civil servant, who reported a message from the ambassador. 'You will see that the declaration of war has finally clarified the relations between our two countries. It has created a situation which, at the final count, will come out as a great good.........'

De Gaulle then went in to see the Prime Minister, where the American ambassador was already present. Had he brought some encouraging messages from the United States? No! There was no note of encouragement or support from President Roosevelt. He was there to take his leave. He would no longer represent the United States as ambassador: the presence of Mr. Biddle, Charge d'Affaires to the refugee governments, gave the impression that the United States was giving up on France.

Paul Reynaud, in his duty as Prime Minister, was preparing hastily a statement to be broadcast that day, after consultation with de Gaulle. General Weygand arrived. The Prime Minister seemed surprised but General Weygand said that he had been called. "Not by me, not by me!" exclaimed the Prime Minister. "Then I must have misheard" replied General Weygand. "But it is a useful error, for I have an important declaration to make. It is clear that without delay we must ask for an armistice." He put a paper with this statement upon it into the hands of the Prime Minister.

The Prime Minister quickly arranged to discuss the statement by the Commander in Chief. It was clear that the battle in metropolitan France had been lost and capitulation was essential. De Gaulle intervened, pointing out that there were other views. Weygand asked if he had an alternative proposition. De Gaulle replied that the government had no propositions to make but had orders to give: he was awaiting those orders. It was with a heavy heart that the Prime Minister sent the Commander in Chief away.

The last hours of the government in Paris were filled with the arrangements for departure. Many preparations had already been made, but much was still left to last minute improvisation. The imminent arrival of the Germans at the walls of Paris presented some cruel problems. De Gaulle had expected, on taking up his government appointment, that Paris would be defended and he demanded to know what were the details of the plans for the defence of Paris. Soon it was clear that Paris would not be defended: it would be surrendered without a fight, as an 'open city.' Even so there was a mass of material to be evacuated, and also a crowd of government officials. The rest of the day was spent in frantic efforts to sort out the mess and answer the deluge of desperate telephone calls.

Towards midnight de Gaulle and the Prime Minister left Paris in the same car. The journey was slow, over crowded roads, and dawn found them at Orleans. On entering the prefecture contact was made with the army headquarters, which had moved to Briare. Shortly after their arrival General Weygand telephoned, to speak to the Prime Minister. The Prime Minister took the telephone and was surprised to learn that Mr. Churchill would arrive in the afternoon. General Weygand insisted that Mr. Churchill would have to be told about the true situation at the battle front. Why was it that the General Weygand was concerning himself about the movements of the British Prime Minister? Was Weygand abandoning his military duties to become embroiled in politics? Was he hinting that he did not expect the government to remain long in office? Reynaud saw the problem and realised that Weygand would have to be replaced by Huntziger. This task Reynaud left to de Gaulle and Reynaud prepared to receive Churchill for a meeting at Briare.

De Gaulle found General Huntziger at his headquarters at Arcis sur Aube, where he was in command of the Army of the Centre. At that very moment the Army of the Centre was being broken through in the Champagne region by the armoured corps commanded by German General Guderian. Despite this de Gaulle was impressed by the calm control of Huntziger, who told him about the poor military situation. De Gaulle spoke of the Government's assessment that the battle for France was lost, but that the Government wanted to evacuate to Africa to continue the war. This would need a total change in strategy and organisation and above all it would need a different Commander in Chief.

Would Huntziger be ready to take the post? Huntziger agreed immediately; De Gaulle told him that he would soon receive the orders.

De Gaulle returned to Briare by way of Romilly and Sens, making contact with many of the commanders on this journey. Everywhere there were signs of disorder and panic and on all sides the troops were moving southwards among the columns of refugees. He was delayed in getting back to Briare because the road was blocked at Mery, where a strange fog, as if it were a gas cloud, added to the anxiety of the fleeing columns, making them behave like a flock of sheep.

Back at Briare de Gaulle gave Huntziger's reply to Reynaud, but de Gaulle could see that the prospect of replacing Weygand by Huntziger was no longer a viable choice, and that Reynaud wanted to follow the advice of a Commander in Chief who wanted to sue for peace. He found Marshal Petain, whom he had not seen since 1938, at the headquarters. Petain discounted de Gaulle's promotion to the rank of general and refused to congratulate him. What good would such a promotion do in time of defeat? De Gaulle reminded Petain that his own promotion had come about at the time of the reverses of 1914: only a few days later there had come the victory of the battle of the Marne. Petain dismissed this, and on reflexion de Gaulle considered him right to do so. The arrival of the British Prime Minister prevented any further discussion.

In the course of this meeting there came into the open the ideas and the passions which would dominate this next phase of the war. The solidarity of purpose between England and France, the strength of the French army, the authority of the Government, the loyalty of the high command, would now be tested. Each person present would play their part, singly or in unison, and would act eventually for their own cause.

General Weygand wanted to see the speediest end to the battle and the war. He was supported in this view by Generals Georges and Besson, Army Group Commanders in the north of France, who had explained that the military situation was without hope. The Commander in Chief, who had also been in post from 1930 to 1935, demonstrated the reasons for the defeat of the armies under his orders, but without admitting responsibility. His view was that the struggle had to be ended before there was a sudden military collapse, which would lead to anarchy and revolution.

Marshal Petain intervened to support this pessimistic outlook. Mr. Churchill, to lighten the atmosphere, reminded the company "Marshal, do you not remember the battle for Amiens, in March 1918, when all was going so badly? I came then to your headquarters, where you showed me your plan. A few days later the front was re-established."

Then the Marshal replied, heavily: "Yes, the front was re-established. You, the English, were in your trenches but I, I had sent 40 divisions to get you out of the mess. Today it is we who are in pieces. Where are your 40 divisions?" The French Prime Minister repeated that France would not withdraw from the struggle, but needed the British to send most of her air force, so that Petain and Weygand would see that it would be possible to rally their forces. Mr. Churchill was unmoved. He hoped that France would not come to see and take satisfaction in a Great Britain having to stand alone in her island. Having heard these discussions de Gaulle concluded that the only possible further action was for France to regroup overseas.

After three hours of discussions, which came to nothing, they sat down to dinner around the same table. De Gaulle sat next to Churchill. Their conversation strengthened his confidence in Churchill's willpower. He alone, without doubt, shared with de Gaulle an unbreakable resolve. What good fortune placed them together at that time is unknown, but in de Gaulle's assessment lay the start of an alliance that was to keep alive the Allied cause. Admiral Darlan, head of the French navy, who had not been at the conference, appeared after the meal, pushing in front of him General Vuillemin, the Chief of the Air Staff; he went up to Mr. Reynaud. The purpose of this interruption gave serious food for thought. A combined air and naval operation had been prepared to bombard Genoa and it was to take place that night. Darlan wanted the operation cancelled, because General Vuillemin's air force would not be able to defend the petrol depot at Berre if the Italians counter attacked. Darlan wanted the support of the government. 'What do you think?' Reynaud asked de Gaulle. "From this point on" de Gaulle replied, "the operation should continue. You must carry on with the attack."

Darlan left, but the counter order was given. In the end, Genoa was bombarded, but by a weak naval force and then only three days later. This showed de Gaulle that from this point on Admiral Darlan was not whole heartedly in the struggle.

On the 12th June de Gaulle was working at the Chateau de Beauvais, with General Colson, in charge of transport, on the plan arranging transport to North Africa. De Gaulle hoped that the events which he had seen did not mean that the spirit of despair had gained too much ground and he hoped that the government would still retain overall control.

After making these preparations de Gaulle returned to Chissay to see Mr. Reynaud, who was late. Reynaud had left a meeting of the cabinet and arrived at about 11 o'clock in the evening, accompanied by Baudouin. During dinner de Gaulle sat near the table. He raised the question of North Africa as a future base for the government, but they would not consider it. The only thing they would consider was where the next immediate move of the government should be. The Germans had already crossed the Seine and would soon be at the Loire. There were two possibilities: Bordeaux or Quimper? It was clear that everyone at the dinner was too tired to see the problem of the choice of the next site of government clearly, so no decision was taken and the discussion was put off until the morning.

De Gaulle favoured Quimper; he had no illusions about there being any possibility of holding a last redoubt in Brittany. The choice of Quimper would keep the government close enough to the coast to escape abroad by sea. If the Germans occupied the Brittany peninsular they would not leave any unoccupied 'free' area, because they would be preparing to attack England, but once aboard ship the French government would have a choice of destination - North Africa or some other overseas territory - reached either directly or after stopping for a while in England. At least the choice of Quimper would have the advantage of a quick decision. On entering government de Gaulle had been told by

Reynaud about the possibility of creating a 'Breton redoubt.' This idea had encouraged de Gaulle that there was a core of resolution to fight on, but all these ideas were oppose by Petain, Weygand and Baudouin, who were pushing hard for capitulation.

Early on the 13th June de Gaulle returned to Chissay. After lengthy debate Reynaud decided to move the government to Bordeaux, saying that this was on the advice of his ministers. De Gaulle was not allowed to issue the orders to prepare for transfer of the government to North Africa. It came as a great shock to realise that Reynaud had become swallowed up in the general gloom of universal despair, for in the Government, all hope had gone.

Despite this, Reynaud sent Weygand, at mid-day on the 13th June, an order to resist as long as possible in the Central Massif and in Brittany. He assured Weygand that in any case the struggle would continue from the Empire and across the freedom of the seas. This letter was full of good intentions, but it was not couched in really decisive terms. The lack of will showed itself in that the letter, although signed, was not sent until the next day. With events moving so swiftly the delay was fatal.

On the morning of the 13th June French political leaders went to see Reynaud. Mr. Jeanneney, President of the Senate, was resolute amongst the confusion. He quoted the example of Clemenceau, with whom he had served from 1914 to 1918. They were opposed to capitulation and were in favour of taking the government to Algiers. De Gaulle understood from the meeting that whatever the arguments, Paul Reynaud was still in charge of decisions. On the afternoon of the 13th De Gaulle went to Beauvais, where he was telephoned and told that a meeting would take place later that day with Churchill, who would arrive with several of his ministers. He was warned that he should hurry to the meeting, for Baudouin was in control and this was not good news.

De Gaulle went to Tours. He had severe misgivings as Reynaud had not been in touch to discuss matters. When he arrived at the headquarters at Tours he found the corridors and courtyards full of members of parliament, officials and journalists. It was a tumult for a tragedy! The conference with Churchill had been adjourned and the British ministers had been in discussion in the garden.

At that moment Churchill and his ministers were about to return to the meeting. De Gaulle was told that the British ministers, after their discussions in the garden, would give their reply to a question which had been put to them by the French. Despite the agreement of the 28th of March 1940, which prevented either side making a separate peace with Germany, would the British now agree that in France's desperate condition she could seek a separate armistice?

Mr. Churchill sat down. Lord Halifax, the foreign secretary, Lord Beaverbrook, Sir Alexander Cadogan and General Spears, who was Churchill's special envoy to France, took their places. There was a moment of complete silence and then Churchill started to speak in French. In a measured and sad tone, inclining his head and with a cigar in his mouth, he started to express his sympathy and that of his Government, and that of his people, with the people of France.

"We can see," he said "how France is placed. We can see that you feel crushed. Our friendship for you is undimmed. In any case, be certain that England will not withdraw from the struggle. We will fight on 'till the end, no matter how, no matter where, even if you leave us to the task alone."

There was for discussion the possibility of an armistice between France and Germany, where de Gaulle thought England would bind France to the agreement not to separate, Churchill explained that his view was to the contrary; he understood France's plight. Suddenly, passing to the subject of the French fleet, he became focussed and forceful. Irrespective of the agreement of the 28th March he could not allow the French fleet to fall into the hands of the Germans. That was the final word of this frightful conference.

Churchill left the room, but outside he insisted that, if France did withdraw from the struggle, that the 400 German pilots who were prisoners in France must be sent to England. They could not be allowed to be released to fight again. He was given that assurance, but this was false. Eventually the German pilots were released by the Vichy Government to the Germans.

Led by Mr. Reynaud, the British went into the next room, where they found the President of the French assembly and several ministers. There, the tone was very different and the French spoke only of continuing the war. De Gaulle went up to Reynaud and asked, excitedly "Is it possible that you are considering that France should seek an armistice?" "Certainly not!" Reynaud replied. "But I must press the English to obtain a better agreement." De Gaulle could not understand the purpose of this. Leaving Reynaud, in the middle of a hubbub in the courtyard of the prefecture, de Gaulle returned to Beauvais. Reynaud then telegraphed President Roosevelt, asking him to intervene and stating that without his help at that time, France was lost.

In the evening Mr. Reynaud spoke on the radio. "It will take a miracle to save France. I believe in miracles." De Gaulle was certain that whatever might be said, France was heading for an armistice. In that case, his position in the cabinet would become impossible. He was about to write his letter of resignation, when, in the middle of the night, Georges Mandel demanded to see him.

As Minister of the Interior Mandel spoke in a serious and measured tone. He was certain that the honour of France could only be safeguarded by continuing the war. Because of this he wanted de Gaulle to remain in the government. "Who knows?" he said "if in the end the Government will not be set up in Algiers." He told de Gaulle that after the English had left, the council of ministers had considered the latest situation. At that moment the advanced German formations were entering Paris. "Are we not at the start of a world war? You have the absolute duty to stay in your position, General! You have the advantage, of all of us, of remaining resolute. Do not think that what must be done for France is possible if you will not do it." This argument convinced de Gaulle to delay his resignation.

The 14th of June dawned. De Gaulle was surprised to find himself still in the Government! He left his host, the Provost of Launay. The Provost would not be leaving his home and surroundings but would await the arrival of the invader. After a difficult and sad journey, along roads crowded with refugees, de Gaulle reached Bordeaux. At the headquarters the deputy mayor told him of the discouraging news he was taking to the Prime Minister. De Gaulle saw Reynaud and told him "For the last three days I have seen the speed with which we have rushed towards capitulation. I have given you my modest opinion, and it is to continue the war. I will refuse to submit to an armistice. If you stay here you will be crushed by the defeat. You must go to Algiers at once! You must decide, yes or no, now!"

"Yes," replied Mr. Reynaud.

"In that case," de Gaulle told him "I must go at once to London to arrange a meeting with the English about our transport. I will go tomorrow. Where will you be?" "In Algiers," he replied.

It was agreed de Gaulle would leave during the night and go to Brittany to see about embarkation. He was asked by Reynaud to arrange a meeting for him the next morning with Admiral Darlan, because he wanted to speak to the admiral about the fleet. The admiral was en route to La Gueritoulde, but that evening de Gaulle got through to him. He put the request for the meeting, but a sour reply was the only response that he got. "Me! Go to Bordeaux tomorrow. I do not know what good I can do, meeting the Prime Minister. I have my command to care for and I have no time to waste."

The tone taken by Darlan showed a depressing attitude. Several minutes later de Gaulle had a brief conversation with Jean Ybarnegaray, the Minister of State, who had been in favour of continuing the struggle overseas. He came to see de Gaulle at the Hotel Splendide, where he was having a hurried meal in the company of Geoffrey de Courcel. "For me," he said "'nothing counts but to obey my old chiefs, Petain and Weygand!'" "Perhaps, one day," de Gaulle told him "you will see that duty to the state outweighs such sentiments." To Marshal Petain, who was dining in the same room, de Gaulle went and made a silent salute. They shook hands without a word. They never met again, never!

Where was this road to disaster leading? All his life Marshal Petain had strained for dignity. Too proud for intrigue, too good to be mediocre, too ambitious to be an opportunist, he nursed a lonely passion to lead. This came from a true bravery, unwavering under the doubting of others. And here, in the winter of his life, events had offered him a proud duty, for which he was ready. Power without limit! Only on one condition could he accept this – if it added to his glory. De Gaulle's assessment of Petain was severe condemnation.

In all respects the Marshal was for the party of defeat. This old soldier, who had seen the events of 1870, when Paris was occupied by the Germans in the Franco-Prussian war, was not able to consider that this was a new Franco-German war. Having lost the first, France had won the second, 1914-18, without doubt with the help of Allies, but with them playing a secondary role. France was now losing the third. Tough, but that is life. After Sedan and the fall of Paris, there was nothing left but the end. All government would cease. That was the judgement of the Marshal. There was no consideration of a world war, the possibilities of using the overseas territories, the idealogical consequences of Hitler's victory. None of these matters impressed the Marshal. The defeat of France was all.

De Gaulle was convinced that at another time the Marshal might not have been so defeatist. He had set out on the road to war and had been defeated. If victory had still been possible France could have played her part. But alas! Overtaken by age he had lost the will to fight. A gentle lassitude had come with age: the senility of Petain was linked to the collapse of France. De Gaulle had these thoughts while he travelled through the night to Brittany. At the same time, he strengthened his resolve to continue the war, wherever such a decision would take him.

Arriving at Rennes on the morning of the 15th June he met with General Rene Altmayer, who commanded troops to the east of the Mayenne and General Guitry, military commander of the region and Prefect of the l'Ille-et-Vilaine Department. They were determined to do their best to defend the region. Then de Gaulle went on to Brest, where more British convoys were ready to re-embark troops. In the afternoon he boarded the French destroyer *Milan*, which was to take him to Plymouth. Also on board was a delegation of chemists led by General Lemoine and Mr. Dautry, Minister of Armaments, taking to safety in England the secrets of France's heavy water programme.

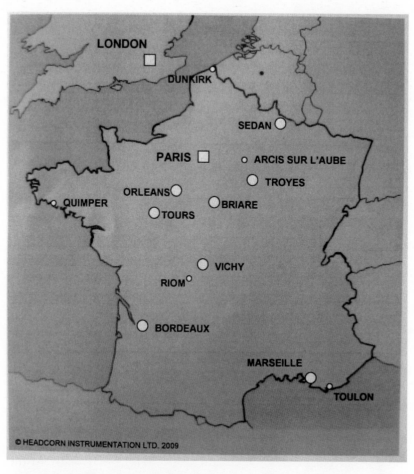

MAP OF FRANCE SHOWING PLACES OF PRINCIPLE IMPORTANCE AT THE TIME OF GERMAN INVASION OF FRANCE STARTING ON MAY 10TH 1940

As they left Brest the battleship Richelieu saluted de Gaulle as it left for Dakar. From Plymouth he went to London, arriving at dawn on the 16th June. In the early morning, in the Hyde Park Hotel, he was visited by Mr. Corbin, the ambassador, and Mr. Monnet, the French economist who had just returned from Washington. He was told of various meetings that had been arranged for that day, and transport arrangements. He was also told that there would be a meeting later in the day, at Concarneau, where Mr. Reynaud would ask Churchill for permission for France to make a separate armistice. They then turned to another subject.

The Government in Bordeaux had already sent a telegram to Churchill recalling the meeting of the 13th June and definitely asking for permission to abandon the agreement not to make a separate peace, signed on the 28th March. They did not yet know what reply would be received from the British, but they thought that the request would be accepted, provided there were guarantees concerning the fleet. Depending on the reply received a meeting of the cabinet would be taking irrevocable decisions that day.

They thought that a new drama on this scene would occur if Mr. Reynaud decided to take the government to Algiers. A totally new idea was that there should be a total union of France and England, making it one country, with common citizenship. The two countries would combine all their structures and their powers, and would share their destiny. It was left to de Gaulle to try to persuade Churchill to the idea of the union, as he would soon be having lunch with Churchill.

De Gaulle examined the text of the proposed agreement. However grandiose the idea, if it were to be put into effect it would have to be done speedily. He saw that it proposed that by an exchange of notes England and France would combine their institutions, their interests, their empires, their laws and there would be a common citizenship - requiring complex negotiations. The British Government would express and apply complete solidarity with France. De Gaulle thought that such a project would have to be brought forward by Reynaud himself, but de Gaulle agreed to put the proposal to Churchill.

That morning was very busy. The first task was to alter the

destination of the liner Pasteur, which was carrying about a thousand 75-millimetre artillery guns from the United States. The liner was bound for Bordeaux, but de Gaulle re-routed it to a British port. It was crucial to prevent such a cargo falling into the hands of the Germans. Eventually these armaments made a large contribution to British re-armament, replacing much of the material which had been abandoned at Dunkirk.

When it came to providing transport, de Gaulle found that the English were keen to provide ships and to guard the convoys. The Admiralty co-operated with the French naval mission, but it was clear that in London there was no confidence that the French position had reverted to one of continuing the battle. It was clear that they expected France to withdraw from the struggle imminently. Above all, fears about the destination of the French fleet were paramount. During these dramatic hours, every Frenchman felt the burden of the inquisition with any English they met 'What will happen to your fleet?'

De Gaulle lunched with Churchill at the Carlton Club. "What will happen to the French fleet?" Churchill asked. De Gaulle replied: "Petain himself will not agree to give it up. Besides, the fleet is the territory of Admiral Darlan. A lord will not give up his fiefdom, but one thing is sure, the enemy will never get his hands on our ships, but to ensure this we will have to stay in the war. I am surprised at the position you took at Tours. You appeared to cheapen the value of our alliance. Your resigned attitude to the situation gave support to those who are in favour of capitulation."

"But you could see that our hand was forced," Churchill replied. De Gaulle told him that he would have had to take a different attitude to prevent a collapse. Churchill appeared astonished. He broke off for a discussion with Morton, the cabinet secretary. De Gaulle supposed that Churchill was looking to change, at the last minute, a decision already taken. Perhaps this was the cause, a mere half hour later, of the British ambassador withdrawing the note which had been given to the French Government in which approval had been given to France asking about the conditions for an armistice.

They then discussed the question of the union of the two

countries. Lord Halifax told de Gaulle that it would be an enormous step and De Gaulle agreed, but pointed out that if it were to be brought into effect action had to be immediate. They had reached the point where everything had to be done to maintain the Alliance. After more discussion Churchill agreed with de Gaulle's advice. He called an emergency cabinet meeting to consider the union of the two countries. De Gaulle went with Churchill to Downing Street and waited in an adjoining office during the cabinet meeting. De Gaulle telephoned Reynaud to tell him that he hoped, before the end of the afternoon, to give him a very important communication from the British Government. Reynaud replied that he would prepare to put it to the French cabinet at 1700 hours, but de Gaulle was warned that there could be no change of position.

The British cabinet meeting lasted two hours. During the meeting several ministers came out to discuss separate matters with de Gaulle and the other French officials. Suddenly Churchill appeared at their head. "We are agreed!" he exclaimed. In effect the text was that which had already been agreed. De Gaulle telephoned Paul Reynaud and dictated the document to him.

"It is very important," he said. "I am going to use this document at the meeting shortly." De Gaulle gave Reynaud some quick words of encouragement. Churchill grabbed the telephone. "Allo! De Gaulle is right. Our proposal can have enormous consequences. You must hang on!" Then, after listening to the reply, he said "Until tomorrow then, at Concarneau."

De Gaulle took his leave of the Prime Minister and flew straight back to Bordeaux. He was ready for the journey to the next conference. Churchill took a special train to Portsmouth to board a destroyer to cross the channel to Concarneau for the next day's meeting. De Gaulle reached Bordeaux at 21.30 hours, where he was told that Reynaud had resigned and that the President of the French Republic, President Lebrun, had asked Marshal Petain to form a government. Capitulation was certain. De Gaulle made his decision; he would leave in the morning.

De Gaulle went to see Reynaud. He found him with no doubt as to what would happen when Petain was in charge. Reynaud was at the end of his tether, without hope; only he could really understand what the outcome of these terrible days would be. Following long days and sleepless nights he had carried the burden alone. For, as always, the leader has to carry the final burden.

Reynaud had been close to every event in the fall of France: the German break through at Sedan, the disaster at Dunkirk, the fall of Paris, the collapse at Bordeaux. He had presided over a government that had been rushed into a defeat it could not avoid. He had faced this torment with a brave soul that had not faltered during those dramatic days and he had never lost control of himself. He had never flinched, appeared undignified, or complained. It was a tragic outcome as a reward for such courage, an injustice brought about by overwhelming events.

In the end, Mr. Reynaud's personality rose to the occasion and if it had been in any way possible he would have achieved a different outcome, but it was impossible. All around him he saw the collapse of the regime, fear in the populace, withdrawal by his Allies and failure by the highest commanders. From the day that the government left Paris, the exercise of power had been nothing but agony; delayed on the way, with all services dislocated, discipline and devotion to duty gone. In such conditions his courage, his intelligence, the authority of his position, counted for nothing. He could not control the avalanche of events.

To regain control he would have to stop the whirlpool and leave for Africa, and start anew from there. He saw this, but it would take extreme measures. It would mean a change of high command, dismissal of Petain and half his ministers, discarding certain influences, resigning himself to the occupation of the whole of metropolitan France. It was a situation without precedent, to escape from the current risks and the normal processes.

Reynaud believed that he could take upon himself the weightiest decisions, beyond any normal calculations. He had tried to achieve these ends by manoeuvre. From there, he could see, would emerge conditions from the enemy to which Great Britain would never agree. He knew that even those who were pushing for an armistice would recoil when they received the conditions imposed by the enemy, but the events leading to defeat were too harsh to be borne. To try to make war without adequate means could only end in one of two ways. If he could not succeed in winning, he would have to give Petain the role of overseeing defeat.

The regime gave no choices to the head of the last government of the third republic. Certainly many in control found capitulation repugnant, but many of those in power, struck by the disaster for which they felt responsible, could not summon courage anew. And so, what was the problem which faced France and which would control her present and her future? Parliament was powerless and the President of the Republic would not raise his voice. Even the council of ministers could not promote the country's cause. At the end of this drama was the annihilation of the state. In the final collapse the administration showed frightened weakness and was without cohesion for the defence, the honour, and the independence of France.

When General Spears, Churchill's special representative to the French Government, last saw Reynaud, and left his study, he looked for de Gaulle. Before the interview with Reynaud de Gaulle had whispered to Spears that he expected Weygand to arrest him. Spears had told de Gaulle to wait exactly where he was until after the interview with Reynaud. He reassured de Gaulle that everything would be all right. On leaving Reynaud's study Spears and the British ambassador found de Gaulle, who said that he wished to go to England. To get back to the Hotel Montre de Gaulle could not travel in the ambassador's car. Their purposes could be easily guessed by anyone who saw them, so he would have to go on foot.

Late that evening de Gaulle went to the hotel where the British ambassador, Sir Ronald Campbell, was staying. He told Sir Ronald of his intention to leave for London. General Spears, who had come into the conversation, said he would accompany de Gaulle. De Gaulle sent to warn Reynaud, who sent 100,000 francs from secret funds. Arrangements were made for de Gaulle's wife and children, who were at Carentec, to be given passports for England and berths on the last ship to sail from Brest. In the event they missed that boat, which was sunk with total loss of life. They reached England safely by another boat.

De Gaulle had clearly become overwrought by the situation. The shock of the news that the French government was to seek an armistice was particularly severe as de Gaulle had been in London settling the agreement for the two countries to unite and fight on. De Gaulle agreed with General Spears that at the moment of the announcement of the French government seeking an armistice the banner of resistance must be raised in England. With Reynaud's resignation in favour of Petain de Gaulle had ceased to be a minister and his junior status as a General was beneath the authority of any head of a regional authority. De Gaulle could not raise the flag of resistance from any part of the French empire.

From the hotel Spears rang Churchill and explained that de Gaulle expected that he would be arrested if he stayed in France and that he wished to come to England to fight on, Churchill agreed that de Gaulle should come. The die was cast. But how to get de Gaulle away without the plan becoming known and thence stopped? De Gaulle would need a safe refuge overnight. It was agreed that he should come to the hotel at 7 a.m. and then they would then go to the aerodrome by car.

The next morning Spears was up at 6 a.m., waiting for de Gaulle in the hallway of the hotel. By a quarter past 7 de Gaulle had still not arrived and Spears was genuinely worried. At nearly 8 o'clock de Gaulle arrived with his A.D.C., Geoffrey de Courcel, a tall, thin young man. There was a large amount of luggage, which was fitted into the car with difficulty. To give the impression that de Gaulle was merely driving around Bordeaux on his normal business they went to two separate buildings that were being used by the Ministry of War. Without leaving the car de Gaulle told officials to make a series of appointments for him later in the day. He hoped that they had not heard that the government had fallen and that he was no longer in his post.

They then drove quickly to the aerodrome. Since the R.A.F. Dragon Rapide biplane had landed many other aircraft had arrived and the place was so overcrowded that it was difficult to taxi or take off. The plan was for de Gaulle to appear as if he was seeing General Spears off, and then to jump aboard the 'plane at the last minute. Before they could take off the pilot insisted that the luggage should be lashed down firmly, to prevent it moving on the flight and destabilising the aircraft. There was nothing with which to tie the luggage down. De Courcel sprinted off and in ten minutes was back with some strong string, which the pilot accepted. While clearance for take off was being obtained they chatted on the tarmac and then Spears got into the 'plane. As the aircraft started to move they hoisted de Gaulle aboard and de Courcel scrambled in. The aircraft manoeuvred through the other aircraft and took off.

De Gaulle left France at 10 o'clock on the morning of the 17th June, 1940. Of the moment of de Gaulle's departure from France Churchill wrote 'he carried with him, in this small aeroplane, the honour of France.'

They flew over La Rochelle and Rochefort. In these ports were burning ships set on fire by German bombing. They passed above Paimpont, where his mother was living, seriously ill. The forest was on fire and ammunition depots were burning. After landing at Jersey to refuel they arrived in London early in the afternoon.

He telephoned the ambassador and the consular offices. Already there was a coolness in their response.

LONDON

When de Gaulle arrived in England on the 17th June 1940 he had resigned from the French war cabinet. He had been promoted to the rank of Brigadier General and the command of the 4th armoured division but he was then brought into the war cabinet, by which time the situation had deteriorated. The French premier was seeking permission to break the agreement with Britain not to seek a separate peace.

De Gaulle was not prepared to tolerate this. When he was brought to England in a De Havilland Dragon Rapide of RAF Transport Command he said that he carried only a general's baton and the honour of France in his knapsack.

The disaster of the battle for France had destroyed the ability to resist the German invasion. Churchill had asked General Weygand, the French commander in chief, "What reserves are there?" The reply had been simple and devastating - "None."

On the very next day de Gaulle was given the opportunity to speak on the BBC to the French nation. He was a comparatively junior general, with no legal authority to speak for France, so that his speech had to be carefully drafted.

He spoke of the army chiefs who had formed the government, facing the defeat of their armies, seeking agreement with the enemy to end the conflict. Certainly, the French had been submerged by the mechanised enemy forces, on land and in the air. It was the tanks, planes and German tactics that had surprised the French generals and brought about their need to seek an armistice.

But was this to be the last word? Must all hope disappear? Was the defeat to be final? No!

He called for belief that the cause of France had not been completely lost. The same means that had brought defeat to the French forces could be used to defeat their enemies and bring eventual victory.

For France was not alone! And this he repeated twice, with great force. France had a great empire. The French empire could join with the British Empire, which controlled the seas, and continue the struggle.

And so, in his first broadcast to the French people, on his very first complete day in England, he launched the Allied cause anew. France, like England, could use the immense industrial might of the United States. The war was not limited to the unhappy land of metropolitan France. The war was not finished by the end of the battle for France.

"It was a war involving the whole world. All the failures, all the delays, all the suffering, will not prevent us from one day destroying our enemies.

Hard struck today by their mechanised forces, we will be able to conquer in the future with a greater mechanised force. That is the destiny of the world!

It is I, General de Gaulle, already in London, who invites French officers and soldiers who find themselves on British territory, or wherever they are, with or without their arms; I call upon the engineers and the specialist workers who find themselves on British territory or wherever they are to come and join me.

Whatever happens, the flame of French resistance need not die and will not die. Tomorrow, as today, I will speak on the radio from London."

On the 19th June 1940 the minister of war in the government in Bordeaux sent a message to the French military attaché in London to demand that General de Gaulle should report back to the commanding general in Bordeaux without delay.

So the battle for the control of the French forces overseas was set. On the same day, June 19th 1940, de Gaulle sent a telegram to all French commanders overseas. It invited them to appoint a representative to get into direct touch with him and to notify him by telegram the name and rank of the representative. It ended with the word 'Sympathies.' The meaning here was not one of sympathy as to the predicament of France, but the meaning of expressing friendship towards them.

A special message was sent to General Noguès, Commander in Chief of French forces in North Africa, based in Algeria. It stated that in London de Gaulle was in direct contact with the British Government. He held himself available, under General

Noguès orders, to take part in combat or to make himself useful in any possible way.

Later that night, still the 19th June 1940, his next broadcast to the French people stated:

"At this hour all France understands that our normal power has gone. Seeing the confused soul of France, the destruction of our government by the enemy and its enslavement by the enemy, seeing the impossibility of continuing to run our institutions, I, General de Gaulle, soldier and head of the French people, have the conscience to speak in the name of France.

In the name of France I declare the following:

All Frenchmen who are still carrying arms have an absolute duty to continue their resistance.

To lay down your arms, to surrender a military position, to accept the giving up of any portion of French territory to enemy control, would be a crime against our country.

At this hour, I call above all on those Frenchmen in North Africa, to the undefeated North Africa. The Italian armistice is a great trap. Amongst the generals in North Africa there are those who will not submit to the conditions imposed by the enemy. It is intolerable that the panic which has consumed Bordeaux should cross the Mediterranean Sea. Soldiers of France, wherever you are, arise!"

And so, what was the situation for de Gaulle? He had been given the opportunity to speak on the BBC to French people everywhere about the fall of France and the duty to continue the struggle from the French empire, joined with the British Empire.

He had rejected a call to return to France and place himself under the control of the government established in Bordeaux at that time.

The difficulty of his position was solved by two declarations by the British Government on the 23rd June 1940 and broadcast worldwide by the BBC.

The first declaration:

The Government of his Majesty considers that the terms of the armistice which has been signed, in violation of the solemn accords concluded between the Allied governments, places the Government in Bordeaux in a state of complete subjection to the enemy and denies it all liberty and any right to represent free French citizens.

As a consequence, the Government of His Majesty cannot consider that the Government in Bordeaux represents an independent country.

The second declaration:

The Government of His Majesty has taken official notice of the intention to form a Provisional National French Committee, which will represent independent French forces who are resolute in following through the war to its end to fulfil the international obligations which France has given.

The Government of His Majesty will recognise this French National Committee and will deal with it in all respects relating to the continuing of the war, so long as the Committee continues to represent those French forces that are resolute in continuing the struggle against the common enemy.

On the 24th June de Gaulle was in contact with French commanders, representing the now forming French National Committee.

On the 25th June the British government issued a communiqué:

"The signature of the armistice by the French government has put an end to resistance by the French armed forces in metropolitan France. However, in the French empire there are encouraging signs of resistance.

In Syria, General Mittlehauser, French commander in chief, has indicated a willingness for French forces to continue in battle. In Indo-China the Governor General has stated that he will not lower the flag. In Tunisia the Resident General remains firm that he will continue the struggle. From Morocco, from Senegal, from Djibouti have come assurances of loyalty to the cause from both the military and civil authorities.

36

The British Government is ready to conclude financial arrangements to enable the French empire to fulfil its role. As the British Prime Minister has already stated, the aim of Great Britain is the complete restoration of the colonial and metropolitan territory of France."

What were the French forces which could come to the aid of the Allied cause? There had been a chance to join the two nations to bolster the resistance to invasion - a genuine but belated and frustrated attempt to breathe life into French resistance when all was going to disaster. De Gaulle states that at this time France was not without a sword, a means to fight. There were in England some units of the light alpine division, returned from their brilliant campaign in Norway under the command of General Bethouart. There were major forces of the French navy – totalling about 100,000 tons – anchored in British waters, having escaped from Cherbourg, Brest and Lorient, and all having aboard their full fighting equipment and some 10,000 sailors. There were also in Britain several thousand wounded soldiers, recovering in British hospitals. The French military mission organised all these elements to maintain authority, for their purpose had been to organise the repatriation of these forces under the control of the government in Vichy, which had become the seat of the Government in the unoccupied zone of France. The north of France and the Atlantic coast were under the control of German occupation forces.

De Gaulle had great difficulty in getting into contact with all the various elements of the French armed forces. He used a large number of subalterns who were keen to join the Free French cause, but who were impeded by higher military authority. What they could do and what they did do was to spread the word to the men of all ranks with who they were in contact. The results were not very encouraging. Eight days after the radio broadcast of the 18th June, the number of volunteers assembled at Olympia, which the English had put at their disposal, amounted to only a few hundred.

The British did not look very kindly on this level of support. They had told the French troops who had wanted to be repatriated about the call to rally to de Gaulle and to join the British armed forces.

**DE GAULLE'S FIRST MEETING WITH
KING GEORGE VIth, 24th AUGUST 1940**

Certainly by the British attempt to reach all available troops they had done their best to conquer inertia and opposition.

The press and radio had also done their best to spread the message. But the British commanders, awaiting day by day a new German offensive, and even invasion, had no time to give detailed attention to the Free French cause. In any case, they were not accustomed to such upheavals, and were not organised to deal with such extra-ordinary events. The normal course would have been to deal with the government now stationed at Vichy. They also could not fully trust yesterday's allies who had, as they felt, fallen apart in the stress of battle. What would they to do if the enemy flooded in? Surely the wisest would get back to France while there was an opportunity. What importance and reliance could ever be placed on groups who had no leaders and no equipment and which this General de Gaulle was now attempting to rally?

De Gaulle's position was not made clear until the 28th June. On that date the British government announced:

"The government of His Majesty recognises General de Gaulle as the leader of the Free French, wherever they are, who rally to him for the defence of the Allied cause."

De Gaulle had arrived in London on the 17th June. It took only eleven days for him to emerge and be recognised as the leader of the French part of the Allied cause. After the long decline and the rancour which had accompanied the attempts to bolster the resolve of the French leadership under the crushing blow of German arms in May and early June the speed of this resurrection of the French cause and new contribution was startling. Only eleven days! The faith and confidence placed in this junior general is amazing. With all the delays which usually would accompany such negotiations no such speedy a decision would normally be expected.

De Gaulle's leadership was not received well by the French authorities. In a letter dated the 30th June the French Chargé d'Affaires in London passed on a message from the French military authorities.

This message stated:

"By an ordinance issued by the Chief Judge of the Military Tribunal of the 17th Region dated the 27th June temporary

Brigadier General de Gaulle (Charles Andre Joseph Marie) has been arraigned before the Military Tribunal of the 17th Region for the crime of refusing orders in the presence of the enemy and by failing to act in military duties as part of this refusal. An arrest warrant has therefore been issued against him on this day.

The President of the Tribunal has signed, on the 28th June, an order requiring him to present himself for arrest to the Prison at Saint-Michel at Toulouse within five days from the date of the 29th June 1940. Failing this he will be judged in his absence." De Gaulle replied on the 3rd July. "I return herewith the text of the document which you have sent me. I would be obliged if you would make it known to those who have sent me this communication that to my eyes it does not contain a speck of interest."

And so he broke with the old French authorities. In this repudiation of the attempts to bring him under the jurisdiction of the old authorities the death of the Third French Republic was certain. Here, in this repudiation of the authority of the regime of the Third Republic, was the birth of the Fourth Republic! Quelle audace! What bravery!

In the meantime de Gaulle had been busy organising the Free French forces. On the 29th June he had visited Trentham Park, to inspect the Light Mountain Division. The general in command wanted to return to France, with the intention of returning to the battle later. Arrangements had been made for de Gaulle to inspect each battalion individually. Thus it was possible to rally a large part of two battalions of the 13th Brigade of the Foreign Legion, with their commander, Colonel Magrin-Verneret. He also reviewed two companies of the Chasseurs d'Alpins and two-thirds of a tank company. There was also some artillery, and other specialised units.

When de Gaulle had left the parade two officers from the War Office addressed the troops. They told the soldiers that they were free to serve under de Gaulle, but if they did so they could be considered in rebellion against their government. The next day de Gaulle wanted to visit the camp at Aintree, where there were several thousand French sailors. When de Gaulle arrived the

British admiral in command advised de Gaulle that there was not good order in the camp and that the men were not ready for inspection. So de Gaulle left empty handed.

Despite this many naval officers were keen to join de Gaulle. Those first to rally to him were the submarines Narval and Rubis, and the patrol-trawler President- Honduce. When Vice Admiral Muselier joined de Gaulle there was a recognised leader for the naval forces. Several dozen French airmen were at the St. Athan base, in Wales, ready to be formed into squadrons.

All the time isolated volunteers were reaching England. Many had escaped from France on the last vessels to leave. Eddy Florentin, in his book about the French Commando Forces, reports that from a tiny port on the Cotentin, St.-Vast-la-Hogue, to pass into history, sailed two trawlers. Among the small group on board was the man who would lead one of the important Commando assaults on D-day, Philippe Kieffer. Others had had great difficulty in reaching England by crossing through Spain. Some airmen, who had been ordered to return to Vichy from North Africa, diverted instead to Gibraltar to reach de Gaulle. Some French merchant officers came with their ships to join the Free French armed forces.

There were also Frenchmen living abroad who reported for duty. From 2000 troops who had been wounded at Dunkirk de Gaulle obtained sign up papers from 200. A colonial battalion, which was serving on Cyprus at the time of the capitulation, joined de Gaulle on mass, with their chief, Colonel Lorotte. In the last days of June fishing boats brought all the eligible men from the Ile de Sein, in Brittany. To assemble all these varied groups General Spears showed great ingenuity in the organisation of transport.

THE TRAGEDY OF ORAN

The great danger, which de Gaulle wrote about, was the future of the French fleet. Admiral Darlan had given his word, on the 18th June, that the French Fleet would not be given up to the Germans. The terms of the armistice gave no immediate direct control over the French fleet to the Germans. Because of the attitude of the French government after capitulation the British feared that the French fleet would one day fall into German hands. With Italy's entry into the war the position of the British became impossible, because the French ships could not be left unguarded. The Italian fleet, with four battleships and eight heavy cruisers, could seize the French ships. The Italians were not in the French first thoughts at the time of capitulation and retained treaty independence to act on behalf of the Axis. British ships would need to be kept guarding the French ships, taking the whole of the Mediterranean Fleet and half the Home Fleet out of the war. The ships on guard would be very vulnerable to air, submarine, and mine attack.

Were the French ships such an important fighting force? The battleships *Dunkerque* and *Strasbourg* were new vessels, completed in 1937. They had 13 inch guns and their design speed was over 30 knots. They were better gunned than the German pocket battle ships such as the *Graf Spee*. They could out run any British ship they could not outgun and they could outgun any ship they could not out run. Heavy cruisers, such as the *Algerie*, of 10,000 tons, had a design speed of 31 knots, but this was considerably exceeded on trials. Carrying eight 8 inch guns, many lighter weapons, and both torpedoes and aircraft, this class of vessel was better equipped than the equivalent British heavy cruisers. French light cruisers, such as the *La Galissonière*, were of 7,600 tons and had a maximum speed of 31.5 knots. They carried four aircraft and could tow a special mat astern to aid the recovery at sea of the aircraft. This greatly increased their range of reconnaissance. Destroyers, such as the *Mogador*, were designed for a speed of 38 knots, but this was also exceeded on trials. They carried eight 5.5 inch guns. Under the terms of naval treaties they counted as light cruisers. Only the British fast minelayers *Abdiel*, *Welshman*, and *Manxman* could keep up with them. The submarine *Surcouf* was the largest submarine in the world. Carrying two eight inch guns as well as anti-aircraft guns and twenty two torpedoes she could surface suddenly and bombard any port with a quick and devastating burst of fire. Amongst merchant shipping she could wreak havoc.

Then, on the fourth of July, came news of a sudden and shocking event. On the previous day the British Mediterranean fleet had attacked the French fleet at anchor at Mers-el Kebir, the naval harbour adjacent to the city of Oran. At the same time the British took control of French naval vessels which had taken refuge in British ports, disembarked the crews, and not without some bloodshed. English aircraft had torpedoed the battleship *Richelieu* at Dakar.

The British press reported these events as though they were a significant naval victory. It was clear, that the British Admiralty, recalling an old naval enmity, had taken advantage of the sad situation since the fall of France, and the armistice concluded by the Vichy government, to fall upon their recent allies. This was not the attitude of the officers and men of the Royal Navy. They detested their orders and the senior officers did everything possible to avoid conflict. British as well as French tears were shed. The French fleet had never undertaken any hostilities against the British. It was also certain that Admiral Darlan would never have allowed the French fleet to fall into German hands. General de Gaulle had repeatedly informed and reassured the Admiralty of this.

He had written to Churchill on the 3rd July 1940, before he heard of the news of the attack. He noted that the grave need to prevent the French fleet falling into German hands had required the British government to extend the blockade, not only against metropolitan France but also against the as yet unconquered territories in Africa. This action required de Gaulle to make certain observations. The British Government, on whose shoulders lay the main burden of the struggle, had decided the whole of the necessary measures to be taken. He brought to the government's attention that during the last war, to co-ordinate the best resistance to the Germans, it had been possible with the aid of American philanthropic organisations, to bring some aid to the people of Belgium. Might it be possible to organise something similar to maintain the physical and moral strength of the French people? It should be possible to bring some aid to those French people living in the unoccupied zone. He reminded Churchill that behind the failed governments lay the soul and the needs of the people of France. Although the French people would understand the need for Britain to take severe measures there must be found a way to help mothers and children to escape the worst privations. If it were useful, he would try and persuade the Government of the United States to organise a committee to bring humanitarian aid to those enduring the greatest suffering. Later that day came the news of the attack by the British fleet on the French fleet.

What had led to the attack on the French fleet at Oran? Why had Churchill not trusted totally the assurances he had received that the French fleet could never fall into German hands? The answer lay in the fate of the 400 German aircrew that had been captured in the fighting of 1939 and up to June 1940. They were held as prisoners of war in France. When the question of the French Government seeking a separate armistice had been considered Churchill had raised the question of their future with Reynaud and insisted that they should be sent as prisoners to Britain. Reynaud had agreed and given his absolute assurance that this would be done. With the sudden collapse of the French Government and the installation of Marshal Petain in control this promise was forgotten. Eventually, under German pressure and to appease the Germans, these German aircrew were handed over to the Germans by the Vichy government, enabling them to fight anew against Britain in the desperate air struggle in August and September 1940. Some were shot down again. Here lay the treachery which made the attack on the French fleet at Oran so sadly necessary.

The determination to fight on after the fall of France, which Churchill so eloquently explained, was against the background of whispering dissension amongst the appeasers. In the background,

**FRENCH FLEET UNDER ATTACK BY THE BRITISH
AT ORAN 3RD JULY 1940**

**3RD JULY 1940, AT ORAN, THE BATTLESHIP
BRETAGNE BLOWN UP AND SINKING**

out of the Cabinet but not out of Parliament, were those with less stout hearts who were ready to make peace under the banner 'The war-mongers have had their chance and failed.' Churchill reassured the Prime Ministers, MacKenzie King in Canada and Smuts in South Africa, of Britain's determination. 'We have command of the seas' he wrote to Smuts. This was the key. The Atlantic lifeline must be held open, but that command of the seas was to be sorely tested. Losses of destroyers in all theatres of war reduced the total number available to only a hundred when, eventually, the United States supplied fifty old destroyers from their reserve. So close was the balance and so near the destruction of the Royal Navy.

There was no doubt about the honour of Admiral Darlan. At a dinner given for him by Churchill at the Admiralty in 1939 Darlan had reminded the company that his great-grandfather had been killed at the Battle of Trafalgar. It was clear that he had no love for England and that his professional position was undermined by the poor quality of his relationship with the Minister of Marine. When the French government collapsed he became Minister of Marine. His assurances about the French fleet were not forthcoming. Had he sailed with his ships to a British port he would have become the natural leader of French resistance, supported by a massive fleet which obeyed him implicitly. Instead he faltered, so that the French cause was left to be championed by de Gaulle, whom Churchill described as having no fleet or army, but an 'unconquerable spirit.'

Article 8 of the Armistice stated the French Fleet in home waters would be demobilised or disarmed under German or Italian control. The Germans would obtain control of the vessels while they were still fully armed. The section outlining German promises not to use them in the war could not be trusted. The Armistice might at any time be ended on the pretext of some minor failure of observance by the French. The decision to attack the French fleet at Oran was the most hateful that Churchill had to make. Churchill's fears about the Germans being able to suddenly take control of the French ships were vindicated by the ease with which French ships in British ports were taken over in a coup de main - overwhelming force with surprise.

Sadly, at Oran, Admiral Gensoul would not comply with any of the alternative actions offered to him. The British emissary, Captain Holland, out of long friendship and sensitivity, wore only one decoration as he visited the French admiral on the battleship Dunkerque, the Legion d'Honneur. When the French Government met to consider the British demands, which Admiral Gensoul had transmitted, one alternative was omitted – the possibility of the French ships sailing to the French West Indies.

When the French dallied about accepting any of the alternatives the British were totally reluctant to open fire. It required a firm and definite direct order from the Admiralty to force them to do so –'French ships must comply with our terms or sink themselves or be sunk by you before dark,' Admiral Somerville was commanded. When the action started the battleship *Bretagne* blew up, suffering the great majority of the nearly 1,300 casualties. This was a tragedy, but it did show the rest of the world the determination of Britain to fight on.

With the death of some thirteen hundred French sailors in the action, how did General de Gaulle deal with this in a broadcast to all France?

In a broadcast on the 8th of July 1940 de Gaulle described the frightful bombardment at Oran on the 3rd July.

"I am going to speak frankly and without detour about those things which each people holds most dear. There is no Frenchman who can speak without grief and without anger about the way in which the French fleet was destroyed by our Allies. This grief, this anger, comes from deep within us. There is no need to hide our feelings about this. I call upon the English to spare themselves and to spare us from calling this a naval victory. To do so would be unjust and out of place.

The naval forces at Oran were out of action at the time. They were at anchor and without any possibility of manoeuvre or dispersal. Their commanders and crews had for fifteen days been demoralised and in despair. They had allowed the British vessels the chance of the first salvo, each one of them knowing that the first salvo would be decisive at such close range. Their destruction is not the result of a glorious naval battle. So it is that a French soldier declares to our English allies that there was no need to prove their prowess in naval conflict."

Then, speaking to French people. "I ask them to consider the final and most essential point of importance, taking the view as to what is necessary for final victory and deliverance.

By a dishonest action the government at Bordeaux had agreed to put our fleet at the service of the enemy. There is little doubt that, out of sheer necessity, the enemy would one day have used our fleet against England and against our own free empire. What was to be done! I say that it was certainly better that our fleet were destroyed!

I would like better to know that even *Dunkerque*, our marvellous and powerful *Dunkerque*, should be beached at Mers el Kebir, than to see her one day crewed by the Germans bombarding English ports and even our own Algiers, Casablanca or Dakar.

In unleashing this fratricidal bombardment, then turning it against the allies and to the irritation of the French, the government at Bordeaux has taken up this role and shown its position of servitude.

In exploiting these events to try to excite hostility between the English and French people, the enemy has taken up the role of conqueror.

In showing this drama for what it is, I want to say that it will not undermine the moral strength of the unity between the British and French people in their patriotic role.

The English who reflect on the matter cannot ignore that for them there will be no victory if the soul of France passes to the enemy.

The French worthy of the name cannot avoid knowing that an English defeat will lead to their enslavement forever.

Whatever happens, even if one of us, for a time, falls under the yoke of the enemy, our two peoples, our two great peoples, have a united cause. We will go down together or we will win together.

When, to those Frenchmen still living in freedom, they rise up to restore the honour and interests of France, I declare in their name that they will act with firm resolution.

They have taken, once and for all, the decision to fight."

And so, in one speech, de Gaulle spoke of the anguish and sadness of France for what had been done at Oran. He warned the British press not to consider it a worthy victory. He then told the French that it had to be done to prevent the Germans gaining eventual control and use of the fleet, which would have led to British defeat and the loss of all hope for the future of France. He blamed the need for the action on the weakness and defeatism of the French Government, which had failed to secure the safety of the French fleet. He ended in expressing the unity of the French and British people to fight and to win together.

He had not been consulted about the attack on the French fleet and he had not been warned of the imminent action. And yet at this time of great disaster and sadness he was completely resolute in joining the futures of the two nations together to win through to eventual victory. There can be no greater proof of his strength and courage as an ally than his actions at this time. It is important to understand the attitude of the British press, which was such that the action at Mers el Kebir was viewed in a very different light. De Gaulle had told Churchill that there could be no absolute guarantee that the French fleet would not fall into German hands in the event of French capitulation.

These events are well described in Admiral Cunningham's autobiography 'A Sailor's Odyssey.' At the time of the action he was in command of the fleet in Alexandria. The Mediterranean fleet had been moved from Malta to Alexandia to avoid possible Italian air attack.

Admiral Cunningham had accompanied the Commander in Chief, in the battleship *Barham*, to Oran in 1937. The French Admiral in the Mediterranean was Esteva. Cunningham describes him as a small, very alert man, with a square-cut beard, turning grey. He always started work early, he spoke English well, and was keen to co-operate.

In November 1937 the French Commander-in-Chief, Admiral Abrial, visited Malta in the cruiser *Algerie*. Cunningham describes the French as being very pleasant, most speaking English, and they got on very well together.

In July 1939 Admiral Ollive came on an official visit to Malta. Cunningham describes this French Admiral as having a great sense of humour and their conferences were most useful. He found the French were thinking on the same lines as the British for offensive action if war were to break out.

During April 1940 General Weygand passed through Malta on his way to take command of the French army. He was a very alert little man and a real live wire, flying prodigious distances in a day for a man of his seventy-three years. He had a great sense of humour. When Cunningham asked him why he was going to Paris Weygand replied "The new prime minister must have heard that I was very old, and sent for me to see if it was true."

Also in April 1940 discussions with Admiral Esteva showed how there would be joint operations if Italy entered the war, though the French did not expect this, at least for some time. The French fleet at Mers-el–Kebir (Oran) included two battleships, *Dunkerque* and *Strasbourg*. On May 1st 1940 a British battleship sailed near Malta. Its escort included four cruisers, three of them being French. The second part of this fleet was headed by three French battleships. All were headed for Egypt and berthed in Alexandria harbour.

Early in May the British fleet commanders heard of General Weygand's appointment as Commander-in-Chief in France. He was admired and his energy, youthfulness and confidence, together with his victorious record, brought new hope to Cunningham and his officers.

At that time Lady Cunningham received a letter from Admiral Esteva, whose home was at Rheims, where he was a great supporter of the cathedral. The city had been heavily bombed and severely damaged. The admiral's sister and brother, the latter severely wounded in the previous war, had had to be evacuated. Esteva wrote 'If our house and all our goods are destroyed, we know that many people are to be severely ruined or hurt and that it is an honour to suffer for high ideals and civilisation and not agree with the coarse brutality of those criminal Germans anxious to rule the whole earth.' Esteva's sentiments were impeccable.

As the war on land, in France, was being lost the combined

French and British fleets in Alexandria were immense – four British and three French battleships, nine British and four French cruisers, and twenty-eight destroyers. This fleet was too large and tempting a target and so two of the French battleships sailed west to other bases.

On June 20th an Allied force under Sir John Tovey, including the French battleship *Lorraine*, sailed to bombard Bardia. Three British destroyers and two French cruisers sailed from Alexandria as reinforcements. After Marshal Petain had asked the Germans for an armistice Admiral Godfroy, commanding the French ships at Alexandria, faded out as a belligerent. The French naval officers in Alexandria had great faith in Petain and Weygand, and none at all in de Gaulle. There was a split in the French naval officers, some junior ones wanting to fight on. One destroyer's crew wanted to fight on under the British flag, but most of the French sailors wanted to return to France. The capitulation of France on June 24th knocked the fight out of the French generals in Syria and North Africa.

The capitulation also brought the problem of the French fleet at Alexandria. If the British fleet sailed into action the French fleet might sail to Beirut, or even back to France, in which case it would fall into German hands. It was this danger which brought about the action at Oran. That fleet was given the alternatives of sailing to a British port to continue the allied fight, to sail to British ports with reduced crews and the crews would then return to France, to sail to French ports in the West Indies, where the ships would be demilitarised, to sail to the United States to be interned in a neutral country, or to sink the ships. The essential was to prevent the modern ships, *Dunkerque* and *Strasbourg*, which could outrun any British battle cruiser, from falling into German hands. At the same time the French fleet at Alexandria might have to be seized.

Admiral Cunningham describes that idea as entirely repugnant, for the men of the French fleet were their friends. They had great faith in Admiral Godfroy, whom they regarded as a man of honour. The idea of suddenly attacking and boarding his ships, inflicting many casualties, would be an act of treachery by the British which was as injudicious as it was unnecessary. Cunningham writes of the attack on Oran as being inept in its unwisdom.

Admiral Godfroy was invited on board H.M.S. *Warspite* at 7.00 a.m. on July 3rd. The unusual hour was a warning. He was invited, in a message from the British Government, to fight on as an ally, and he initially appeared to accept this offer. The alternatives of de-manning or scuttling were then put. Admiral Godfroy said that he would have to consult his government. French crews could only fight under the French flag. Otherwise they would be deserters.

At the other end of the Mediterranean, Admiral Somerville was negotiating with Admiral Gensoul at Oran. Admiral Godfroy chose the alternative of sinking his ships in open water. Admiral Cunningham tried to persuade Godfroy to demilitarise his ships in harbour, to allow the easy removal of the crews. This suggestion was accepted and the French started to unload oil fuel and torpedo warheads. Shortly afterwards Admiral Godfroy sent a hand written note to Admiral Cunningham. Godfroy had been ordered to sail back to France, but replied that his ships could not. He would be prepared to remain at Alexandria with the crews on board, but if attacked he would scuttle the ships in Alexandria harbour, but in a position to cause as little difficulty as possible for the British. But still no solution had been reached at Alexandria which would allow the British fleet to sail, as the French fleet there had not yet been immobilised.

Early on the morning of the 4th July Godfroy sent Cunningham a personal letter. Negotiations having failed at Oran the British fleet had attacked the French, sinking several ships. The battleship *Bretagne* had blown up, capsized and sunk. 1297 French sailors had died. The French had returned some fire, but no British ships were hit or casualties caused. French forbearance versus British perfidy.

It was clear that the French ships in Alexandria were raising steam, preparing to sail. Before they could raise steam the British, using French speaking officers, appealed directly to the French crews. Each French ship had been 'twinned' with a British ship. The captains of these British ships went aboard their opposite numbers, to reason with the French captains. Some were friendly.

The captain of the French cruiser *Neptune* received Captain Rory O'Conor with the greatest cordiality. He told him "When I saw that under your orders the tompions were being removed from your guns, I immediately ordered the tompions (covers against the entry of see water on passage) to be placed in mine." So the French captain responded to the threat from the British guns being made ready for action in making his unusable.

Many discussions took place among the French naval officers that day. After a meeting on board Godfroy's flagship the admiral came to see Cunningham. Godfroy agreed to yield to overwhelming force. They reached an agreement to disarm and disable the French ships. There was immense relief that agreement had been reached.

Admiral Cunningham had great sympathy for Admiral Godfroy, who had behaved most honourably. The fate of France and the tragedy at Mers-el Kebir were always on his mind. But in the months to come no success of the British fleet passed without his sending a letter of cordial congratulation. Every loss was followed by a letter of sympathy. In 1941, after the fall of Greece, he tried to help. He could not join in the battle but if there were dive bombers attacking the anchorage the French ships would use their light weapons in the general defence.

And so the terrible change from Allies sailing in concert to a difficult standoff interfered with the natural sympathy between the two navies. British sailors who had taken part in the bombardment at Oran were in tears. De Gaulle's assessment and broadcast had made the matter bearable for the moment. What is certain is that those French sailors who stood to their duty and would not damage their ally by forceful opposition to the bombardment when they could have damaged or sunk the British ships were heroes in the Allied cause. Perhaps one day the British will understand and recognise this.

De Gaulle was certain that there was no possibility of the French fleet falling into German hands. He was convinced that Admiral Darlan, quite apart from any other national interest, would never allow the Germans to lay their hands on the French ships. The terms of the armistice kept the French fleet out of German hands. But could and would the British trust the German word? Churchill spoke of German treachery and there lay the source of the mistrust which led to the tragedy of Oran and the air attack on the *Richelieu* at Dakar.

It was necessary to rejuvenate French spirits.

RAISING THE FREE FRENCH STANDARD

On the 13th July 1940 de Gaulle sent out a message for the 14th July national day. 'To all Frenchmen. Understand this! You still have an army in the fight!'

On the 14th July de Gaulle was in Whitehall, surrounded by a very emotional crowd, to review the first organised troops. A young girl, Violette Bushell, went with a friend to the ceremonies at the Cenotaph, where they saw representative detachments of many famous French regiments. The French sailors were easily distinguished from the British by the red pom-poms on their hats.

At ten o'clock precisely General de Gaulle arrived. He was cheered repeatedly by the troops, and also the large crowd of spectators. After a trumpet call the general laid a large wreath with a tricolour ribbon and inscribed 'Les Francais Libres.' He issued the call "Salut aux Morts" and came smartly to the salute. The cry went up 'Vive la France,' and 'Vive General de Gaulle.'

Violette was the daughter of an English father and a French mother. On that 14th of July she would meet a young French officer, Etienne Szabo. After taking him home to offer the hospitality of a meal, their romance blossomed. Married in the haste essential for love to flower in wartime, she soon had a daughter.

Her husband was severely wounded while fighting at the battle of el Alamein and he died the next day. She joined the Special Operations Executive and after parachuting twice into France to organise Resistance groups she was captured by the Gestapo. After torture by the Gestapo she was shot at Ravensbruck concentration camp in early 1945. Their daughter, Tania, received the George Cross on her behalf from King George the Sixth.

They then marched to the statue of Marshal Foch, where a tricolour floral tribute was placed. The excitement was so great that the civilians watching broke through the police cordon and mingled with the troops.

On the 21st July de Gaulle met several French airmen who had taken part in the bombing of the Ruhr. He announced that the Free French were back in the battle.

This was when the Free French adopted the Cross of Lorraine as their symbol.

By the end of July the troops who were fully organised amounted to 7,000. A great effort was made to recover the arms of those French troops who had been repatriated. The urgent need to organise the Free French forces stimulated an exchange of letters on the 7th August 1940.

Churchill wrote to de Gaulle about the conditions of service for the Free French forces. They would be under de Gaulle's command and His Majesty's Government would recognise de Gaulle as their Commander in Chief wherever the Free French forces might be found. He set out an accord for the recognition by His Majesty's Government that there would be a united Allied victory and there would be a restoration of the territorial integrity and the grandeur of France.

De Gaulle's immediate reply, on the same day, accepted the memorandum and he undertook to bring to the Allied cause, as commander in chief, all Free French forces wherever they might be. He undertook to use Free French forces in all the theatres of war in the Allied cause.

And so, in the course of six frantic weeks of effort, Britain found herself not alone, but with comrades in arms for the common cause. Where the French Government had surrendered and vanished from the battlefield, under de Gaulle the French empire and those forces which had escaped and continued to find their way to British shores would swell the ranks against the common enemy.

The immense difficulties in getting the French forces organised into effective and controlled fighting units would tax both leaders' ingenuity and patience. Neither was free from competition and dissention within their own ranks, but the cordiality of their exchanges and focus on the essentials showed how much they respected each other.

Perhaps the greatest tolerance of all was when de Gaulle spoke to the French people about the attack on the French fleet at Oran.

By converting the speech from its start, where he expressed grief and anger, to its triumphant concluding call to join the Allied forces for the eventual victory, he showed a mastery of psychology and political skill that has not been surpassed. This speech set the whole Allied cause rolling. Here was a new hope and defiance arising out of defeat and betrayal.

De Gaulle himself was to be subjected to the severest personal and professional attacks. At Clermond Ferrand, in his absence, he was court martialled. He was sentenced to death, stripped of his nationality, and all his property and belongings were seized by the state. He was deprived of any possibility of legal authority under the old rules of the French state and he had to start anew. The result was that there was no possibility of resurrecting the Third Republic. At the conclusion of the war a new start would have to be made and this led to the foundation of the Fourth Republic. It is a sign of the power of the character of the man and his unflinching devotion to both his country and the Allied cause that he was able to command respect, devotion, and admiration so widely.

On the 24th August King George VI visited the nucleus of the new French army. The inspection was something of a trial. The main thing de Gaulle remarked upon was how short the King was.

At this stage there was a great difficulty in encouraging French people everywhere out of the sad melancholy which, after the capitulation, gripped them. It was necessary to rekindle national pride and to give hope for the future.

In setting up the Free French forces it was necessary to act in strict cohesion with the British. The legal position of French troops had to avoid conflict with the British authorities. From the first de Gaulle advised Churchill that he would be forming a 'National Committee' to co-ordinate the Free French war effort. By this time a good number of senior French officials had rallied to de Gaulle's flag. De Gaulle speaks very highly of the contribution of General Spears at this time.

Starting from offices in St. Stephen's House, by the Thames, the Free French offices expanded into Carlton Gardens as a permanent headquarters. There were difficulties of deception by those who were supposed to be helping, but also great encouragement from other quarters.

From France, despite the difficulties of evading the censorship, they received letters and messages. There was a photograph, taken under the noses of the Germans, showing a group of men and women overcome by grief at the tomb of the Unknown Soldier. It had been sent on the 19th of June, with the words 'De Gaulle, we have heard you! Now we await you!' There was also a picture of a grave smothered with flowers. It was the grave of General de Gaulle's mother, who had died at Paimpont on the 16th June, as if she had died offering to God her life and suffering for the honour of her country and her son's mission. Thus the Free French started to get the measure of the feelings of the people about their refusal to accept defeat.

These messages also showed that it was possible to hear de Gaulle's broadcasts from London throughout France. French people living abroad echoed these feelings. Many got in touch to join the Free French cause, from countries such as the United States, Brazil, Argentina, Egypt, India and Japan, as well as very strong support in England. There was pride and there was hope; in England there was sympathy and support. The King, in his own way, showed this. Each member of the Royal Family joined him in this. For their part ministers, and officials, never failed to express their best wishes. It was impossible to imagine the generous kindness shown by the British people everywhere, and their kind consideration.

All sorts of help was given to aid the Free French volunteers. De Gaulle could not count the number of people who came to his offices offering help, time, and money. Everywhere de Gaulle went he received a generous welcome. When the British papers revealed that the Vichy government had condemned him to death and had confiscated his belongings, numerous jewels were left anonymously at Carlton Gardens for his benefit. Several dozen widows sent their wedding rings to be added to the Free French effort.

Some French officers, arriving in London with only the clothes they stood up in, were surprised to be taken to a London outfitters and kitted out down their underwear. The bill was paid by a Frenchman who had lived in England for eight years. He was determined to do everything to further the French cause. Later he was to serve in the anti-aircraft defence with the batteries on Hampstead Heath. His mathematical skills as a Maitre Pointeur, adding and subtracting three figure sums faster than they could be entered into the calculating machine, were put to the aid of the defence of London.

A really active atmosphere was growing in England. The German air attack and the possible invasion were awaited, at any moment. The whole world was shown a united nation. De Gaulle was very impressed by the way each citizen seemed to behave in a focussed manner, as if the whole country depended on them personally. It was very moving to find that each person took responsibility upon himself or herself, whereas in reality at that crucial time survival depended on only a small number of fighter pilots.

The enemy needed control of the skies for the invasion to take place. If the navy could be bombarded from the air it would not be able to stop an invasion fleet. The army, with a dozen divisions, most of whose equipment had been left behind in France, was in no fit state to oppose successfully any landings. After overcoming these depleted units the German army would have little difficulty in occupying the country, despite valiant resistance by the Home Guard. The King and the government would have to escape to Canada. It was certain that there would be those who would dance attendance on the Germans to gain advantage.

But this type of speculation did not touch the mass of the people, who were fully prepared for the struggle. Each man and woman prepared some defensive measures. Everyone was involved in the construction of shelters, distribution of arms, organising rationing, working in factories and in the fields. There was no lack of effort or discipline. The only thing lacking was the means. This was the effect of the many years of disarmament.

Certainly there was no lack of humour. One newspaper cartoon showed the German army stopped on the road. With all its tanks, guns, generals and men it was halted by a wooden barrier. A note on the barrier demanded the price of one penny to pass, but because the Germans would not pay a penny for each vehicle to pass the barrier would not be raised and the invader could not enter.

Meanwhile, the Royal Air Force was ready. The ordinary people found the tension of waiting for the attack almost unbearable. Mr. Churchill, always the leader, was impatient with waiting. One day in August, at Chequers, the prime minister's country house, de Gaulle saw Churchill shouting at the sky 'Why won't they come?' 'Why are you in such a hurry to see your cities destroyed?' de Gaulle asked him. 'Because if Oxford, Coventry, Canterbury come under attack the United States will be so outraged that they will come into the war on our side,' he replied.

De Gaulle expressed doubts about this. Two months after the fall of France the United States had shown no sign of abandoning its neutrality. "That is because France collapsed!" replied Churchill. "Sooner or later the Americans will come. But it will only happen if we are unbeaten. That is why I think of nothing but our fighter aircraft!" he exclaimed. "You can see that I was right not to send everything to the battle for France. If we had done so all would be lost for you and for us." De Gaulle replied that if the fighters had been sent it would have helped the Alliance and allowed the war to be continued from the Mediterranean and from Africa. The British would then be less threatened and the Americans more likely to come to the aid of Europe and Africa.

They agreed that these were sad times. In the end there was a difference. France was the edge of a continent, England was an island, America another world.

AFRICA

By the end of August 1940, the Free French had the means, an embryo organisation, and a certain popularity. It was time to bring it into use. De Gaulle was uncertain how and where to launch some offensive enterprise. Hitler had, in Europe, won the first round. Now it was time to start the second, and on a world scale. It was necessary to strike wherever possible and it would be to Africa that the Free French would have to turn. It was there, a few weeks earlier, that de Gaulle had tried to get the banner raised. He was convinced that it was in Africa that the next battles would be fought.

In the vast wastes of Africa France could, under its own control, raise a new army and continue the struggle. It would enable France to come back into the Allied line of battle. If metropolitan France were to be liberated the prior reconstruction of a French administration and a French community with a vibrant spirit would make recovery in metropolitan France much easier and much more sure. In any case, German aggression into Africa was designed to help their Italian allies. French forces in Africa could oppose and even prevent this. French action on a notable scale would impress Britain and the United States. It was necessary for the Free French to establish their authority over the French African colonies.

Because of the control of the Vichy government de Gaulle could do nothing immediate in Algeria, Tunisia and Morocco. He had received some messages of support from isolated areas, some administrators, and old soldiers in those territories, but this was not nearly enough to have any prospect of gaining control. The British action against the French fleet at Oran had severely damaged the Allied position. Time and other means would be needed to win the major territories to the Free French cause.

There could also be problems in West Africa. A few days after the British attack on the French fleet at Oran British aircraft from a carrier had attacked Dakar, in an attempt to put the French battleship *Richelieu* out of action. Nevertheless, an expedition should be mounted to try to gain control of French forces in West Africa.

It was in the equatorial territories of France that there was the best chance of raising the Free French flag. In Chad the governor, Felix Eboué, had shown a will to resist. As a black African he had shown every opposition to the triumph of the evil Nazi racist regime. At the first challenge, with his secretary General Laurentie, they opted to support de Gaulle. They had the support of the French part of the population and the military garrison was keen to join battle and looked for support with whatever de Gaulle could supply. The commercial interests knew that their business relations would certainly suffer if there was hostility to the adjacent British colony of Nigeria. These approaches were made on the 16th July. They were followed by a public announcement that de Gaulle had granted the authority for the government of Chad to continue thenceforth under the flag of the Cross of Lorraine.

In the Congo the situation was more obscure. There were still those in power who owed allegiance to the government of Vichy. There was also uncertainty about which direction Gabon would take. This old French colony had always been conservative in its attitude and would certainly not take the lead. De Gaulle was certain that whatever the views of individual governors of France's African territories, he would have to move quickly to establish his authority. The Vichy government had sufficient forces to enable it to keep control of nearly all the territories and had sent Admiral Platon on a tour of the territories to emphasise Vichy's control.

De Gaulle emphasised to Lord Lloyd, British Minister for the Colonies, the danger of these Vichy interventions to the stability and security of the British colonies of Sierra Leone and Nigeria, the Gambia and the Gold Coast. Lord Lloyd agreed the danger and supported de Gaulle's mission to gain control of the French territories by providing him with air transport for his envoys to start their mission from Lagos, in Nigeria.

The first task was to gain control in Chad. Three officials and one military man were to form the party. The military man was Captain Hauteclocque, who had arrived from France via Spain. This man was to change his name to protect his relatives still in France and would rise to great prominence. He would be better known as General Leclerc. He would be at the head of the second

French armoured division, which would lead the liberation of Paris.

But if there was to be a real power base it would also be essential to seize control of three other French African colonies, and especially to take over Brazzaville, capital of French Equatorial Africa. This task de Gaulle entrusted to Colonel Larminat. This brilliant and courageous officer had arrived from Cairo. At the end of June 1940, as head of the Army of the Levant, he had tried without success to persuade his over-all commander, General Mittelhauser, to continue the struggle. He had urged that those French forces that did not want to accept the armistice would withdraw to Palestine to join the British, but Mittelhauser would not allow this. This position was assisted by the attitude of General Wavell, the British commander, who did not think that the French troops could be of any value. Despite this opposition, some French forces did manage to reach the British lines. For his daring, Larminat was placed under arrest, but he escaped.

With assistance from a sympathetic governor of the Belgian Congo, Ryckmans, Larminat prepared an expedition from that direction into Brazzaville. Sir Bernard Bourdillon, Governor General of Nigeria, provided the French party with his active support. On the 26th August Governor Eboué and Colonel Marchand declared that Chad had joined de Gaulle.

On the 27th August Leclerc and Boislambert succeeded brilliantly in taking over the Cameroons, managing this with very little in the way of practical strength. It had not been possible to provide them with military support. De Gaulle had found, in camp in England, about a thousand black French troops, from the Ivory Coast. They had arrived in England too late to re-enforce their units fighting in the battle for France. It had been arranged that these troops would return to Africa via the Gold Coast, but they were such good troops that the British commanders kept them in the Gold Coast to re-enforce the British garrison.

Without this military support the small party travelled to Douala by night, took control with the support of a few local Gaullists, and by morning Leclerc was in control as commander and governor of the territory. All this was accomplished without any major problem and with no bloodshed.

On the 28th August, at Brazzaville, Commandant Delange took over the governorship from Husson, without resistance but not without protest. Husson was replaced and sent back by boat to Leopoldville. At St. Mart the governor expressed his allegiance but some of the military threatened to fire on the town.

And so the greater part of French Equatorial Africa sided with de Gaulle and joined the Free French, but at Dakar the Vichy authorities had reacted quickly. They undid the work which had been achieved, removed some of those who had declared for the Free French, and put their own supporters back in power. Overall, however, the result was favourable for the Free French.

There would be a much greater difficulty in taking control of West Africa. It was under the control of the Vichy supporters in the North African territories and they had under their command strong military forces. Dakar was well fortified, with strong coastal batteries and there was also a strong air force detachment there. The Governor General at Dakar, Boisson, was a man of burning ambition and had thrown in his lot with the Vichy government. He had shown his determination in this direction when, on arrival in mid-July, he had imprisoned the governor of Upper Volta, who had declared in favour of de Gaulle.

The Free French did not have sufficient forces to contest the matter at that time. In any case, it would not have helped the Free French cause if they had started towards the liberation of France by engaging in all out conflict in Africa. De Gaulle found this setback, at Dakar, particularly hard to bear, after the progress which had been made. There was the possibility of a direct attack on Dakar. The alternative was a landing at some distance, with the possibility of gaining troops on the way to Dakar. If the more distant landing were to be tried and the troops brought up along the coast by train, their journey would have to be covered from the sea by vessels of the British fleet.

De Gaulle saw Churchill and put the plan to him, in the last days of July. Initially Churchill was doubtful about the plan, but on the 6th August, in the large room at Downing Street, which served as office and Cabinet meeting room, they pored over the large numbers of maps assembled on the very large table.

Churchill told de Gaulle that the idea of taking over Dakar had very great possibilities. It would be a tremendous advantage for the British. It could become a very important base in the battle of the Atlantic. After discussion with the Admiralty and the army chiefs of staff it had been agreed that the British would provide support for such an expedition. A large force would be provided, but this large force could not be spared to remain for long on the west coast of Africa. It would have to be quickly withdrawn for use in the defence of England and for use in the Mediterranean sphere of battle. Because of the need for a quick result from the use of such a large force it would not be possible to land the troops at a distance, so that Dakar would have to be taken by a frontal assault.

Churchill went on to elaborate in picturesque terms and he painted the following picture for de Gaulle. "Dakar will awake one morning, sad and uncertain. In the gold of an eastern sunrise the inhabitants will see an immense fleet, covering the sea into the distance, composed either of naval vessels or transport ships. Approaching slowly, the fleet will send a radio message to the military personnel and the people of Dakar, expressing friendship. Many ships will be bedecked with the tricolour. Others will fly the flags of Britain, Holland, Poland and Belgium. A small ship carrying a white flag will approach the shore first. General de Gaulle's envoys will step ashore. The governor will be made to understand that if he co-operates with the Free French the Allied fleet will retire, but the alternative will be a battle in which he will be destroyed."

And then Churchill went on to describe to de Gaulle the interview as he saw it. "During the conversation between the governor and your representatives some Free French and British aeroplanes will overfly the city, scattering leaflets expressing friendship. The military and civil authorities will discuss among themselves the advantages of taking up your cause and the alternative of a major battle, which would be with France's allies. The governor will know how badly the affair will turn out if he resists, but will seek the best terms. Perhaps, to maintain his honour, he will launch a few salvoes, but in the end he will dine with you and drink to a final victory."

Beneath Mr. Churchill's eloquence de Gaulle detected some sound thinking. The British could not detach such a large fleet for anything other than an immediate and speedy approach to Dakar. The British Admiralty might well decide, with or without the Free French, to take over Dakar. The need for an Atlantic base and the presence of the French battleship *Richelieu* could not help but excite British attention, interest, and action.

De Gaulle concluded that if he were to play a leading part in the action, there would be a good chance of rallying support for the Free French cause. Without the Free French, the British would eventually strike on their own account. If there were no Free French participation the battleship *Richelieu*, the coastal defences, and the air force squadrons would make it a bitter and bloody battle. The transports would be in very great danger, with no adequate defence so far from a friendly port. Even if eventually the British were to overwhelm Dakar's defences, they would be left with severe damage to Anglo-French relations which would affect every other theatre of war.

After a short delay de Gaulle accepted Churchill's proposal. The details of the plan were discussed with Admiral Cunningham. De Gaulle found him to be sometimes unwell, but an excellent naval officer and a good-hearted ally. The forces which could be gathered by de Gaulle were weak. The Free French fleet could muster only three small warships and two armed trawlers. The army contingent was also small, and carried on two Dutch ships. With all their supporting troops, the Free French mustered only two thousand men. The tanks were not on the same ship as their crews and the aircraft were to be brought still in their packing cases.

The British fleet which would support the operation would comprise two old battleships, *Barham* and *Resolution*, four cruisers, the aircraft carrier *Ark Royal*, several destroyers, and a tanker. In support, there would be two battalions of British infantry, with their means of unloading. The Polish brigade, which it had been arranged would form part of the force, was excluded. It seemed that the Prime Minister had become less aware of the importance of the expedition.

A few days before the expedition's departure the British raised the question of the destination of a store of gold which would be captured. There was some doubt as to whether it belonged to the Bank of France, the Belgian National Bank, or the Polish National Bank. When the Germans invaded France much of the French gold reserves had been sent to Senegal and another portion had been deposited at the United States Federal Reserve. The Belgians and the Poles, quite legitimately, wanted their portion to be safeguarded. But the British wanted to use these funds for the purchase of armaments, to be used in the united Allied cause, in the United States. At that time the United States would not supply anything unless the payment was made in advance. These disagreements over the ownership and destination of the money threatened the whole expedition. To undo the impasse de Gaulle agreed that the gold which belonged to France could be used by Britain in the United States, but only for the purchase of arms which would be used by the Free French. It would all be in the Allied cause.

Just as the troops embarked came the news of the rallying of Chad and the other French territories to the Free French cause. De Gaulle felt that even if the expedition to Dakar were not successful the Central African territories would form the base for action by French forces in the war and for French independent sovereignty.

The expedition sailed from Liverpool on the 31st August. De Gaulle himself was with the French troops and a reduced general staff on the *Westerland*. The atmosphere on board was one of great friendliness. The Free French staff left behind in England continued the assembly of an administration to cope with the growing numbers and strength of the Free French forces. General Catroux was expected to arrive shortly in London, from Indo China. De Gaulle left behind for him a letter of instructions and an outline of his plans. De Gaulle felt the enormity of the task before him as he left with his tiny force of small Free French ships, sliding away into the night, all lights extinguished, under an aerial bombardment. The fortunes of France hung by a thread.

The force reached Freetown, in Sierra Leone, where they

regrouped and obtained the latest information. But the voyage had taken nearly three weeks, to the 17th September, with a course having to be taken far out into the Atlantic to avoid aerial reconnaissance by the Germans finding them. The delay in the voyage had given the Vichy government a vital advantage. From Toulon, the French Mediterranean naval base, they had sent three heavy cruisers, three light cruisers, and supporting vessels. These had passed through the Straights of Gibraltar without the British navy intervening. After calling at Casablanca this fleet had already reached Dakar, joining the French battleship *Richelieu*. A further cruiser, the Primouguet, re-enforced the now very powerful fleet at Dakar.

De Gaulle received the very serious news that this fleet, observed at a distance by a British destroyer, had left on a southerly course. This could only mean that they intended to try and regain Vichy control of French Equatorial Africa, which de Gaulle's envoys had won over to the Free French cause. This possibility was confirmed when the captain of the cargo ship *Poitiers*, en route from Dakar to Libreville, was stopped by the English and scuttled by her captain rather than be taken. It was clear that the Vichy government was launching a major expedition to regain the French territories which the Free French had taken. Admiral Cunningham agreed with de Gaulle on this. The British ships were too slow to overtake the French force, but if battle were to be joined they should be able to overpower the French fleet. Admiral Bourrague was surprised by British cruisers, so that the French fleet returned hastily to Dakar when the news of the presence of the Anglo-French fleet became known. This about turn by the French fleet removed the danger to the Free French African colonies, but it increased the difficulties of taking Dakar. The authorities there were now fully on guard, and were re-enforced by a powerful fleet. They replaced the colonial forces manning the coastal batteries with naval gunners. The chances of success at Dakar were much reduced.

In London, Churchill and the Admiralty considered that these events should cause the expedition to be abandoned. They suggested that the large escort fleet should take the Free French ships to Douala, and then perhaps elsewhere. De Gaulle thought this to be the worst solution. If everything was left unchanged at Dakar the Vichy authorities could await the withdrawal of the British fleet to the north and then have a free hand to retake the other African colonies. The Free French in Central Africa could be blockaded and all their efforts nullified. They would be prevented from taking any effective part in the struggle against the Germans or Italians.

However difficult things were in West and Central Africa there was better news elsewhere. The French Oceanic territories and the French territories in the Indies declared for de Gaulle. Then St. Pierre and Miquelon, the tiny colony off Newfoundland, came to de Gaulle's side. Other small oceanic colonies later declared for de Gaulle. With these favourable sets of news, how could Dakar resist?

Churchill later said that he was pleasantly surprised at the proposed action, and readily agreed. Because of the small size of the Free French forces Admiral Cunningham tried to take command of them, and to soften the blow he offered hospitality to de Gaulle on board the battleship HMS *Barham*. De Gaulle then declined to accept both the take over and the hospitality. At this the admiral sent over a letter late at night renouncing his takeover intentions. They upped anchor on the 21st September and at dawn on the 23rd approached Dakar in thick fog.

The fog greatly hampered the enterprise. Instead of Churchill's intention of making a great show of force as the fleet approached, to over awe the garrison and the population, the fleet was quite invisible from the shore. It was impossible to delay: the plan had to go ahead. Promptly at 6 o'clock de Gaulle used the radio to address the armed forces and the inhabitants. He announced the arrival of the fleet and their friendly intentions. Soon after the broadcast two small French light civil aircraft took off from the aircraft carrier *Ark Royal*. They were carrying three officers who were going to land at the airfield at Ouakam, where their mission was to make friendly overtures to the garrison. De Gaulle received the message 'Success, we have landed safely.'

Then the shock. Suddenly artillery and naval gunfire opened

up. The battleship *Richelieu* started to fire on Free French and British planes that were flyng over the city. The planes had been dropping leaflets expressing friendship. De Gaulle sent two small craft carrying the politicians in to the shore. The larger ships carrying the Free French forces then approached the port through the fog. As the ships approached there was no reaction and the leading ships tied up and started to unload their troops. Their commanders sought out the commander of the port. They were carrying a letter from General de Gaulle to the Governor General, written in the general's own hand.

However the envoy who received them told the officials that they were under arrest and at the same time he called out the guard. Seeing this Free French withdrew to their ships, but they were fired on. Two of the Free French were seriously wounded in this contact and were brought back aboard the *Westerland*.

The shore batteries then started an intermittent fire on the British and Free French ships. The *Richelieu* had manoeuvred in the harbour to better train her guns and she now opened fire. By about 11 o'clock the cruiser *Cumberland* had been severely damaged. Admiral Cunningham then radioed "I am not firing on you. Why are you firing on me?" The reply he received was "Retreat twenty miles." The English reply was several salvoes. It was clear that there was no serious intention on either side for serious combat. Up until midday no Vichy aircraft had taken to the air. De Gaulle did not think that the Vichy forces wanted to put up a very serious opposition. Perhaps they were looking for some pretext for a reconciliation. At midday Admiral Cunningham sent de Gaulle a message expressing the same view. He wondered if it would be possible to land the Free French troops at the nearby small port of Rufisque. This was not possible because of the shallow water. It would mean landing without any heavy weapon support.

At about three o'clock the *Commandant Duboc* entered the port. Locals were waiting to greet them but the Vichy forces opened fire. A few moments later two Glenn-Martin bombers flew low over the British and French ships to show that they could bomb at will.

Admiral Cunningham telegraphed that the French cruisers *Georges Leygues* and *Montcalm* had left the harbour in the smoke and were only a mile away. The British warships were otherwise engaged and could not cover the invasion force. It was clear that surprise and with it every chance of success had been lost. It would not be possible to land an invading force and there was a danger that a few salvoes from the Vichy cruisers would destroy the Free French forces. De Gaulle decided to withdraw to the open sea to avoid serious losses.

The next day the British fleet had received orders from Churchill to press home the affair with an ultimatum to the Vichy authorities in Dakar. They replied that they would not give in. There followed, through the smoke, a lively exchange of fire between the British ships and the land batteries and the ships in the harbour. By the afternoon it was clear that there would be no certain outcome from these exchanges.

As evening fell the battleship *Barham* came alongside the *Westerland*. De Gaulle went into conference with Admiral Cunningham in a sombre atmosphere. He was upset that he had not succeeded in subduing the opposition. The British could not understand how or why the French forces in Dakar should put up such fierce opposition to their compatriots and their allies when France itself was under the jackboot of the invader.

Admiral Cunnningham assessed the situation. He did not think that continuing the bombardment would produce a satisfactory outcome. General Irwin was ready to disembark the land forces, but there would be great dangers for the landing craft and to the soldiers. What was the Free French advice? De Gaulle replied that the bombardment could settle nothing. To land troops against fierce opposition would damage every advantage that could be gained and he was against it. The attempt to seize Dakar would have to be abandoned lest it become a bloody shambles.

Admiral Cunningham was to announce the cessation of the bombardment and state that it was under the orders of General de Gaulle. But a blockade would be imposed to limit the action of the Vichy controlled ships in the harbour. It might be possible to enter Dakar by an overland attack launched after disembarking at a place which was less well defended, such as Saint-Louis. The Free French would not abandon the enterprise.

During the night a telegram was received from Churchill urging the forces to press on with the enterprise. He was annoyed that the attack had been cut short and that this had given a propaganda victory to the Vichy French and the Germans, which they were exploiting in world-wide radio broadcasts. In any case the fog was lifting and there would be a better chance of an effective attack. In particular the affair had given a bad impression in Washington.

Without consulting de Gaulle further the bombardment was resumed at dawn. Towards evening the battleship *Resolution* was torpedoed by a submarine and had to retire. Several other British ships were also severely damaged. Four planes from the *Ark Royal* were shot down. On the other side the battleship *Richelieu* and several buildings were damaged. The destroyer Audacieux and the submarines *Persée* and *Ajax* were sunk. The crew of the Ajax were rescued by an English destroyer. But the guns in the land forts were still firing. Admiral Cunningham decided to break off the battle and the fleet sailed away to Freetown.

The following days were very depressing for de Gaulle. It was as if he had been hit by an earthquake. In London there was fury. In Washington the Anglo- French efforts were derided and de Gaulle was the subject of ridicule. The whole failure was blamed on de Gaulle. He was likened to a Don Quixote. In truth the cruisers which the Vichy government had sent from Toulon had tipped the balance. The knowledge of the impending invasion was thought to have leaked from Free French sources. It was made clear that there was no confidence that the Free French could keep their mouths shut. It was thought that de Gaulle's position had been so damaged by the affair that the British would abandon him and turn to General Catroux or Admiral Muselier.

And Vichy made the most of the affair, treating it as a great naval victory. The might of the British navy had been repulsed. It was as if Trafalgar had, at last, been avenged. Showers of telegrams of congratulation were poured on Governor Boisson for his heroic defence. General Weygand came especially from France to invest him with the Croix de Guerre.

De Gaulle felt abandoned and beaten by this setback. But it soon became clear to him that the Free French were, in truth, unbreakable. When he visited the troops who had taken part in the attack they all were hostile to any idea that he should give up. Their resolution had been re-enforced by the attitude of the Vichy forces. When an aircraft from Dakar overflew the fleet it was met with furious anti-aircraft fire from every side. Soon he received telegrams of support from Generals de Larminat and Leclerc, expressing their every confidence in him. London also expressed support. These messages brought him great comfort at such a difficult time and this showed how firm were the foundations of the Free French.

Back in London the affair gave grounds for malevolence, but it did not disrupt the relationship between Churchill and de Gaulle. In the House of Commons a resolution was passed expressing the British Government's full confidence in de Gaulle. Churchill knew how the British failure to prevent the passage through the straits of Gibraltar of the French ships from Toulon had overturned the invading force's advantage. It had been a devastating failure. Two months later he admitted this to de Gaulle. And yet London had known about the movement of these French ships. A secret message from a Free French sympathiser in Tangiers had brought the news, but the message had arrived during an air raid and it had been delayed and the delay lost the opportunity of intercepting the ships. A similar warning had come from the British naval attaché in Madrid, who had been alerted by the Vichy government's naval attaché there. So two messages had been disregarded. It certainly was not a Free French failure.

The attitude of the public was much less hostile to de Gaulle and this, in turn, softened the attitude of the Prime Minister, Parliament, and the press. It certainly gave the Americans the idea that if at any future date they were to land troops on a shore controlled by Vichy forces that they were likely to be opposed.

There was no possibility of renewing the offensive at Dakar. The Free French were escorted to the Cameroons and then the British fleet sailed away. De Gaulle had travelled in the *Commandant Duboc*. When he arrived in Douala General Leclerc was waiting for him and the French forces which had come from England disembarked. The local population were concerned about trade in and out of the country but the arrival of these forces reassured them and the Free French spirits in Africa immediately revived. It was the saving grace of the whole enterprise. Wherever he went de Gaulle was greeted enthusiastically. The whole experience rejuvenated everyone's spirits.

It was time to prepare an offensive. The French forces could attack from the deserts of Chad and Libya and eventually break through to the shores of the Mediterranean. If this was not immediately possible de Gaulle was keen to prepare a military formation which could go to the aid of the British in the Middle East. In Chad the troops were keen, but poorly equipped. When de Gaulle told them that he expected them to fight their way through to the Mediterranean they were stupefied.

Back in London Churchill, in de Gaulle's absence, had suggested to General Catroux that he should take de Gaulle's place. Churchill had wanted to send Catroux via Cairo to the Levant to mobilise the forces. De Gaulle had managed to deflect Churchill from this proposal. Catroux's action in refusing these approaches caused de Gaulle to raise a glass in his honour and re-enforce their friendship. The loyalty Catroux had shown in these affairs was the fulfilment of every loyal duty. A split in the leadership of the Free French at that time might very well have destroyed them.

In Brazzaville de Gaulle found this poorest of the French empire's African colonies struggling economically. With some useful exports there was a little income, but the lack of manufacturing meant that the colony was short of an adequate income to maintain the full array of services. On the 27th October de Gaulle, in a speech later termed 'The Manifesto of Brazzaville,' chastised the Vichy government for its subjugation to the Germans and the co-operation which followed and stated that the Empire would never accept such servitude. Opposition was a sacred duty. In the Belgian Congo de Gaulle received a moving reception, with the Belgians joining the French inhabitants in the welcome. The Governor, Ryckmans, wanted the Belgian Congo to join the Free

French cause. This would have been against the terms of the Belgian capitulation, but there was a determination across central Africa to support the Allied cause.

In Gabon there was some Vichy resistance, with a small aerial bombardment. In other areas there was also Vichyite resistance. At Libreville possible battles could have been worse. If the British had not agreed to prevent French Vichy ships sailing south from Dakar the Free French position would not have been tenable.

When de Gaulle visited the wounded from these encounters he found that some of the Vichyites wanted to join the Free French. Dakar, Vichy and Paris radio stations denounced de Gaulle's activities in Africa, actions which showed that they at least were having an effect. Atrocities were claimed to have been committed - charges which were made to cover up earlier actions of the Vichy authorities in the region. It was clear that these charges could result in punishment of the unarmed representatives whom de Gaulle had landed by air in Dakar. He therefore proposed exchanging them for Vichy supporters captured elsewhere in equatorial Africa. When de Gaulle pointed out that he held enough Vichy supporters to hold in the balance against the lives of the Free French held in Dakar, the tone of the broadcasts from Dakar softened immediately.

These events in Africa did much to dissipate the temporary euphoria with which the Vichy government had consoled itself after the armistice. They had thought that they had done well to re-establish some form of assembly in Vichy and a supreme court at Riom, a town near Vichy. French generals were able to inspect French troops. In the rump of the country under their apparent control those who had led the country to surrender could pretend some air of normality.

Within France the news of the actions of the Free French was stirring the embers of French resistance and the Germans became aware that their own actions could be a cause of this activity. Stirred into some sort of action on the next day planes from Morocco bombed Gibraltar. In Madrid the Vichy authorities opened negotiations with the British to seek passage from Africa of cargoes bound for the Vichy section of France. The British informed de Gaulle of these meetings. The Vichy government gave an assurance that if the Germans benefited from such trade the Vichy government would transfer to North Africa and resume the war on Britain's side. De Gaulle warned the British to be wary. How could those who had surrendered to the Germans, condemned those who continued the fight, and had placed themselves under the jurisdiction of German laws now be trusted? The Americans and King George VIth had sent encouraging messages to Marshal Petain; contacts had been maintained with French military leaders in North Africa, but under the German pressure there could be no illusions other than that Vichy France was completely under German control. On the 24th October 1940 Petain met Hitler at Montoire. Collaboration with the Germans was officially confirmed. In early November Vichy broke off the negotiations with the British in Madrid.

This finally put an end to any idea that the Vichy government had a legal right to represent the interests of France. De Gaulle solemnly undertook to look after the legal responsibilities of the Republic and to be accountable for his actions at the time of the renaissance of France's full freedom. At Brazzaville. on the 27th October, de Gaulle announced that the people of the Empire would not accept such 'horrible servitude' as the Montoire agreement between Hitler and Petain stated. A new power would have to direct French efforts in the war. "These events charge me with this sacred duty, and I will not fail." He announced the formation of a council for the defence of the Empire, formed of those in charge of the administration in the territories and senior military figures and enshrining the highest values of the nation. On the 5th November de Gaulle formally notified the British government of these arrangements. It was to end any hopes the British had of turning Vichy supporters such as Weygand onto the Allied side.

Not all de Gaulle's aims in Africa had been achieved, but the Free French effort was now firmly established, from the Sahara to the Congo and from the Atlantic to the Nile basin. A military force was assembled to attack the Italian forces in Eritrea. It was the start of Free French activity in the Middle East campaign. To mount such efforts across the vast distances of central Africa was a difficult undertaking, but the enthusiasm of all concerned drove the effort forward relentlessly.

In returning to London in mid-November de Gaulle was acutely aware of the difficulties of the journey to avoid the territories controlled by the Germans and the Italians. It emphasised the difficulties facing the Free French, but the efforts being undertaken showed the unrelenting determination of the Free French supporters.

LONDON, NOVEMBER 1940

When de Gaulle returned to London he found the mood sombre. The British were proud that they had survived the German aerial onslaught preparatory to invasion and the victory of the Battle of Britain had removed that danger. The submarine war was raging and endangering the supplies necessary to feed the nation and continue the war. England's life and England's glory were at risk on the high seas.

Following the fall of France slow convoys could no longer survive in the Mediterranean. Troops and supplies for Egypt had to take the long and dangerous route round the Cape of Good Hope, while the routes to India, Australia and New Zealand had been greatly lengthened. The need for convoys to zig-zag to avoid submarines lengthened the voyages even from the United States and Canada. These longer voyages made ever greater demands on the convoy escorts, but none of these actions had succeeded in persuading the Americans to enter the war. American opinion was certainly hostile to Hitler and Mussolini, but the political climate was still isolationist and focussed on neutrality, and neutrality was their law. This was the law. Britain was having to pay in gold for its purchases from the United States. Shares owned by British citizens were taken over by the British government and sold to defray the costs of armaments. It was coming to a situation where Britain would no longer be able to afford to stay in the war.

A Russo-German pact was signed in January 1941. This added to the pact Germany and Italy had signed with Japan in October 1940. Hungary and Romania joined the Axis in this period. Franco had met Hitler and the actions of the Vichy government further enhanced the German position.

Against this progress in Hitler's cause the British people mobilised, to the armed forces, to the factories, and to the production of food. Rationing was strictly enforced and penalties for taking part in the black market were severe. Many British cities were badly damaged in the Blitz. The people had to leave their beds every night to take shelter and in London this meant for many going down to sleep on the platforms of the Underground stations.

Pre-occupied with survival, the British Government had little time to attend to the Free French cause as a separate issue. Everything needed to be incorporated in the overwhelming struggle. It was difficult for the British to see the point at that time of dealing with the Free French as a special and separate entity. In such desperate circumstances the future possibilities of a growing ally were not in the forefront for attention. The needs of the Free French for equipment and support to start more aggressive involvement would be an additional drain on British resources and would be a cause of friction. The Free French, hastily recruited from many sources, man by man, would not quickly have the stable organisation to make them an immediately available fighting resource. All the functions of a government to control not only military affairs but also all the administration of a full nation's organisation were in a disordered state. The difficulties for the Free French caused some resignations of those who found the tasks too daunting, causing disquiet amongst both the Free French supporters and the Free French allies.

De Gaulle had to take a very firm control of the Free French affairs, but in the midst of this turmoil the British government was brutally misled in an 'intelligence' matter. The British intelligence at this time was of variable quality, and this led to a serious mistake. On the first of January 1941 de Gaulle was summoned from his home in Shropshire by Anthony Eden to the Foreign Office. Eden presented a report that Admiral Muselier had been in secret contact with the Vichy government and that he had sent to Admiral Darlan details of the expedition to Dakar. Churchill had given orders that Admiral Muselier was to be arrested. This decision had been approved by the whole British Cabinet and the Admiral had indeed been arrested. Eden had rushed to inform de Gaulle of these sudden events, but the urgency of the affair had prevented de Gaulle being informed before the action.

Eden showed de Gaulle documentary evidence to support the charges. The damning messages had been passed to Vichy through a South American embassy in London. When these documents had been intercepted by British Intelligence they had been assessed as genuine and had led to the British action. This appeared to be too trite to de Gaulle. The Camembert smelled too strong! De Gaulle treated what he had been told with the greatest reserve, because it all appeared to be a cleverly contrived Vichy plot. After considering the matter for forty eight hours de Gaulle told the British Government that the documents produced were highly suspicious, not only because of their content but also because of the sources from which British Intelligence had obtained them. The documents themselves did not contain any substantive proof and there was nothing in them to justify the outrageous action of the British in arresting a French admiral. De Gaulle had not been shown the proof. It was essential that Admiral Muselier should be released form prison and treated honourably until the matter had been fully explored and the truth brought into the open.

This produced a great quandary for Anthony Eden. The charges were most serious, involving treason. De Gaulle issued a formal note of protest. He invited the First Sea Lord, Sir Dudley Pound, to intervene in the matter, as a fellow Admiral. Suddenly the British started to vacillate and they seemed much less sure of their ground. It was arranged for de Gaulle to meet Admiral Muselier at Scotland Yard, not in a cell but in an office and without any guard present. This showed to the world that de Gaulle did not believe the allegations. It came to light that two officers taken into the Free French intelligence service in London while de Gaulle was in Africa had laid the false trail. Unfortunately it was the British who had insisted that these officers should be employed by the Free French. Investigations revealed that their background in intelligence had been falsified.

De Gaulle made this clear to General Spears on the 8th January. He insisted that the British Government should release Admiral Muselier within twenty four hours. If the British Government did not comply de Gaulle would break off all relations with the British Government, with serious long term consequences. Later that day General Spears came to de Gaulle to inform him that the error had now been recognised, the supposed documents had been proved to be forgeries, and that the Admiral had been released. The next day the Attorney General came to see de Gaulle and stated that legal measures were being taken against the perpetrators. These were mainly British officers. The Attorney General wanted de Gaulle to appoint a Free French officer to take part in the investigation. Later that day Churchill and Eden received de Gaulle at Downing Street and expressed their profound apologies over the affair. They would make amends to Admiral Muselier over the gross insult which he had suffered.

This affair could do nothing but sour de Gaulle's view of his British allies. In the event de Gaulle records that the effects were not entirely bad. To compensate for their error the British showed themselves much more ready to make advances in furthering the Free French progress. The Free French were given authority to set up judicial authorities over their own citizens in British territories. They made arrangements with the British Treasury for financial and monetary agreement.

This improvement in relations made possible the formation of a sound Free French organisation to control activities throughout the Empire. It would be possible to organise the financial control of all Free French activities and pay for them. In effect the British would provide financial support and services for the Free French under de Gaulle's command. An exchange rate of 176 Francs to the pound was established, which enabled a Free French Bank and Treasury to be set up in London. It enabled the Free French to set up a full trading position to allow the territories of the empire to support the cause.

All this was excellent for organising the empire, but what about Metropolitan France? Where were the means and the people to start organising action against the German occupation to start towards liberation? What arrangements could be made for the re-establishment of the French State after the Liberation?

The establishment of an organised resistance movement would be a new theatre of war. Some stocks of military supplies had been retained under Vichy control after the armistice. If hostilities were to be renewed these might be brought into use, but there was no foundation on which to build. There was one advantage. The action of the Vichy government in depriving de Gaulle of his citizenship and sentencing him to death had freed him from any need to pay attention to their pronouncements.

GENERAL DE GAULLE AND QUEEN ELIZABETH

They had declared him beyond the pale, but once there he was free to roam, to plot, and to build the machine for their destruction. And he was not alone!

By some strange twist of fate there was a part of the adult generation in 1940 which was ready for clandestine operations. The youth of the inter war generation had shown a special interest and aptitude for intelligence work and secret activity. Many theatrical and film plots had reflected this interest. This psychological focus made it much easier to recruit for these secret adventures than would otherwise have been the case, but it also ran the danger of giving these activities a falsely romantic gloss. What had to be realised was that the Germans would not be idle against such actions. The taking of hostages would be common and the number of innocent Frenchmen shot would run into thousands. It would not be until the liberation that he true cost of these activities would become clear. No one could foresee that each of the near one hundred lamp posts in the town of Tulle would be the gallows from which a Frenchman would die by hanging. The cause of freedom could not flourish without the greatest bravery and sacrifice.

Commandant Dewavrin, code named Passy, was chosen to lead the Resistance. He was seized with a cold passion for the task which the hardships and the setbacks which would be encountered made in every way necessary. An embryo organisation had to be set up in France. The British wanted all secret agents to act independently, so that no spread of arrests due to knowledge of a network could follow the arrest of a single agent. The Free French position was to set up a forceful organisation of great strength. The tasks and purposes were complementary but different.

Day after day, or rather night after night, efforts were made to recruit for the secret army. Infiltration of the organisers into France was done by parachute, trawlers landing them secretly on the coast, small aircraft landing at night, or by infiltration across the borders from Portugal or Spain. With Allied support the men and material grew, but it was still not an effective organisation during the winter of 1940-41. The British still had to be fully convinced that all this effort would produce a useful addition to Allied strength when the time came for invasion. It was difficult for the British to see that if the French enthusiasm were to produce a really effective force it would have to be large, well organised, and therefore would have to be independent. The dangers to be faced by those encouraging the formation of a secret army would need the fervour, the idealism, and the hope of the restoration of a liberated France. As the force grew it could not achieve the support it needed if it were subservient to British command.

The Free French knew that they were dependent on the British for all support and supplies, but for those in France the idea that Great Britain and de Gaulle were the same thing could only cause difficulties later. Free French demands were taxing Britain's abilities, but a good cause was never refused. But there would also be some serious disputes. De Gaulle well understood the value of making broadcasts on the BBC wavelengths. The British also understood the value to the Allied cause of nationals of the occupied countries speaking to their own peoples, but the British also wanted to retain control. De Gaulle would not submit to any British control of his broadcasts.

These were seriously differing points of view. They were accommodated by the Free French being given broadcasting periods of five minutes each, twice a day, while the BBC employed French journalists to provide a service of programmes 'Frenchmen speaking to Frenchmen.' With de Gaulle's approval many Free French contributors took part in these BBC programmes. Free French journals were also published, with the assistance of the British authorities. When there were later quarrels about the contents of the programmes there was still a channel for independent Free French broadcasts from central Africa.

De Gaulle paid great attention to the short five minute Free French programmes broadcast by the BBC each day. Maurice Schumann was the most frequent broadcaster in these programmes. De Gaulle himself broadcast about every eight days in these programmes, understanding well the large audiences and their wide geographical spread. He kept his message simple. He described the course of the war and the mistake of the capitulation. He expressed national pride and the way in which continued actions against the enemy were keeping the French cause alive. It expressed the hope of final victory and the need to re-establish the grandeur and glory of France.

These broadcasts were so effective that Parisian students, on the 11th November,1940, formed a solemn procession to the Arc de Triomphe which German troops had to disperse with gunfire. Under de Gaulle's influence, on the 1st January, a large part of the population and in particular in the occupied zone, stayed at home, leaving the streets empty, and observing an 'hour of hope.' But in the Vichy controlled area there were few who contested Marshal Petain's authority. The Marshal was still popular, for he had kept the German troops out of a large part of France. Films of his visits to numerous towns and cities and of his taking part in such activities as the reopening of school classes were widely shown. Many in the population thought that Petain and de Gaulle had a secret accord which would save and restore France. Such propaganda had no basis.

The most pressing battle was the one in Africa. It was agreed with General Wavell, the British commander, that French troops from Somalia and Cyprus would join the Allied forces in the battle for Tobruk and Derna. A French battalion fought well at Sidi Barrani. But the main task was to form a full division in the French territories on the Red sea. This was done, but it was only lightly armed.

The British had first to deal with the Italian armies in Ethiopia and Eritrea. A French force, after orders from de Gaulle to Generals Larminat and Catroux, played a part in the action. The French forces had some tanks available. Other forces were drawn from Chad, with Spahis coming from Syria, and with some troops from the Foreign Legion. Four battalions from Senegal were also brought into the battle. French pilots, equipped with Blenheim bombers sent from England, were based in Khartoum. French Somalia had a garrison of 10,000 well equipped troops. De Gaulle was keen to bring them into the battle, but they had already declared allegiance to Vichy.

In London the British supported de Gaulle's moves to bring more French troops into the Allied fight. It was agreed with

General Wavell that the French troops would fight under his orders. At the same time de Gaulle urged Churchill to acknowledge the French contribution. From Chad, General Leclerc had crossed the desert and taken the Italian outpost at Mourzouk, linking up eventually with a British patrol which had come south from Egypt. Spreading out over 1000 kilometres of desert Leclerc's troops attacked Italian outposts and on the 1st March 1941 forced an Italian surrender. At this time the British were advancing in Libya. The Allies were on the march!

But it was still the enemy who was controlling the direction of the war. Would the Germans invade North Africa in the west via Gibraltar and in the east coming down from the Balkans and through Suez? The Free French troops were still very weak and unable to counter any such major attack.

In November 1940 Italy had attacked Greece, while on the 1st March 1941 Germany invaded through Bulgaria, attacking Greece and Yugoslavia. As soon as Greece was invaded de Gaulle sent General Metaxas, the Greek Prime Minister, a message of support on behalf of France. But de Gaulle could not obtain transport to send a small but symbolic force, nor could General Wavell spare any substantial forces to help the Greeks.

At the start of February 1941 a German mission arrived in Syria. Their purposes were to stir up trouble to facilitate any later German advance into southern Russia. In the Far East Japan was threatening and this put additional demands on the already over-stretched British forces. It also threatened a whole range of French territories, from Indo-China to New Caledonia. This was a threat that de Gaulle had no means to counter. He was informed of the Japanese take over of Siam and Laos, and of pressure on Indo China, by both the British and the Dutch in London. Messages from everywhere showed that there was no force able to prevent the Japanese taking over French Indo China. America was in no way ready to enter any conflict. If nothing could be done to save Indo-China it was clear that Australia and New Zealand were keen to prevent any Japanese take over of New Caledonia or Tahiti. In discussions with Prime Minister Menzies, of Australia, de Gaulle agreed that common defence would not undermine French sovereignty.

These difficulties strengthened the alliance between France and Britain and De Gaulle was better regarded. De Gaulle thought that the King was always very well informed; the Queen and all members of the Royal family were keen to keep in close touch about current affairs. These good relations existed with all government ministers and in particular Mr. Churchill. But nothing could divert their attention from the primary needs of Britain. Nothing could undermine their full focus on their public duties, but equally they were not without flashes of humour in these darkest hours. These were qualities which de Gaulle often, and greatly, admired. This also produced a forceful British cohesion which de Gaulle sometimes had to counter.

Sometimes these were difficult pressures from the British side and the atmosphere was often soured by unhelpful comment in the British press. Amongst these doubts and difficulties there was one thing that was certain. It would always be possible for some accommodation to be reached. It would never be necessary to give a blunt "No." This was a time when the British could not see any clear direction for the progress of the Free French cause. "Where do you want to go?" they asked de Gaulle. But de Gaulle had severe difficulties. Not every Frenchman with whom he now made contact rallied to his support. Frenchmen were still split between loyalty to what was the nominal legal government in Vichy and the hope of French restoration under de Gaulle's leadership. But de Gaulle had been convicted, condemned and sentenced to death by a court martial. Did he have any legal authority? Would anyone associated him in any way be subject to a similar sentence? These were serious doubts at a time when the Allied cause was suffering so many reverses. What might be the punishment meted out to relatives still in France?

If these doubts assailed those in French territories overseas and particularly in Lebanon, Syria and North Africa they did not seem to dismay in any way those Free French assembled in London. There was a burning desire to further the cause by getting into action. There was tremendous loyalty to de Gaulle as the sole inspiration for the resurrection of France as a free and great country. A French officer, known as 'Andre the Zouave' from his military command, was desperately keen to return to his unit in north Africa and get quickly into battle. To maintain contact with what was happening in London he wanted a radio which would work in the desert to allow him to retain contact by listening to the BBC. He found a portable radio which would do the job in the possession of a French supporter in London. In those days such long range radio receivers worked on a high tension battery of about 90 volts and a low tension lead acid accumulator which was usually recharged every few weeks at a local garage. The high-tension batteries lasted about six months of reasonable use. He swapped a large Philips mains receiver for this little battery model. He managed to obtain several of the high-tension batteries. The accumulator could be recharged from a vehicle's circuits. And so, with his new means of retaining contact he went off to war.

After these difficulties there was a sudden lack of liaison between the French and the British. No telephones rang. There were no meetings. There were no dinners - only an impenetrable silence. It was as if a chapter had closed.

And yet there were great opportunities to work together. Such misunderstandings could not be allowed to get in the way of the joint purpose. The press reversed their previous hostile attitude and were more benign. And so the common cause was recognised and the British freeze thawed. The real base reason for the problems remained obscure, but such mistrust had no virtue or value.

It was clear that at the start of March 1941 that the war was going to become more active. This would be in the face of the obstinate opposition of Vichy and dissention amongst the allies.

But all was not gloom. While a guest of Churchill at Chequers, at dawn on the 9th of March, de Gaulle was woken by a Prime Minister dancing for joy. The news that the American Congress had passed the 'Lease-Lend' Bill was a massive relief after weeks of anxious negotiations. At last there could be confidence that the armaments and supplies with which to fight the war would be made available. The United States would earn the title 'The Arsenal of the Democracies.'

In such an exuberant mood Churchill took the opportunity immediately to mend his relations with de Gaulle and to ask him to go to the Orient and Africa to take care of affairs. He asked it of de Gaulle as a personal favour and de Gaulle could do nothing but comply. In this way they parted on renewed good terms.

So by the 14th March de Gaulle was on his way to Africa. The original agreements entered into by the British Government on the 24th December 1940 with the Free French Council for the Defence of the Empire were fully re-instated and re-affirmed. French political leaders were now in support of the Free French cause and several middle ranking French officers had arrived from South America to add strength and experience to the Free French armed forces.

In every area of the Americas Free French diplomatic representation was firmly in place. There was something to look forward to. The introduction of the Order of the Liberation had given the Free French a means of recognition of the highest quality of service for the cause. On his journey, firstly to Africa, de Gaulle was received as a Head of State in the British territories on his route. In the French African territories all doubt had gone and confidence was growing. It was time to go on the attack and start out on the road to the liberation of France.

THE ORIENT

De Gaulle clearly understood the importance to the British Empire and the Allied cause of the Suez Canal. Control of this vital waterway could allow the re-enforcement of the troops who would have to fight their way westwards along the North African coast towards Tunisia and then use that control as a springboard for an attack on Italy and the south of France. Free France could not stay idle in such a struggle. The French Central African territories were a springboard for attack and a passage for aircraft to be delivered across the Atlantic from the United States. It would avoid the perils of a long journey round the Cape.

There was a severe danger that the Germans would attack through the Balkans to the oil centres of the Middle East. The attack on Italian forces in Eritrea was, under the command of General Platt, assisted by French troops and air forces, but the British were loath to employ too many French forces. If the British re-enforced the French and the French played a large part in any victory the defeat of the Italians would not be entirely a British triumph and the French would claim their share of the territorial spoils. If French forces out of Djibouti were part of the victorious troops France could claim too large a share of control of Eritrea, Ethiopia, Abyssinia, Somalia and the Sudan. Such an attitude only supported Vichy attempts to divide the British and the Free French.

De Gaulle visited a French brigade, which, with a Hindu division, formed the left flank of the Allied assault on the Keren. When de Gaulle asked the successful French commander, who had come across the desert from Algiers to take part in the combat, for his thoughts the reply was "If only those in the west could see how well we have done, they would have no doubts." By the 7th April French forces had taken the capital of Eritrea and received the surrender of the Italian naval forces in the Red Sea. A total of 14,000 Italian prisoners were captured in this campaign, but still French Somalia stayed out of the war, denying the French troops a direct route along the railway line from Djibouti to Addis-Ababa.

At this time the British situation in Cairo was somewhat unstable. There was an underground current of hostility from

Egyptian nationalists who were waiting to see if a German victory in the desert could open opportunities for independence for Egypt. Their trust in Germany as an ally would have been badly misplaced.

British successes in Libya were short lived. The introduction of the Africa Korps under General Rommel would lead to the loss of Tobruk and to the British being pushed back almost to the gates of Cairo. The number of British prisoners taken in the fall of Tobruk would be disastrous, and this would so undermine Churchill's authority that he would face censure in the House of Commons. Only the lack of any other shining knight for the field of battle would leave him in power, but the wound to his pride and the damage to his position would be everlasting. Worse, the wound would not heal with a scar: it would be a painful, persisting and powerful damage whose effects would last forever. His hostility to those Labour members of parliament who were the focus of the rebellion would be life long and the hatred of them for their political treachery would persist beyond fifty years. These were the type of men who would pull the bung from the bottom of a lifeboat.

In these difficult times de Gaulle appreciated the strengths and qualities of the British Commander in Chief in the Middle East, General Wavell. He understood fully the folly of sending insufficient forces to support the Greeks whilst the desert battle was being lost. Too little, too far, and too weak: there was just not enough strength to do the job. Add to this German intrigues in Syria and unrest in Iraq and the situation in the whole of Middle East threatened to disintegrate, with the loss of the Suez canal threatened and the need to withdraw the British fleet from Alexandria.

The Allied forces in the Middle East at that time had many Australian, New Zealand and South African units. Their governments were pressing to see victories for their efforts. The Indian troops also wanted and needed to see some sign for victory. General Wavell found himself in a hotbed of intrigue and political doubt in Cairo. Throughout he kept a steady nerve and firm control, but it was the shortage of forces to keep the enemy at bay on any front but the Ethiopian, and above all to secure a victory over the Germans anywhere, which undermined his position.

De Gaulle could do nothing to help in Egypt, but in Syria and Lebanon he put General Catroux to the task of taking control of these countries, or at least blocking any German advance there. If the Germans gained control France's cause would be lost and if there was a vacuum Britain might take France's place in the area. But the French forces in Syria and Lebanon were still chained to Vichy authority. Many of the French troops who had been in these countries at the time of the armistice in June 1940 had been demobilised and sent back to France. 'Gaullists' had been arrested. In short, Free French progress in the two countries would not be quick.

In Alexandria Admiral Godfroy's agreement with Admiral Cunningham that French ships in the port would be neutralised left one battleship, *Lorraine*, four cruisers, three destroyers and one submarine at anchor. Few of these naval forces were willing to fight on the Allied side. They were holding to their instructions from Vichy. It was appalling for de Gaulle to see, on a visit to Admiral Cunningham in Alexandria harbour, these fine French warships lying quiet and useless to the Allied cause.

De Gaulle had tried to convert some senior French generals, such as Weygand to the Allied side by secret messages of friendship, but these approaches had been rebutted. In a broadcast on the 28th December 1940 de Gaulle had spoken on the radio to all French officers. He urged them to draw forth their swords and join those of the African empire in resuming the fight. In January he had asked the Defence Council what should be their attitude if the Vichy government, or at least part of it, would decide to renew the struggle. The view of all was that any who wanted to join the cause of French liberation would be welcomed.

None of these approaches were successful. Weygand replied that de Gaulle ought to be shot. From Beirut came a correct but cold reply and the enemy were already in position in Syria. The best the Free French could do was to put their small force at General Wavell's service. The British also incorporated the small French air contingent. Despite the small size of the French force they made a good impression. The French were received particularly well by the Egyptians. The old ties, initiated after the contribution of Champolleon to the appreciation of Egyptian historical culture, were rekindled. In contrast the British were received coldly, for they were the occupiers. De Gaulle himself was well received by the Egyptian Monarchy and Government. There were many French scholars, dignitaries, businessmen and workers on the Suez Canal integrated into Egyptian society. In Egypt de Gaulle found firm and strong support for the Free French, but a mere expression of support was not a firm springboard for effective action.

De Gaulle returned to Brazzaville, to strengthen his base there. The danger of defeat in the Middle East might mean that the African territories would have to be the starting point for the renewed battle. There were still many shortages of equipment, but none of discipline or determination. The first military task was to fully equip General Leclerc's Saharian column. Everything that could be spared or scrounged was provided.

Defeat would descend from the Balkans. On the 24th April 1941 the Greek front crumbled and Yugoslavia succumbed. The British would defend Crete, but could they hold it? German troops were descending on Syria, from whose bases they could bomb Alexandria and the Suez Canal. De Gaulle sent General Legentillhomme, but with only the very few forces available, to try to oppose the German take over of Syria. The British were not in favour of these moves. They were facing the full might of Rommel's advance and the Syrian danger appeared as an annoying side-show. Certainly General Wavell, with three fronts in battle, could not contemplate a fourth. The British Government, to appease Vichy, allowed the steamer *Providence* to sail from Beirut to Marseille, taking some Gaullists into internment. Djibouti also continued under Vichy control. This was the price the British were prepared to pay to keep these territories quiet.

Some degree of interference was apparent from the Americans. They were keen to see if Vichy could be used as a conduit to Hitler to alleviate the condition of some of the subjugated countries. The United States was keen to stay out of the combat but her industries were waxing rich on the proceeds of the British purchases and an American re-armament programme which faced its target towards Japan. The Americans tried to persuade the British to be more accommodating towards the Vichy government. De Gaulle wanted to mount an operation to take control of Syria and Lebanon, but this would have interfered with Anglo-American relations, and so he was asked to return to London.

De Gaulle protested violently about this cutting off of supplies to assist the Free French in taking over Djibouti and the Levant from Vichy control. Such interference might make it easy for the Germans to take control of Syria. De Gaulle stayed away from Cairo and returned to his headquarters in Chad. He recalled General Catroux from Cairo, because his presence there was useless. Further telegrams were sent to Eden protesting about this British approach to Vichy and likening it to the agreement which Admiral Darlan had made with Hitler at Berchtesgarten, that German planes could be based in Syria.

Provoked by the Germans and Vichy the Iraqis threatened to open hostilities against the Allies in early May. On the 12th May German aircraft arrived in Syria. General Dentz, the Governor in Syria, had allowed German troops to disembark on orders from Vichy. This altered the view in London about de Gaulle's warnings. Churchill asked de Gaulle to return to Cairo and not to withdraw General Catroux. This change of heart by the British pleased de Gaulle and his reply, accepting, was made, as an exception, in English.

When de Gaulle returned to Cairo on the 25th May he found General Wavell ready to launch an attack into Syria. The collapse of resistance in Greece and the loss of Crete had altered his attitude. The original plan for General Catroux to take Syria using only Free French forces had to be abandoned. The activity of Vichy, with the Germans, meant that the Vichy troops there had been stiffened in their resolve to oppose the Free French. Vichy troops had been moved to the Syrian frontier. Behind this defence the Germans could manoeuvre at will. The Vichy troops alone numbered 30,000, with Syrian and Lebanese forces in addition. This force also had aircraft, artillery, and armour.

MECCANO MAGAZINE

Editorial Office:
Binns Road, Liverpool 13
England

Vol. XXVI. No. 7
July 1941

With the Editor

These Summer Days

I chose the subject for this month's cover for its beauty and for its atmosphere of peace. Until this war is won and the world made safe from madmen of the Hitler type we must all concentrate to the utmost on meeting every call made upon us; but at the same time we must not allow the sordid misery of war to fill our lives. Even those of us who live in the "blitzed" areas still have the sunshine, the trees and the flowers.

We shall win the war; the brute beast that is Nazi Germany will be trampled underfoot. But to do our share in this we shall need all the health and energy we can build up in the woods and fields these summer days.

* * * *

Next month's issue will include a thrilling account of life-boat rescues at Dunkirk and elsewhere, and the first of two fine articles by *"Railway Engineer"* on railway working in Australia. Other articles will describe the building of a modern United States airport, and an interesting early steam carriage. All the regular features will be there.

Leaders in the War

XX.—General de Gaulle

General Charles A. J. M. de Gaulle was born at Lille in 1890. He was educated for the French Army at St. Cyr Military Academy and the École de Guerre.

In the war of 1914-18 he served on the Western Front. While a Lieutenant he was wounded when leading his men in a counter-attack on Dinant, was awarded the Legion of Honour and promoted to Captain. He was again wounded on two occasions, on the last of which he was taken prisoner by the Germans. He

General Charles André Joseph Marie de Gaulle, leader of the "Free French" Army.

made five unsuccessful attempts to escape; once he was free for a fortnight before being recaptured.

After the war he returned to France, and later fought in Poland, where he was awarded two decorations. For a time he was a professor at St. Cyr, and afterwards was appointed to the French General Staff.

De Gaulle was one of the first in France to realise the great possibilities of army mechanisation, and he was Colonel of a French Tank Regiment at the time the present war began. He wrote a notable book stressing the importance that mechanised units would play in the next war, but although this attracted widespread attention it failed to lead to any practical results. When France collapsed last year de Gaulle refused to serve in the French Army that accepted the Vichy Government, and by a court martial he was deprived of his nationality and sentenced to death. He was in London at the time, however, and there he began the formation of his now great army of "Free Frenchmen" who have allied themselves to Great Britain to carry this war to a victorious end.

* * *

Readers will be interested in the appointment of Air Marshal Sir Philip Joubert de la Ferte as Air Officer Commanding-in-Chief, Coastal Command, R.A.F. Most of us remember his striking broadcasts, which unfortunately he was unable to continue. We hope to reproduce his portrait next month.

Sir Philip has succeeded Air Chief Marshal Sir Frederick William Bowhill, who after four years as head of the Coastal Command has been appointed to command the organisation ferrying American aircraft across the Atlantic. The work of this organisation will increase as aircraft deliveries are accelerated.

EDITORIAL PAGE OF THE JULY 1941 MACCANO MAGAZINE. THROUGHOUT THE WAR THIS MAGAZINE WAS EXPORTED TO ALL PARTS OF THE BRITISH EMPIRE AND COMMONWEALTH

The Free French force numbered only 6,000 men, 8 artillery pieces and 10 tanks. Air support was two dozen 'planes. British interference had greatly worsened the situation.

Information from Beirut and Damascus indicated that if the Allies came in great strength they would not be opposed, but if the force was weak it would be fought fiercely. This position was discussed with General Wavell. It would be a campaign that required an attack both from the south through Palestine and from the east through Iraq. It would need one armoured and three infantry divisions. It would also need, for a short time, a large involvement of the Royal Air Force. The infantry would need additional transport and artillery support.

General Wavell was already deeply involved in Libya and under great pressure from Churchill in London, where the political climate was hostile in Parliament. He therefore gracefully declined the Syrian project on the terms offered. He would provide, under General Wilson's command, one Australian division and a British cavalry brigade, marching by the coastal route. Small additional forces were also offered. A further two Australian battalions were later added. Sixty aircraft were available and naval support would be provided from the coastal waters. With this small force disaster was likely.

On the 26th May de Gaulle inspected the Free French troops. He found them poorly equipped. There were seven battalions, a company of tanks, one battery of artillery, a reconnaissance regiment and a squadron of Spahis. To prevent news of the start of the campaign reaching Vichy headquarters small groups of Jewish irregular troops from Palestine crossed the border and cut telephone communications. In a fight with Vichy forces one of these soldiers lost an eye. Moshe Dayan was to become the Israeli Commander in Chief in later years. On the 8th of June the Franco-British force advanced. The Germans had taken over the aerodromes in Syria. There were threats that Axis forces would try to re-conquer the Free French strongholds in Equatorial Africa. The British promised aid if such an attack were mounted. The Americans also became interested in preserving the Free French position in central Africa, with offers of material support. All these threats in Africa made a quick campaign against the Germans in Syria more urgent.

Even if British and French troops were marching together, political rivalries continued behind the scenes. At the end of the Syrian campaign the British intended to be the masters. It was clear that after the war France's mandate in the Levant would not be re-instated. The Free French had stated that there would be changes to the status of Syria and Lebanon and that they would be granted independence. It was clear that there was British military dominance in the Middle East and that it was also clear that the Foreign Office in London had a clear purpose to impose British leadership throughout the Middle East. The Free French would give independence to the Arab countries, the British would not.

There was then a change of mind on the part of the British. Independence would be granted and the statement of this intent would be jointly guaranteed by the Free French and the British. De Gaulle refused this suggestion - a guarantee by the French had never needed confirmation by the British. De Gaulle received a warm message from Churchill and in response De Gaulle thanked Churchill for the warmth of the message but not for the British idea. To de Gaulle it was clear that the granting of independence could be turned to British advantage. It would be the French who gave up influence and the British who would gain the glory.

And so there was disagreement at the start of the campaign. The Free French suffered some severe casualties, with General Legentilhomme being severely wounded. Frenchman was firing on Frenchman. It was a tragedy that this fratricide had been brought about as a result of Hitler's actions. All those fighting should have been on the same side, and some of the casualties should have been German.

It was hoped that General Dentz would soon cease opposition to the Allied advance. Vichy sent Benoist-Mechin as an envoy to Ankara to try to get neutral Turkey to allow the passage of Axis re-enforcements to Syria. The request was refused. In Iraq the Axis ally, Rachid Ali, was overthrown and fled to Germany. This opened the way for the Allies to enter Syria from the east. It was expected that the Germans would use their air power based in Syria, to oppose the invasion. Instead, their aircraft were withdrawn to Greece. The only new support the Vichy French received was two squadrons of French aircraft from North Africa. On the 18th June the Vichy High Commissioner for the Levant asked the American consul in Beirut to find out the terms the British and Free French would require for a cessation of hostilities.

Already, on the 13th June, de Gaulle had been in touch with Churchill to agree the terms which would be demanded for an armistice. The terms should include fair treatment for all combatants and officials and a restoration of France's control in the Levant, operated by the Free French. Those French who wished could remain; the rest would be repatriated. There would be no retribution against those officers who had followed Vichy's orders. These terms were agreed on the Allied side. But the next day the text which appeared had been altered. The British wanted to repatriate the whole lot. De Gaulle wanted to use those who could be incorporated into the Free French. The difference would be large numbers and the balance of power.

There was also great delay by Vichy. They waited more than three weeks before responding to the terms for an end to the fighting. Why had they delayed so that the only effect was to suffer greater losses? The reason was the start of the German offensive against Russia. Hitler wanted to keep the Allied forces embroiled in Syria to give Rommel, in the west, an easier task. The Vichy French could do Hitler's dirty work and take the casualties.

Free French forces, under General Catroux, entered Damascus on the 21st June and de Gaulle arrived in the city on the 23rd. That night German 'planes bombed the Christian part of the city and thereby showed their support for the Vichy French. It was necessary to show that what had happened had not undermined French authority in the region. It was merely a change from Vichy French to Free French control. There was to be nothing British about it.

On the 24th June de Gaulle appointed General Catroux as effective Governor of the Levant. His task was to restore economic and civilian life to as normal as possible a state as the external war would permit. He was to ensure the defence of the region against external threats and to work with the local population towards setting up conditions for their independence based upon a continuing alliance with France. The negotiations were to start from the basis of the treaties signed in 1936. The importance of this was that it would underline the continuity of French control.

While in Damascus de Gaulle received the heads of all the local political, religious and commercial organisations. These people treated his visit as that of a head of state. This underlined the acceptance of the continuity of French rule. It certainly put paid in local minds to any prospect that Germans would be in control in the Levant.

General Legentilhomme, who had continued to command his troops, although severely wounded, repulsed a major counter-attack on the 26th June. On the 3rd July an Indian column entered Syria from Iraq as the British were advancing up the coastal route. On the 10th July the Vichy warships withdrew to Turkey, where they were interned. General Dentz then agreed to a cessation of hostilities, with an agreement to be signed three days later.

On the 28th June de Gaulle sent a warning note to Churchill, concerning Britain's attitude in French territories. General Catroux's presence had to be insisted upon at the signing ceremony. There were serious changes afoot elsewhere in the region. General Wavell had been relieved of his command and sent off to be Viceroy of India. He was replaced by General Auchinleck. In this turmoil the armistice for the Levant was signed between General Wilson and General Verdilhac, the Vichy representative. The effect of this document was to transfer the Levant to Britain. There was no mention of the rights of France and no mention of the future of the area. Vichy had completely abandoned French interests. The agreement also led to the repatriation of all the troops, so that de Gaulle was denied any opportunity of adding to his forces or of protecting the interests of France in the Levant. The French of Vichy had produced an effect which would always give de Gaulle cause to return to the phrase "Albion perfide." The Free French were denied any opportunity to contact the Vichy French forces. These were repatriated speedily on ships sent by Admiral Darlan. The armaments left behind were seized by the

English. The Syrian and Lebanese troops, which had always been loyal to France but had not been used by Vichy, were put under British command.

De Gaulle repudiated the agreement the British had made with the Vichy French. He returned to Cairo, at each stop on route explaining to the senior officer of the British authorities the seriousness of what had been done. The alarm bells rang loudly. Oliver Lyttleton, Minister of State for foreign affairs, flew out to Cairo. Lyttelton did not want to start his mission with a disaster and he was smoothness itself in his approach. The campaign had produced a great strategic advantage. Vichy power in the Levant had been defeated, and most importantly authority in the Levant would not pass from France to Britain. Power would remain only with the Free French, and they would control Beirut and Damascus.

The only British purpose had been to win the war, but the British had been worried that there would have been dangers of later insurrection if the Vichy forces had not been removed. The British purpose in joining with the Free French in guaranteeing independence to these states had been to reassure them that a hand over of power from the Free French would not lead to their being immediately swallowed up by the British. It would take military control to maintain public order for the duration of the war. The purpose of embarking the troops quickly for repatriation was to avoid any possibility of disorder, which they did not have the troops to control. There should be no doubt about the common cause.

De Gaulle replied that he well understood the common cause, but the British action had divided them. France and not Great Britain held the mandate, and France alone could decide the conditions and timing of independence. The maintenance of civil order in Lebanon and Syria was a French and not a British responsibility. Lyttelton reminded de Gaulle of the accord of the 7th August 1940. De Gaulle reminded Lyttelton that it referred only to the direction of the war against the common enemy. It in no way referred to control of French territories and their political disposal. The agreement was for fighting and not for playing politics, and it was certainly not to allow Britain to put messy fingers into the pot of French colonial affairs. Did the British intend to use the agreement to decide who should govern France when Allied troops landed on French soil? De Gaulle reminded Lyttelton that the British had made contact with Vichy without his knowledge. Sending the troops back to France, where they could be re-equipped, meant that they might return, to be fought again, this time in Africa. In any case, the French equipment which had been seized should be returned to the Free French authorities.

Lyttelton stated that the armistice had been signed and the terms could not be changed. De Gaulle reminded him that the Free French had not signed it and he would not ratify it. Lyttleton was perplexed. De Gaulle stated that he would withdraw all Free French forces from British command as of the 24th July, effectively in three days time. General Catroux would be ordered to take full control of Lebanon and Syria, effective immediately. Free French forces would be ordered to make contact with all other French forces, wherever they were, and to take over control of all their equipment. The Free French would re-organise the native Lebanese and Syrian troops and take command of them. De Gaulle then handed Lyttelton a note outlining these terms.

In taking his leave de Gaulle told Lyttelton "You know how much I myself and those who follow me have done for our alliance. You will therefore know how much it would vex me if we now have to work together on different terms. But neither we nor those in France who are filled with hope could allow an alliance to continue which damaged France. If it were to come to that we would suspend our alliance with England. Whatever happens we will continue the fight against our common enemy with all our vigour. In three days I will go to Beirut. I will be available for negotiations."

As he left Lyttelton de Gaulle considered that he was troubled. De Gaulle himself was severely upset. That afternoon he drafted a document announcing that from mid-day on the 24th July Free French troops would cease to act under British command. There would be a new style of collaboration with the British. De Gaulle telegraphed Churchill. "We consider that the armistice signed by the British with the Vichy French is so against the interests of the Free French, and that is to say France herself, that it offends French dignity. I trust that you yourself will understand that such a British attitude, on a vital issue for France, will greatly increase our difficulties and will severely damage our cause."

Later that same evening Lyttelton asked to see de Gaulle. He stated that it was clear that there was the impression that Great Britain intended to take France's place in the Levant, but this was a severe misunderstanding. Lyttelton was ready to make this clear in a document. De Gaulle said that this would be a good re-instatement of the principles, but it would not rectify the situation of the armistice. It would cause confusion about whether or not the terms of the armistice were to stand. As the Free French were not a party to the agreement and as it involved French territories the legal basis of the armistice was unsound. Lyttleton asked for de Gaulle's proposals. De Gaulle replied that the text of the armistice had to be effectively amended by agreement. It was also necessary for British troops to cease military activities in the Levant.

The atmosphere eased. After further discussions and assessments an 'interpretation' of the armistice was agreed. The Free French could contact troops in the Levant to rally them to their side. French military material would be handed over to the Free French and the Free French would take control of the Lebanese and Syrian forces. If the Vichy forces broke the terms of the armistice both the British and the Free French forces would take action against them and they would do everything possible to bring such forces over to the Free French side. As some substantial violations had already taken place the agreement would allow the destination of some of the Vichy troops to be altered.

De Gaulle had no reason to doubt the integrity of the British minister, but how would General Wilson and his Arab allies react? De Gaulle telegraphed Churchill that he did not wish a complete Vichy army with its equipment to escape. It would be better to halt the repatriation and to give the Free French a chance to convert these poor troops who had been misled by enemy propaganda.

On the next day, the 25th July, Lyttelton gave de Gaulle an official note. "We recognise the historic interests of France in the

Levant. Great Britain has no interest in Lebanon and Syria, other than to win the war. Great Britain has no wish to diminish the position of France. The Free French and Great Britain, together and separately, promise independence to Lebanon and Syria. We voluntarily state that in all ways France will have in the Levant the dominant and privileged position amongst all the nations of Europe. You already know the Prime Minister's recent assurances in these matters and I am now happy, today, to reaffirm them."

In the same letter Lyttelton enclosed an agreement which de Gaulle had suggested concerning the co-operation of the British and Free French Military authorities in the Middle East. The British would not meddle in French politics and the French would work under British command. This agreed, de Gaulle left for Beirut and Damascus. There he took control and in a speech in the University to those in authority he outlined France's position. In Beirut, on the 27th July, he received a great reception, both from the troops and the population. When he met many of the French officials he was among those who had served Vichy. Their service had been to the job and not to the cause. All pledged their support and loyalty for the Free French cause. This was France, and not under German domination.

It was there that de Gaulle found urgent work to do. He found how little General Wilson and his political officials had held to the accords agreed with Lyttelton. In agreement with the English, General Dentz had concentrated his troops at Tripoli, where he remained in command. The individual units still retained their flags and their arms. They were still taking Vichy's orders and were ready to embark for repatriation for France. The ships to take them were already on their way from Marseilles. Admiral Darlan and the Germans were making haste to get their hands on the troops and their arms, and the British were assisting them. There was no chance to rally these troops. They were set on embarkation and the British police would not allow the Free French to reach their potential comrades.

The agreement with Lyttelton was dead. At Jezirah Major Reyniers was treated by the British like an enemy. He was prevented from re-forming squadrons of Syrian troops. In the desert the British officer, 'Glubb-Pasha,' was collecting the Arab Legion to serve under King Abdullah of Transjordan. From every area there were alarming reports of British interference. The British took over command of Druze troops, who then rejected French authority. In one place the Tricolour was lowered and the Union Jack raised, but over a French government building.

On the 29th July de Gaulle ordered General Catroux to go with a strong force and take back the French building and resume command of the Druze forces. General Wilson had been warned and sent a message to stop General Catroux's column. De Gaulle replied with a firm message that he expected full co-operation and that anything less would be treated as a gross insult to the sovereignty and dignity of France. The French threatened to fight, if the British wanted a fight. On the 31st July the French took back the building and hoisted the Tricolour. The French took over command of the Druze troops and shortly afterwards the British withdrew from the region.

Wilson then threatened to impose martial law and assume total power. De Gaulle threatened full opposition. Lyttelton would not intervene, but he did demand that General Spears should be present at all General Catroux's negotiations in Beirut and Damascus. Such a demand was intolerable. De Gaulle telegraphed Eden that the British attitude made co-operation impossible, and that the affair threatened a total break between the Free French and the British.

Such a quarrel was far from the British Government's purposes. On the 7th August Lyttelton went to see de Gaulle in Beirut. It was a meeting which could prove decisive for Allied relations in the Middle East. Lyttelton admitted frankly that the British Military had not kept to the agreements of the 24th and 25th July. He put it down to difficulties in transmission of the orders leading to a lack of comprehension. The error was much regretted. He seemed unhappy when General Catroux outlined the whole range of incidents. Lyttelton declared that the Vichy forces had broken the terms of the armistice. 52 British officers who had been taken prisoner in the recent engagements should have been released immediately but this had not happened and there was no word yet about their release. As a result General Dentz would be transferred to Palestine and matters would change.

De Gaulle did not hide from Lyttleton the Free French anger at the way in which the British were behaving. Lyttelton complained about the manner of Free French co-operation. Speaking directly de Gaulle stated that General Wilson had used the pretext of defending the Levant to usurp French authority. If there were any further Axis attempts to enter the Middle East from the north how could General Wilson expect French co-operation after his actions?

Lyttleton tried to smooth matters but de Gaulle would not receive General Wilson. He agreed that he should visit General Catroux in Beirut. De Gaulle was convinced that British intentions in the area had little to do with opposing the Germans and much more to do with displacing French influence in the area. Lyttelton re-assured him that this was not the case, but de Gaulle would not be moved. He was certain that the difficulties would be renewed. So bad was the relationship at this time that de Gaulle sent a message saying that the British attitude was so intransigent that the Free French would have to oppose them right up to the Rhine.

These were not the only difficulties. In trying to contact the forces whom the British had intended to repatriate no adequate time was given for the approach to be made. Eventually, from a total of 30,000, 127 officers and 6,000 troops were persuaded to join the Free French. In the end some 25,000 French troops who might well have come over to the Free French side went back to France. When de Gaulle saw their ships depart for France he knew that a great chance of aiding their country had been lost, and deliberately so, by the British.

It is clear that these quarrels greatly undermined the relationship between de Gaulle and the British. But was it the British in the Middle East or the British in London? It seems clear that in London the Middle East was a military problem. Greece had been lost, and then Crete. The evacuation of Crete had left a lot of the defenders in German hands, despite the Navy's great efforts and at the cost of several ships sunk. The battle in the western desert was also being lost. To London, Syria and Lebanon were unimportant side shows which posed only low level threats. The whole Middle East was only a small part, and not the most threatening part, of the war effort. Britain was being savagely blitzed every night. The Battle of the Atlantic was going badly. The Far East threatened to erupt as a whole new danger against which there were no adequate resources to aid resistance. Australian and New Zealand troops were fully committed in the Middle East and might have to be withdrawn to defend their own territories.

So what was causing such a storm among the Free French? From London it did not seem so important and definitely not so urgent. To de Gaulle and the Free French any idea that their Allies were undermining the honour, dignity and the future independence of France would make it impossible to rally the necessary support. Vichy could thrive on the Allied split. What of the future if the war was lost? Both views had virtue, but the disagreement was volcanic. What was Churchill, with such a vast field of battle to oversee, to make of what he was told about de Gaulle's repeated protests and threats from and about a small corner of the war zone? Churchill's exasperation is understandable. The whole war would not be lost in the Levant. In the Atlantic it could be.

General Catroux had to put in place an administration from top to bottom in Syria and Lebanon. Fortunately the local population were sympathetic. The Free French had come in like shining knights. Their courage in taking on much larger forces was recognised and it stopped the chance of a German invasion. It brought the day of independence nearer. All arrangements for control of internal functions, such as finance, economic control and public order had to be put under local control. Only defence and foreign affairs were to be retained as mandated functions.

In 1939, when Paris refused to ratify the treaty of 1936, the French governor had dismissed the President of the Republic and dissolved the Syrian parliament. De Gaulle wanted to re-instate them, but they could not see an early route to independence, and declined. In Lebanon the situation was different. The parliamentary term had long expired. Political and religious rivalries surfaced and intrigues abounded. Without the British intervention the process of achieving independence could have gone smoothly.

The re-establishment of Free French authority in Syria and Lebanon prevented the Germans gaining access to the Arab territories. It also stopped Turkey coming under such severe German pressure that it might have abandoned neutrality and joined the Axis camp. With a combined force of French, Syrian and Lebanese troops guarding the eastern Mediterranean coast Free French forces could largely be withdrawn to Egypt. De Gaulle returned to Cairo and saw the new British commander, General Auchinleck. He put most of the Free French forces at Auchinleck's disposal for the coming battle with Rommel. Auchinleck replied that a major battle was certain to take place soon. With the Middle East situation stabilised for the moment the focus of the war would move to the Russian front and the Pacific.

THE ALLIES

If the Allied cause were to advance the Free French would have to become more active, particularly militarily. The United States had not entered the war, despite Churchill's hopes. The Americans admired Britain's pluck and were providing some assistance. American naval ships were taking an increasing role in defending Atlantic convoys in their half of the ocean. In Russia the Germans would soon find that General Winter would come to the Russians' aid, as it had done to frustrate Napoleon's campaign.

The Free French would also have to woo the United States. The American government was still in close contact with the Vichy government and in particular with General Weygand. There had been no meeting between de Gaulle and Roosevelt and American attitudes towards the Free French could be regarded as no more than cold reserve.

From May 1941 de Gaulle sent Pleven as permanent representative of the Free French to the State Department. Not only would he be a representative but he would be authorised to make purchases of war material. He would be a customer and he would not arrive with an empty wallet. In return he could also offer air bases in Cameroon, Chad and the Congo. There was the same offer for the French territories in the Pacific if there was war with Japan. The Americans had already asked for service facilities in the New Hebrides and New Caledonia, under the guise of facilities for Pan American Airways.

The Americans were not slow to make allies of the Free French once the threats became clear. In August 1941 an American air force officer arrived in Chad and in September the Secretary of State, Cordell Hull, stated publicly the community of interest which existed between the United States and the Free French. On November 11th President Roosevelt extended 'Lease and Lend' to the Free French, on the grounds that the defence of territories owing allegiance to the Free French was vital to the interests of the United States. There is some evidence that Churchill had a hand in recommending this. In London diplomatic relations between the Free French and the United States were formalised. There was a gradual change of attitude everywhere in favour of the Free French. Radio broadcasts were more favourable and a French Institute was founded in New York.

If there had been troubles in the Middle East these could not be allowed to undermine the alliance in the common cause. On the 10th October 1941 de Gaulle wrote to Churchill:

'Dear Mr. Churchill,
Once more affairs are most stormy. Once more you are at the centre. I am, permit me to say, more than ever certain of your destiny, which is to achieve victory. Please believe, dear Mr. Churchill, my feelings of the deepest devotion.'

The need to improve the co-operation between the Allies in the North African battle was evident and on the 8th December 1941 de Gaulle wrote to Churchill:

'My dear Prime Minister,
I have received the letter which you sent me on the 7th December. It was not necessary for you to tell me of the keenness of the Free French forces in the Middle East to join the battle against the Germans in North Africa, side by side with the valiant troops of the 8th Army. According to my information, General Catroux is already in rapport with General Auchinleck on this subject.'

On the 7th December 1941 there was a massive change in the situation. The Japanese attack on Pearl Harbour catapulted America into the war. It would have been expected that the Free French would immediately have been recognised as allies, but it was not so. On the 13th December the U.S. Government requisitioned the liner *Normandie*, in dock at New York, and 13 other French ships. There was no discussion about the takeover, the use of the ships, or their armament. A few weeks later the liner *Normandie* was destroyed by fire, while in dock in New York.

Later in December 27 nations signed a pact of alliance, but the Free French were not included. An odd affair occurred with regard to the tiny French territories in the mouth of the St. Lawrence River in Canada, St. Pierre and Miquelon. The population had wanted to join de Gaulle, but Vichy retained control of these tiny islands so close to Newfoundland. The British were concerned that these islands, almost on the convoy routes across the Atlantic, could become a base for German submarines. The radio station on the islands could send messages about convoy sailings to alert the U-boat wolf packs. When the Americans wanted to neutralise the islands de Gaulle decided to act.

The situation was more serious and more involved than the Allies knew. The Vichy French were running an intelligence service from their embassy in Washington. German submarines were being re-fuelled at the islands. Allied cable routes across the Atlantic passed through the islands. If the Free French invaded the islands Hitler might use it as a pretext to invade other French territories. The fear of provoking Hitler and therefore a reason for appeasement had been shown to provide no protection against Hitler's aggression. The British, Canadians and Americans were powerless to intervene in the islands. The Canadian Prime Minister, Mackenzie King, was fearful that any Anglo-Saxon intervention would be a propaganda victory for Vichy and Hitler. It would give French Canadians a reason for splitting Canada in two.

President Roosevelt called the incident a tempest in a teapot. Secretly he approved of de Gaulle's action. He had recognized the government of Vichy France in order to provide a window of access into Europe. Vichy's new ambassador to Washington, Gaston Henry-Haye, was pro-Nazi. On arrival at the embassy he told his staff "Our prime objective is to establish the fact that Britain betrayed France and is therefore the real enemy. Every means at our disposal must be used to convince American officialdom and the American public that this is true."

In the United States Vichy supporters were reporting on the activities of those supporting de Gaulle. De Gaulle's supporters were threatened with reprisals against relatives still in occupied or Vichy controlled France. These Vichy supporters burgled offices to obtain lists of anti-Nazis. Pierre Laval, in the Vichy government, was using his daughter, José, as a courier to the Washington embassy. Her husband was employed in the French embassy and she claimed diplomatic immunity. When she was returning to France her flying boat had to land at the British colony of

Bermuda. Secret intelligence warned Bermuda that some of the papers she carried were wrapped in out of date French Foreign Office wrappers. When the aircraft landed at Bermuda these papers were seized on the pretext that they were addressed to the Quai d'Orsay, in Paris, and not to Vichy.

In the captured papers Pierre Laval was offering that the French people would join Germany. He assumed that Britain was finished and that American business and industry would take the opportunity of the European market, which Germany could control. He offered the services of French airmen to join the Germans in bombing Britain. Pictures of the bombing of Britain had already appeared in the French journal 'L'Illustration.' The French huge gold reserves were held in the French island of Martinique and Laval offered to use them for German purchases in the Americas. They totalled 50 million ounces of fine gold. The gold had reached Martinique in the French cruiser *Emile Bertin*. In the capital, Fort de France, the gold had been unloaded into the old fort and was stored in the underground ammunition stores.

All this was the background to the position of St. Pierre and Miquelon. The control of these islands was essential for the safety of Allied convoys. Politically it had to be the Free French who did the deed. An opportunity came when Admiral Muselier was visiting Halifax, in Nova Scotia, to inspect the heavily armed submarine *Surcouf* and the French escort vessels which were sailing on guard duty with the Atlantic convoys. He wanted to visit Saint-Pierre and Miquelon but had to ask Canadian and American permission. The secret of the visit was out. De Gaulle had to inform the British to avoid any impression of duplicity. When Washington refused permission Admiral Muselier gave up the attempt. The British Government had no objection to the visit but in view of the American opposition thought that the visit should be abandoned and De Gaulle had to accept the situation.

A few hours later the Canadian Government, under pressure from the United States, decided to make a landing and take over the radio station. The Free French protested in London and Washington. As the invasion was into French territory French permission should be sought. De Gaulle ordered Admiral Muselier to go at once to the islands, where he arrived on Christmas Eve, amongst great enthusiasm from the inhabitants. A plebiscite was held and the Free French gained a crushing victory. The young people joined up to form a defence force for their islands. Savary was named as administrator to replace the governor.

It would be expected that this little operation would be regarded by the Americans as a resounding success. Here were French people making a democratic choice, but it was very poorly received by the Americans. There was a real storm and Cordell Hull returned from his Christmas break to deal with the crisis. The expedition to the islands by the Free French was denounced, and, not only that, the Americans demanded that the Canadian government restore the status quo ante i.e. put Vichy back in power.

The uproar in the American press during the next three weeks was unbelievable. The Americans could make a decisive choice between Petain and de Gaulle, while just at that moment Churchill and Roosevelt were meeting at the Quebec Conference. De Gaulle telegraphed Churchill informing him of how badly the American attitude was affecting French public opinion. Churchill replied that he would do his best to deal with the problem. The Americans stubbornly refused to alter their attitude and tried to browbeat the British. In their turn the British tried to persuade the Free French to accept the neutralisation of the islands. When de Gaulle refused this suggestion the United States threatened to send a cruiser and two destroyers.

"What will you do if this happens?" asked Anthony Eden. "The American ships will be stopped as they enter French territory and the American Admiral will be invited to dine with Admiral Muselier, who will charm him" replied de Gaulle. "But what if the cruiser crosses the boundary?" asked Eden. "Our troops will assess the situation." "But what if the Americans continue?" pressed Eden. "They will be unhappy, because we will fire on them." Eden threw his arms in the air. "I understand your alarm" went on de Gaulle, "but I have faith in the democracies."

Cordell Hull saw the Free French representative in the United States and when Churchill returned from Quebec to London he asked to see de Gaulle. At the meeting Churchill and Eden proposed that the status of the islands should remain unchanged. In exchange the three governments would publish a communiqué which would save the face of the United States. The Free French accepted this suggestion. In the end no such statement was published. The Free French retained control of St. Pierre and Miquelon and nothing more was said.

Elsewhere in the world matters were moving to require a closer co-operation between the Free French and the Americans. Japanese aggression had made the French pacific territories of New Caledonia, the Marquises, the Tuamotus, the Society Islands and even Tahiti strategically important. The Free French were equally keen on the alliance, for they could not defend these territories. The only condition was that the Americans would respect French sovereignty.

These territories had in part been stripped of their normal garrisons. They had been brought across the seas to join the Free French forces in equatorial Africa. There were consequent difficulties in some of the oceanic territories; civil authority was breaking down. De Gaulle appointed and promoted to Admiral Thierry d'Argenlieu as Pacific High Commissioner. He was to restore order and put all the territories on a full war footing to support the Allied cause. The light cruiser *Triomphant* and the escort vessel *Chevreuil* were put at his disposal. The British consul had been one of those imprisoned in Papete and his release was one of the first actions of Admiral d'Argenlieu. This action was well received in London.

In December 1941 the Vichy government gave approval for the Japanese to take control of all French territories in the Pacific. By this means they hoped to regain control of them. From Saigon Admiral Decoux urged the inhabitants of the French islands to revolt against the Free French government. De Gaulle ordered the auxiliary cruiser *Cap des Palmes* and the submarine *Surcouf* to go as re-enforcements to Admiral d'Argenlieu. Unfortunately on the night of the 19th February 1942, near the Panama Canal, the *Surcouf* was in collision with a cargo vessel and went straight to the bottom with Captain Blaison and 130 men.

In early 1942 the Japanese onslaught had taken Malaysia, Singapore, Hong Kong, Wake Island, Guam and most of the Philippines. In London de Gaulle met the American ambassador John Winant. He expressed fears that General MacArthur would not leave the Philippines. If such a great general were lost he could not be replaced. De Gaulle was later pleased to learn that MacArthur had reached Melbourne safely.

On the 15th January 1942 the State Department sent a message to the Free French delegation in the United States in which it recognised French sovereignty over all French territories in the Pacific. All bases which were established would remain French property. Reciprocal rights would be given to France to continue to use American bases if American bases on French territory remained in use after the war. It expressed the hope that the good co-operation which existed with the Free French High Commissioner would continue in the future.

There were immediate practical results from this mellifluous rapprochement. On the 25th February de Gaulle announced that General Patch would be the American commander in the Pacific and that he would be based at Noumea. In March the Free French were invited to be represented on the War Committee for the Pacific, based in London. American bases were also established in the Tuamotus and the Society Islands. It greatly improved the chances of these scattered French islands avoiding invasion, but there were still problems to overcome. The presence of American troops, American Dollars, and American Intelligence was disturbing the populations of these islands. Some of the local police wanted to come under American control and payment rather than remain under French terms. Governor Sautot, unhappy at his subordination to Admiral d'Argenlieu, sought local popular support which amounted to an uprising. De Gaulle called Sautot to London.

Sautot tried to postpone his departure and the Americans became somewhat embroiled in the affair. De Gaulle warned them off but instructed d'Argenlieu to restore his personal relations with Patch and to restore the situation by that route. After three days of riots d'Argenlieu restored order and took over the reins of command. It was urgent to restore order and control. On the 6th May at Corregidor and on the 10th May at Mindanao the Americans surrendered their last hold on the Philippines. The Japanese were moving south to the Coral Sea, just north of Australia. At any moment Noumea might be invaded.

Following the unrest in the Pacific islands troublemakers were despatched to serve in Syria. De Gaulle telegraphed notice of his confidence to Patch and hoped that very close co-operation would be established with d'Argenlieu. In the end it was the Japanese defeat at the Battle of the Coral Sea which ended the Japanese threat to Australia and New Caledonia.

The American people were mobilising fully for war, but they still did not regard their Free French allies with favour, but there was co-operation. The United States wanted a bomber base in Africa and this was granted in exchange for 8 Lockheed aircraft to be used for communication purposes. Gradually the recognition of the Free French was accepted.

Russia had, through radio Moscow, attacked "The imperialist English" and "Their mercenaries, the Gaullistes." This had continued until the German tanks had crossed into Russia in June 1941. One hour later Churchill and de Gaulle were heroes. Russia's entry into the war on the Allied side brought new hope. German armies would be swallowed up in the Russian plains, but Russian resistance would need to be strengthened by the provision of armaments until Russian production could expand. This would drain some arms from other theatres of war. De Gaulle ordered a statement to be issued, as Churchill had done, that the Russians were now allies. For the Russians it meant breaking off relations with Vichy and they also recognised De Gaulle as head of the Free French. Their ambassador to the Vichy government transferred accreditation and location to the Free French.

There was some small initial help from the Free French for the Russians. Escort vessels and cargo ships took part in the arctic convoys to Murmansk. So far de Gaulle had not persuaded the British to use two light divisions from the Levant in Libya. De Gaulle offered them to the Russians for duties in the Caucasus, but eventually these troops were used by the British against

Rommel. Later de Gaulle sent other troops to Russia. In the other direction fifteen officers and men who had avoided capture by the Germans were freed by the Russians and turned up in London. Meeting the Russian foreign minister, Molotov, in London de Gaulle found him unsmilingly serious and never ready to depart from a prepared position. De Gaulle remembered that he was dealing with the man who had signed the Soviet-German pact which had given Hitler the safety on his eastern borders to unleash the whole fury of the German army against France.

Both the Free French and the Russians had a common interest in the Allies opening a Second Front in the west by invading France. De Gaulle also sought Russian help in maintaining French authority over all the French overseas possessions. Most importantly at this time he never forgot that the centre of all Free French affairs must remain in London. Above all, London was the closest Allied capital to metropolitan France and it was from England that support for the Resistance and the eventual force to liberate France must come.

In this regard de Gaulle's relationship with Anthony Eden, the British Foreign Secretary, was blossoming. De Gaulle found him to be very European in outlook and very humane in perception. Eden retained for de Gaulle a sense that every civilised thought and activity was preserved as a goal from which the hardships and brutalities of war would never divert him. When there were disagreements and problems to discuss de Gaulle found Eden brilliantly intelligent and able to conduct negotiations with an admirable natural courtesy. De Gaulle detected that, underneath it all, Eden had a special affection for France.

If Anthony Eden, the Foreign Secretary, was sympathetic it was a demeanour which covered the sinister machinations of the underworld of the Foreign Office. In the dark shadows lurked those who had colonial ambitions to grab France's overseas possessions. In all the spirit of Allied co-operation it was these shadowy activities which did much to thwart the progress of the Free French contribution to the Allied cause because of the need to divert effort to thwarting Foreign Office intrigues. A suspicion of de Gaulle was fostered. It was put about either that he was a stalking horse for the communists or that he was tending towards fascism. Clement Attlee, the deputy Prime Minister, came to see de Gaulle on these matters and was reassured about the Free French firm adherence to democracy.

Above all, the position of the Free French depended on the attitude of the Prime Minister. When there were disagreements Churchill seemed to take them personally. It was as though it was a painful argument in a family. It seemed as though any disagreement with de Gaulle wounded and hurt him as would such disagreement between brothers. And so at times their meetings could be accompanied by severe expressions of anger. It was other events which contributed to making this great man so angry. The Battle of the Atlantic was bringing more and more serious losses. On the 10th December 1941, off the east coast of Malaysia, the battleship *Prince of Wales* and battle cruiser *Repulse* were sunk by Japanese air attack. Their air cover had failed to protect them when they had been sailing to intercept Japanese transport ships bringing troops to land on the coast of Malaya. Then on the 15th February 1942 Singapore surrendered. This bastion of the British Empire, thought to be impregnable, had been taken by a single Japanese division and 73,000 British troops went into captivity.

The bad news was not at an end. In June 1942 Rommel broke through the British lines in the western desert and was nearly at the gates of Alexandria. 33,000 British and Commonwealth troops in Tobruk were taken prisoner. It was this catalogue of losses which were so grievous to Churchill. Where was a victory to come from? He felt these losses as if, as at one period in the First World War, he was in the front line. These losses brought discontent on the political front. Churchill and the war cabinet came in for severe criticism about their conduct of the war. It is in this atmosphere that de Gaulle fully understood Churchill's foul temper. At this time the only strong support could come from Roosevelt, but American aid would come at the price of subordinating the British Empire to the will of the Americans. At this time the voice of the Free French was only dimly heard.

When de Gaulle had arrived back in London in September 1941 de Gaulle found Churchill in a very bad humour. The conflicts in the Levant had been an unwelcome and diverting nuisance from the essentials of the wider picture of the war. On the 2nd September Churchill wrote to de Gaulle deploring his attitude and saying that there was no point in their meeting.

Churchill showed some reluctance in substituting Free French control for Vichy control in the Levant. The cold hostility lasted only until the 15th September. On that day they had a meeting which started badly but improved markedly. By the end of it they had agreed that the Cairo accords would stand.

To emphasise the point the Syrian Republic was declared independent on the 27th September and the Lebanese on the 26th November. Great Britain recognised the two new republics and their new status was widely notified by de Gaulle. Not only did the British not object to these announcements, they suggested them. Making and supporting the declarations was one thing, but the British were still loath to avoid interfering. They recruited – quite illegally – Druze troops and declared a state of siege. Taking this step produced a revolt in Iraq. General Wilson tried to expel some French officials.

General Catroux tried to accommodate the British demands, but there was no settling of the matter. In May 1942 the British tried to force through elections in Syria and Lebanon. This was accelerating the pace of change and causing instability. De Gaulle thought that the elections would be better postponed until the end of the war, when conditions were more normal. But elections were promised in the newspapers. The British were also trying to negotiate a treaty to gain control of Ethiopia. And then British troops, without warning, landed on Diego Suarez, at the northern tip of the French island of Madagascar. It was like a Pearl Harbour to de Gaulle. The entry of Japan into the war threatened Madagascar. It could become a base for enemy submarines. The governor was in two minds as to whether to support Vichy or the Free French. The British had good reason to want to control Madagascar, but the Free French wanted to be part of the invading force and take over political control for France.

On the same day as the attack on Diego Suarez a communiqué published by Washington stated that America and Britain agreed that Madagascar would be returned to France and that the occupation had only been undertaken because it was necessary for the Allies. But no reason was given for over-riding the authority of France. When de Gaulle brought the matter up with Eden, Eden appeared embarrassed. He stated that he wanted French administration to continue. "But what French administration?" de Gaulle asked: a modus vivendi in which the French would be left in place while the Allies remained in Diego Suarez was achieved.

De Gaulle opposed this plan. For the Allies to take control of Madagascar would involve a major expedition in such a large island and would take several weeks. Indeed the position would be made much more difficult if the Germans forced the Vichy authorities to fight. Eden said that the Allies counted on de Gaulle to take control in Madagascar to avoid this and this could be declared publicly. On the 14th May the British government declared "On the subject of Madagascar it is the intention of His Majesty's Government that the French National Committee, representing the Free French forces and in co-operation with the United Nations will take over the administration of the newly liberated territory."

This was an important undertaking by the British. The next day de Gaulle spoke on the radio expressing confidence in the Allies. But he also stated that France's empire would be neither divided up nor neutralised. A brigade from French Equatorial Africa would be sent to Madagascar to maintain French authority. Perhaps this was dealing with an imaginary problem, but it would delay the entry of further French territories into the war on the Allied side. And then, de Gaulle's representative was prevented from going to Diego Suarez.

All these activities soured relations between the Free French and the British. In early June 1942 a British mission in the Gold Coast was found to be making secret overtures to the populations of the French territories at the mouth of the river Niger. General Giffard, Commander in Chief in West Africa, expelled the Free French missions in Bathurst, in the Gambia, and Freetown in Sierra Leone. De Gaulle was asked not to go to inspect Free French troops in Libya. The whole scenario in London was one to

115

foster a feeling of mistrust.

It was clear that the British and Americans were planning a vast operation in Africa. General Marshall and Admiral King, Commander-in-Chief of the Atlantic Fleet, had been in London in May, but had avoided seeing de Gaulle. The Free French were being by-passed and the intention was to capture French territories and to parcel them out amongst the Allies. The National Committee was unanimous in forcing the British and Americans to realise that the Free French were their allies and that they were all in the conflict together.

Mr. Charles Peake, a Foreign Office Diplomat, expressed to Churchill and Eden that the Free French had suffered enough improper interference - in Madagascar, Syria, and elsewhere - to lose confidence in co-operation with Britain and the United States. This was damaging the war effort. Despite this the Free French would press the enemy with full force. Messages were sent to Generals Leclerc and Catroux to this effect.

Before this could be put into effect Churchill sent a message on the 10th of June that he wanted to come and see de Gaulle. They spent a very full hour together. Churchill started by complimenting de Gaulle on the stout defence of the Free French troops at Bir Hakeim, in the western desert. This had blunted and delayed Rommel's assault on the British positions at El Alamein, at a time when they were still unprepared and vulnerable. There was no ulterior motive in the Allies' actions in Madagascar and this should be understood. Co-operation was essential and with this de Gaulle agreed. Churchill pointed out that the Free French were not Britain's only allies, and that he would have to tell the Americans of their discussions. When de Gaulle raised the question of Britain's actions in the French territories and the attitude to France itself Churchill reassured de Gaulle of Britain's good intentions. "I am a friend of France!" he cried out. "I have always wanted a great France with a large army. It is necessary for peace, order, and the security of Europe. I have never had any other purpose."

"That is true," de Gaulle replied. "You have the virtue that after Vichy signed the armistice you were still playing France's card.

This card, which is called de Gaulle – don't lose it now! It would be absurd at the very moment that the political climate with the Free French is encouraging French resistance to the Germans."

They spoke of Roosevelt and his attitude. Whereas Churchill was at the head of a united nation, a united empire and large armies, de Gaulle was struggling against disunity and with very limited forces. He had the duty to look after the destiny of France. "It is too hard and I am too poor so I cannot bend "de Gaulle told him. " We still have great difficulties to overcome" Churchill told him. "But one day, we will be in France; perhaps next year! In any case, we shall be together." De Gaulle records that as they parted Churchill showed great emotion and friendship. When they got to the street Churchill repeated "I will not drop you. You can count on me."

Three days later Eden, in his turn, repeated the assurances. Obstacles placed in the way of Free French movements were withdrawn. "Believe me" Eden told de Gaulle, with great warmth, "We wish to march hand in hand with you to get ready for the Second Front in the west." Whatever else happened, de Gaulle was now sure that England would not desert him.

The Greeks and Yugoslavs and the other displaced Crowned Heads and governments in London could see that the success of the Free French in upholding French independence was a beacon to their own hopes of regaining the independence of their countries. So it was in their interests to give the Free French every possible support. They also saw that the eventual restoration of a strong France was essential to peace and stability in Europe. In return the Free French provided these governments with administrative support and de Gaulle met the Chiefs of Staff of all these countries. The one thing they all shared was living in the shadow of the tragedy which had befallen their nations. There was the fear of what reprisals might be exacted for their own absence abroad and the hope that their own efforts would soon bring salvation to their countries. Fear and hope bred the strongest determination.

There was little doubt that their entry on the Allied side would bring eventual victory, and the liberation of their countries. But in what state would they be when they were liberated? The Dutch saw their empire in the East Indies conquered and destroyed, despite the valiant resistance of the forces under the command of Admiral Helfrich and General Ter Porten.

The Grand Duchess Charlotte of Luxembourg and her family took up life in London. The children had piano lessons to maintain some element of normality and they kept in touch for very many years after the war with their piano teacher, Professor Sadie MacCormac of the Royal Academy of Music in London. They were overcome with sadness at the state of their country and could do little to help.

For those governments of eastern European countries in exile the situation was even more tragic. If the entry of Russia into the war was to ensure victory was it also to ensure freedom for their countries? Entry into and exit from their countries was not the same thing with the Russians. In Greece, in particular, there was a significant communist presence. This was to erupt after victory into a vicious civil war.

For the Poles there was no doubt that the Russians would be an adversary, even if for the moment they were allies against the common German enemy. Poland hoped to be allied to the West, but escape from the clutches of their eastern saviour would be unlikely. In July 1941 the Polish government in exile signed an agreement with the Soviets that the Russian-German agreement of 1939, which divided Poland between those two nations, was null and void. The agreement to release Polish prisoners in Russian hands was not properly honoured and the plight of those released was pitiable in their long march to the west. To de Gaulle General Sikorski, head of the Polish government confided "When the final moment comes, who will save Poland? It will be France or nobody." These ideas among the exiled governments re-enforced de Gaulle's authority and standing.

The consequence was that de Gaulle was increasingly recognised as the French personality with whom to do business. It was de Gaulle who signed, on behalf of France, a common declaration in January 1942 about the nature and punishment of war crimes.

To maintain France's prominence with the Anglo-Saxon nations de Gaulle spoke frequently on the radio to the British and American public. He also spoke to many luncheon and dinner audiences, making himself especially agreeable at the subsequent informalities. In this he felt severely frustrated by his inability to command English well. Translations were provided in advance, especially for the radio. He spoke to a wide range of audiences in England, from parliamentary groups to workers in the English Electric tank factory in Stafford, and in many British cities, from Edinburgh to Portsmouth. He had been labelled as one of the war leaders as number 20 in a series in the July 1941 issue of the Meccano Magazine, becoming well known at that early stage in his leadership to thousands of boys, both in Britain and overseas. To these audiences he could explain the idea that France Combattante – Fighting France – would march hand in hand with their allies to victory.

But the United States was still communicating with the Vichy government. De Gaulle described those who would deal with those who destroyed democracy with fascism as poor scribblers who should be drowned at sea. He took a very firm stand. Free France would be steadfast and resolute. By the start of the summer of 1942 the war was coming to a climax of decision. Russia was turning from defence to offence. The British had sent large re-enforcements to the Middle East. The United States was poised to enter the European and African conflict. France, subdued at home and in many places idle overseas, was joining the struggle with increasing strength and confidence.

Where would the next battle be – North Africa or metropolitan France. France Combattante was now strong enough to enter the battle. Would all French people rally to the flag? Could de Gaulle put France back together as a united nation?

FIGHTING FRANCE

Between the summer of 1941 and that of 1942 the strength of Fighting France had grown. De Gaulle himself could not control every facet. He needed a loyal and efficient organisation. In September 1941 the foundation of the National Committee had created the necessary organisation. To organise the African and Middle Eastern regions had taken de Gaulle away from London for eight months. Time would be needed to create an organisation which would be active and efficient.

The demands which de Gaulle made on his office staff in London were immense. Information in and out was a deluge and changes in direction and in directions caused his office staff to refer to him as "General Nuisance." If he was, it was for a great cause. Such was the nature of the man that the greater the demands and the pressure, the greater the loyalty and devotion he inspired. It was as if all recognised that as the general on the charger he had a longer view, and the foot soldiers trusted the accuracy of his view and the wisdom of his orders. He had stood for the honour of France and they would stand by him.

Great changes were taking place. The crew of the battleship *Richelieu*, which had escaped from Oran under British fire in July 1940 and which had then fired on the British at Dakar in September 1940, found themselves by 1943 part of the British Home Fleet at Scapa Floe.

The National Committee was performing the tasks of government, but would not assume the title. To broaden the democratic appeal de Gaulle formed a Consultative Assembly to advise the National Committee. This was the embryo Fourth Republic. In doing this he was not without opposition. Some Frenchmen thought that he was assuming the role of Head of State and preferred to place their allegiance with the Allies; Roosevelt, Churchill or Stalin. Others continued to enjoy the intoxicating pleasure of the cocktail mix of pre-war French politics, their machinations in London and New York distorting the focus of de Gaulle's leadership for their own out-dated ends.

In this regard Admiral Muselier became involved. He was a good organiser of the small Free French naval forces, but he could also become embroiled in intrigues, causing untold trouble. He tried to persuade de Gaulle to adopt the role of a central figurehead and leave the realities of exercising power to him. He even threatened to make the Navy his own special force. Some French personalities refused to join the National Committee under de Gaulle's leadership. Churchill saw these machinations and was appalled. How could a country which was struggling to rise from the mire of defeat still continue with its pre-war dissentions? His own war cabinet had no such disunity. He wondered if de Gaulle would continue as leader of the Free French, but without doubt there was no one else who had the moral right or the force of personality: and there was no one else to whom the Free French troops would be loyal.

At this stage the British Government intervened. If Admiral Muselier was going to take the Free French Navy out of Allied control it would be a significant loss to the Allied cause. It would mean that there was a move towards fascism. Admiral Muselier had to be kept under control.

Muselier would be dismissed from command of the Navy, but any further British interference would make it impossible for the Free French to continue Allied unity. The British waited to see which way the wind would blow in the French Navy. All Free French naval ships and establishments sided with de Gaulle. Only a few officers rallied to the Admiral. Muselier was isolated for a month – a form of house arrest. As he had been judged on British territory de Gaulle asked the British to enforce the order, under the terms of the agreement of the 15th January 1941. All this delayed Allied progress. The British exasperation with the Free French was justified, but de Gaulle was not the cause. The British wanted Admiral Muselier to remain in command of the navy after his one month of isolation.

At the end of the month de Gaulle asked Admiral Muselier to go on a tour of inspection. Instead, a few days later, Admiral Muselier, who had done so much to rebuild the navy, resigned. There was continuing criticism from other elements that should have been loyal. The National Committee continued to meet regularly at Carlton Gardens. De Gaulle found them a loyal and most helpful and efficient group of colleagues.

But it was always de Gaulle who spoke for Free France, and in France resistance was becoming more active, and the separate movements for resistance were starting to see the need for unity of action for the common cause. Secret messages, some carried by those who escaped from France, kept de Gaulle in frequent touch with the mood and feeling in the country. The idea that after the armistice the Vichy government was 'saving the furniture' became more and more discredited. More than 1,500,000 French prisoners of war had not been repatriated. Germany had retaken Alsace and Lorraine for incorporation into Germany. France was raped for its industrial and agricultural production and French troops were forced to fight the Allies. There remained no doubt that Vichy had no chance of rescuing France. The only hope lay with de Gaulle and the Free French. By the summer of 1942 Petain announced on the radio how poor the response was to his appeals for support in all spheres and how a deep malaise was affecting the French people.

From August 1941 German troops in France came under attack and the Germans shot hundreds of hostages in reprisal. They imprisoned and deported thousands as slave labourers. These brave but un-coordinated actions were costing the French people dear. It would need better organisation to make effective attacks with less cost and suffering. The French people were suffering the terrible brutality from which they had expected the armistice to protect them. Acts of resistance were not popular and could even damage the cause of liberation if individual and minor acts prevented the organisation of a controlled uprising by an Army of the Interior when the full invasion came. De Gaulle warned against premature action in a radio broadcast on the 23rd October 1941.

In the meantime the best attack on the Germans would be by Special Forces, with Commando raids on coastal targets. As Churchill commanded, "set the coast of Europe ablaze, give the Germans no peace or respite". Raids such as that in Operation Fahrenheit on the 11th/12th November 1942, when 13

Commandos landed at Plouezec in Brittany and destroyed a radio station, killing three Germans without loss to themselves, would be more productive and less costly. The Germans evacuated the village and never returned. Perhaps Plouezec was the first place in France to be liberated.

German massacres continued, 50 killed at Nantes and Chateaubriant and 50 at Bordeaux on the 25th October. De Gaulle broadcast to the nation. "In killing our martyrs, the enemy believes that he will spread fear throughout France. France will show that she has no fear. I ask all French men and women to stop all activity and stay immobile, wherever they find themselves, on Friday the 31st October between 4 and 4.05. Such a widespread national strike will show the enemy his danger and prove the strength of French unity." The call was followed, particularly in the factories. It emphasised the need to control resistance actions to prevent anarchy.

Amongst the military that had been forced to lay down their arms by the terms of the capitulation there was a desire to return to combat. Even Petain, addressing a crowd in Marseille, suddenly shouted out "Remember, you are always mobilised!" Vichy was losing control and many army detachments were in both camps, with support growing for the Secret Army. But there was no way in which the Vichy regime could be replaced, and there were very few arms and little money to support any formation of an armed resistance. This would have to come from England.

In the occupied zone conditions were much harsher. The Gestapo were in control and the controls were rigid and severe. Letters, movement, habitation, work, were all under the tightest regime. Any suspect was imprisoned or deported and any active defiance was put down with torture and then a bullet.

The communists would not join other resistance movements in the occupied zone, and so the forces against the Germans were dangerously split. They would act to undermine de Gaulle's authority. He would ensure that communism would pass into history, but France would endure.

In October 1941 de Gaulle found that Jean Moulin was in Lisbon, having escaped from France. He had been Prefect of the

Department of the Eure et Loir at Chartres before the German occupation. He had been manhandled, wounded and imprisoned. Vichy apologised for his treatment. He would be certain to serve the Free French movement, but it took two months to bring him to London.

In eighteen months he was to re-organise the whole of the resistance movement and convert its synthetic unity into solid reality. Eventually, on a trip into occupied France, he was captured, horribly tortured, and put to death. He died for France, like so many others. In describing his sacrifice de Gaulle likened it to surrendering the evening of his life so that others may have a new dawn. It was so like the inscription on the memorial at Kohima "Go home and tell them of us and say, for your tomorrow we gave our today."

By March 1942 Moulin had got sufficient agreement to encapsulate the ideas in a declaration 'One struggle, one leader.' It referred to accepting de Gaulle's leadership. It enabled air and sea operations to be properly co-ordinated. Secret flights by Lysander small aircraft were dangerous to fly and dangerous for the reception committees, who marked out the landing grounds in the dead of night. To bolster spirits one of the flights brought back for Madame de Gaulle an Azalea which had been purchased in the Rue Royale in Paris. The information provided for London grew in volume and importance. No German ship left any of the Atlantic coast ports without London knowing of the departure within a few hours. Plans of all major military constructions, such as submarine pens, were stolen and sent to London.

Several Resistance leaders came for a few months to London, to give information and exchange ideas. Among them was Pierre Brossolette. He was later captured in France and died as a victim of the Gestapo. He was a colleague of Yeo-Thomas, code named the 'White Rabbit,' an RAF officer who was a British secret agent who was captured and sent to Buchenwald, but survived. In Paul Brickhill's book about Yeo-Thomas the last sentence outlines his thoughts. 'Perhaps he was thinking of Brossolette, and of Hubble, and of Kane, and of all those other brave men who died that nobility might come back into the world.' These Allies fought together, dreamed and hoped together, and died together. They should be remembered together. In the centre of Troyes, on Brosselette's house, there is an appropriate memorial plaque.

To make clear the peace aims which would follow the triumph of achieving the war aims de Gaulle published them, on the 23rd June 1942. The French people would be united and there would be a revolution in the organisation of French life. Meanwhile he settled with his family in England, moving with his family, first to Shropshire and then much closer to, and eventually into, London. He describes the sympathetic and discrete relationship of his neighbours. He recalls how the kind and reserved attitude of the English people made it possible for him and his family to enjoy a serene life, without any harassment or intrusion. At this time he was often invited to official ceremonies by the British Government, as well as by other Allies. Many organisations were formed to support the French, with help from notable British persons such as Lord Inverclyde, Lord de la Warr, and Lord Ivor Churchill.

In the Albert Hall, on the 15th November 1941, de Gaulle outlined three main political aims. The first was to wage war with all possible force. The second was to change the attitudes and policies which had led to capitulation The third was to outline the principles for the rebirth of the institutions of France. These declarations were greeted by tumultuous and prolonged applause from the ardent crowd in the Albert Hall.

There was now, for the first time, a really coherent structure developing in the Free French forces in Great Britain. De Gaulle went on many tours of inspection and it was here that, for the first time, the phrase "Le Grand Charles" was heard. It was possible to gather together all the arms and munitions which had been recovered from France and from the Norwegian campaign of 1940. Children who had come from France were growing up and were formed, through their special schools, into the Cadets of the Free French. Of 211 who entered the Free French forces 52 were killed in action.

French naval ships taking part in the battle of the Atlantic were dependent for supplies and repairs on Allied bases. This brought an essential unity to the provision of equipment and the training for action. French ships remained under French individual command but obeyed British strategic orders. In this way they could give of their best. In return the British provided full and equal supplies and the most up to date equipment. The Free French were provided with new corvettes, frigates, destroyers and submarines. They gave of their best in the joint struggle.

Some ships remained from the old French navy. By 1942 *Rubis*, *Minerve* and *Janon* remained of the original five submarines. *Triomphan*, *Leopard*, *Melpomene* and *Bouclier* were escorting convoys. *Congre* and *Lucienne-Jeanne* were minesweeping at the entrance to British ports. Other Free French ships were serving off the African coasts and in the Pacific. Six further armed trawlers were brought into service for coastal defence. The old battleship *Courbet* acted as headquarters ship. Nine further ocean going escort vessels were brought into service. Eight torpedo boats formed the 28th flotilla for high speed aggressive action in the channel. Four further escort vessels, the destroyer *La Combattante* and the submarines *Curie* and *Doris* were taken over from British construction. Further expansion was limited by a shortage of trained sailors.

By June 1942 700 Free French sailors had died. Ships companies totalled 3,600 sailors. Further French sailors came from the merchant marine and from the Suez Canal Company. French Commandos commanded by Commandant Kieffer were, after discussion with Lord Mountbatten, to take part in combined operations with the British Commandos. One of their British colleagues described the three commando leaders, Lord Lovat, Philippe Keiffer and Anders Lassen as being totally without fear in their leadership.

The French Merchant Marine which was taking part in the Allied campaign comprised 660 vessels adding up to 2,000,000 tons of shipping. They served with the British Merchant Navy, many of the ships carrying the dual flags of France and Britain. A quarter of the French merchant marine sailors were to be lost in the battle.

Admiral Sir Percy Noble, commanding the Battle of the

Atlantic from Liverpool in May 1942, showed de Gaulle the Operations Room for control of the battle. The Free French contribution was numerous but still small. It was terrible to consider how many French ships remained in port –Dakar, Toulon, Alexandria, Fort de France, Casablanca -, inactive in the Allied cause for the liberation of France. It was with a heavy tread that de Gaulle climbed the stairs from the underground headquarters.

He was determined to redouble his efforts in the Allied cause. French airmen had to fly under British control in British aircraft. There was no real remnant of the original French air force. Some French squadrons had taken part in the battles in Libya and Eritrea. Some, adopted by the English, had taken part in the Battle of Britain. De Gaulle had found the Minister of State for Air, Sir Archibald Sinclair, very helpful and co-operative. French pilots would be British trained, but could form French squadrons. This led to the formation of the 'Ile de France' air group, and then the 'Alsace' air group to fight in Libya. Other air groups followed. Co-operation with the RAF was close and good.

The main focus For Free French co-operation with the British at the end of 1941 and in early 1942 was in North Africa. Whether the British were routing the Italians in Tunisia or defending against the Germans at the gates of Alexandria the Allied cause was common and the Free French would be there. The Saharan columns could come north from Chad, under the command of General Leclerc. The infantry regiments under General Larminat would join the British. In the service of the Axis powers an agreement between Admiral Darlan, on behalf of the Vichy government, allowed Axis troops in North Africa to be supplied through Tunisia.

In the first months of 1942 the situation in Tripolitania stabilised, neither side mounting any major attack. General Leclerc, with his force from Chad, seized several enemy outposts and took numerous prisoners, before returning to base. In April de Gaulle made him Commander in Chief of all Free French forces in Africa, but it would take ten more months of desert hardships before victory was achieved in North Africa.

The British had not used Larminat's forces from Syria. Each

of the two divisions had five infantry battalions, artillery and an anti-tank regiment, anti-aircraft protection, a reconnaissance group and other support. Larminat had taken over the arms left by General Dentz. These were now well-equipped divisions. Each batallion had its own battery of six 75 millimetre guns. De Gaulle reminded Churchill of the availability of these well armed forces. The British declined to use them, citing their dispersal in Syria and their lack of equipment. The British were aiming to beat Rommel on their own, without the need for French help.

De Gaulle then offered their services to the Russians when the African front closed with victory. But then British intentions suddenly changed. Churchill wrote de Gaulle a warm letter expressing the hope that General Auchinleck could use a French force for the attack on Cyrenaica. He said he knew how keen the French were to come to battle with the Germans. De Gaulle replied that he approved the project and sent the necessary orders to General Catroux. Equipped with additional guns the French division, under General Koenig, fought a hard battle against Rommel at Sollum and Bardia. The French were electrified by taking German prisoners. The French troops were incorporated into the British defence on the Gazala line at the southern point of Bir Hakeim.

Later in 1942 the Russians agreed to the French suggestion for sending troops. De Gaulle decided to send the other light division and the air group 'Normandie.' The British rejected the suggestion of sending the 2nd Division to Russia. The British now wanted the French troops and the 2nd Divison reached General Auchinleck in March. When fully assembled the Free French put 12,000 soldiers into the Allied line in the western desert.

Rommel attacked Bir Hakeim on the 27th May. In this ground of 16 square kilometres would be fought one of the fiercest battles of the war. The Italians, in an outflanking move to the south, lost 40 of their 100 tanks. The next day the French destroyed 15 vehicles and took 200 prisoners. Rommel had not expected to meet the British armour and withdrew to mount a new attack. 50 Kilometres to the west a French column took over an Axis position.

On the 2nd June Rommel seized the initiative. By a direct frontal assault on General Ritchie's position German troops broke through a minefield and split the British line. German troops then attacked the French force at Bir Hakeim. For the first time since 1940 French and German troops met in battle. In a skirmish the French took 150 prisoners. Then the Germans unleashed a furious heavy artillery barrage. Four or five times a day the French positions were dive bombed by Stukas. Supplies only reached them in tiny quantities.

Stocks of ammunition and food dwindled. The troops had to keep their wounded with them and bury their dead around them. On the 3rd June Rommel sent a message written in his own hand demanding that the French lay down their arms or be destroyed, as had the British brigade. On the 5th June a German officer came again to make the same demand. The reply was artillery fire. International interest became aware of this battle. Could French soldiers recover any glory?

On the 7th June the French troops at Bir Hakeim were completely surrounded. A German and an Italian division, twenty artillery batteries and several hundred tanks made a furious assault on the French positions. The French had held out for the six days General Ritchie had asked of them. Then the next demand was to hold out for forty-eight hours more. But there could be no relief. The 8th army had been pushed back in disarray, losing contact with the French.

There were even more furious German attacks on the 8th June. Unsuccessful, the Germans tried again on the 9th June. The French 75 millimetre guns were outranged and overpowered by the heavy German artillery. Severe shortage of water worsened the position of the French troops. The world was becoming aware of the heroic French stand. Newspapers in all continents carried headlines announcing the 'Magnificent feat of arms.' It was impossible to allow a surrender. The idea of a column of French prisoners being forced to march past Rommel into captivity was too horrible to contemplate.

With great difficulty the French withdrew through minefields and surrounding enemy positions. By the 11th June the Chief of the Imperial General Staff, General Alan Brooke, sent a message to de Gaulle "General Koenig and a large part of his troops have reached El Gobi after passing through the enemy lines." De Gaulle thanked the messenger and closed the door, alone for a moment, overcome with emotions of pride, relief, and joy. The 1st Light infantry division had lost 1,109 casualties out of 5,500 men. Much equipment had been destroyed and some abandoned.

On the 12th June the Germans announced that they had taken the position of Bir Hakeim. Berlin radio broadcast a communiqué stating that the white men taken prisoner at Bir Hakeim were not regular soldiers and would be shot. Within an hour de Gaulle broadcast on the BBC: "If the German army acts so dishonourably as to shoot French soldiers taken prisoner when fighting for their country General de Gaulle makes it known, with deep regret, that he will be obliged to inflict the same punishment on German prisoners who fall into the hands of French troops." Before the end of the day Berlin radio announced that no harm would come to French prisoners taken at Bir Hakeim "The soldiers of General de Gaulle will be treated like soldiers." There is little doubt that Rommel would not, in any case, have carried out such an order.

General Catroux helped with the re-equipping of the 1st Division at Sidi-Barrani. French air force squadrons continued as part of the Desert Air Force. But the 8th Army was forced out of Cyrenaica and soon after Tobruk surrendered, the Germans taking 33,000 prisoners. The British fell back to El Alamein, where General Cazaud with the 2nd Division formed up in the southern part of the defence line. The losses in the campaign were too much for the British to bear. General Auchinleck was replaced by General Alexander. The original choice for command of the 8th Army, General Gott, was killed when the Bristol Bombay aircraft in which he was flying to take up his command was ambushed and shot down by German fighters. Within 24 hours General Montgomery was appointed to take his place.

Before he left General Auchinleck published a communiqué in honour of the 1st French Division "The United Nations express their admiration and recognition of the French forces and their valiant General."

In London, six days later, to celebrate the second anniversary of General de Gaulle's call to arms of the 18th June, 10,000 French, civilian and military, came together at the Albert Hall. It was a grand and inspiring occasion. De Gaulle received a great welcome and his oration was received with the greatest enthusiasm by the crowd. Free France had survived, endured, and thrived. France was still in the war! France would remain united in the struggle and Fighting France had shown her teeth and at Bir Hakeim her troops had been touched with glory. The whole world had to recognise France. The atmosphere was electric and all present understood that after all the struggles and doubts a new France with a new strength had arisen from defeat. With 70,000 men under arms French strength would grow. Joined with the Resistance movement in France the first real dawn of the possibility of liberation was seen. There was hope and there was happiness.

A NEW DAWN

In the spring of 1942 Free French forces were still small in number. For de Gaulle there were two tasks; the eviction of the invader and the rebuilding of his country. If the French could remain united their strength would grow and with it their influence. The continuation of the Vichy government kept before the world the picture of French disaster. The communist party in France was another problem. Since Hitler's invasion of Russia in June 1941 the communists had provided a vocal, and to a lesser degree an armed, resistance to the Germans in France. It was clear that they would be a danger during the reconstruction of the French State. They were certainly seeking glory in the French struggle.

De Gaulle's task was now doubly difficult. It was not enough to raise the standard in the empire of French armed resistance to the invader. Within France there were political forces which would seize power at the point of victory. The liberation would need as careful timing as the serving of a soufflé.

At this time it was the Americans, with their vast production of military supplies and their great resources of men to be armed, who were deciding policy. Nothing could be done if the Americans did not agree. Large numbers of American troops, ships and planes were starting to arrive in Britain. Everywhere in the streets of the cities Americans were to be seen and their presence felt in the social and economic life of the country. The British, having played the major role in the first two, and the hardest years of the war, were now to be swamped by the American might necessary for victory. Churchill's role was changing to that of almost a lieutenant of Roosevelt, and France's power base was so much less.

Despite all this power the Americans were undecided on policy. The Russians, sorely pressed in the east, urged the establishment of a 'second front' on the western coast of Europe to absorb a great part of the German strength. To land on the coast of France in 1942 or even 1943 with sufficient strength to ensure success was out of the question. Although the build up of American forces in England was accelerating they were not trained and in effective units. There were very few amphibious landing craft at that time. It had been a close decision to persuade Roosevelt that 'Germany first' was the Allied aim rather than concentration on a Pacific victory. After all, the Americans had entered the war because of the Japanese attacks in the Pacific. Eventually the plan of an Allied landing in North Africa was decided upon, for the autumn of 1942. It would involve many of the troops sailing from the United States to make a direct assault on the African shore. Such a long and dangerous journey to a landing on a hostile shore had never before been attempted. It was the first time that the Americans would spearhead a major Allied operation. In the First World War their entry had been to re-enforce fully established positions, and then only in the very late stages of the war. The American Navy, already the strongest in the world, could absorb and use additional forces from the Allies. But the Allied ground and air forces were too weak and disorganised and would find such integration far from easy.

The British were still in great difficulty facing Rommel in the western desert. Tobruk had not been able to be held and the Suez Canal and the route to the Middle East, with its oil fields, were in great danger. What could not be risked was the possibility of another Dunkirk. The 'Battle of the Atlantic' was in its most crucial phase, with shipping losses so severe that the trans-Atlantic lifeline was nearly broken.

The Americans realised that for any direct attack on metropolitan France they would need the co-operation of the French Resistance and this would mean obtaining de Gaulle's sanction. In May 1942 the American ambassador in London asked de Gaulle for his view on a direct attack across the English Channel. The difficulties of such an attack at that stage of preparedness prevented any plan for invasion going forward. On the 13th July 1942 they gave further recognition to the status of the Free French who, as an active fighting force, were gathering all French nationals into a unified force to join the United Nations in the fight against the Axis powers. It also recognised that the National Committee, based in England, would represent all French forces, wherever they might be. Another re-enforcement of de Gaulle's authority was when, on the 14th July, de Gaulle took the salute at a parade of French troops. General Eisenhower and Admiral Stark attended the parade, adding American recognition of de Gaulle.

On the same day Anthony Eden, the British Foreign Secretary, broadcast to the French people:

"I speak to you not as amongst friends but as amongst Allies. Thanks to the decision of General de Gaulle, France has never left the battlefield. England has seen with hope and growing admiration the resistance of the French people. In our eyes, the re-establishment of the greatness and independence of France is not only a promise but a necessity, for without it, it would be vain to try to reconstruct Europe."

Meeting with senior American commanders in late July 1942 de Gaulle assured them that on opening a second front in Europe they would have the greatest support of the French, both from within France and from abroad. De Gaulle was keen to proceed with the invasion of metropolitan France as soon as possible. The Vichy government was under the control of the Germans and it was clear that the Germans would eventually occupy the Vichy controlled territory. The earlier an Allied invasion could be mounted the easier it would be to unite the widely spread French forces.

An assessment of the military position showed that the Germans would have some 40 divisions available to counter the attack. The invasion force, because of the inexperience of so many of the troops, would need an invasion force of some 50 divisions, of which 6 or 7 would need to be armoured. It was clear that the need for air superiority, over the invasion beaches and behind the German lines, would be crucial.

An early invasion, in the autumn of 1942, would not allow the Germans to recall troops from their heavy engagement with the Russians in the east. A 'Green Plan' combining aerial assaults by the Allies and sabotage by the French Resistance would do much to impede any German re-deployment of their available forces.

De Gaulle was able to offer an initial Free French contribution of a division coming from the Orient, a mixed brigade from equatorial Africa, four squadrons of aircraft and a large number of naval and transport ships. When all the Free French forces were assembled there would be an additional eight divisions and 15 squadrons of aircraft, coming from the French empire. Once landed in France, the French secret army would also be added to the Allied cause. He sent this information to Churchill and the other Allies on the 21st July 1942.

It soon became clear that the British and Americans could not assemble the necessary troops for such an invasion in the autumn of 1942. In a North African campaign, which was possible, the Americans did not wish the Free French to take control of Morocco, Algeria, or Tunisia. Indeed the Free French had been cut off from contacting their representatives in these French territories. This was a policy dictated by Washington. The United States was still making contact with the Vichy government and was determined to over-rule any control by de Gaulle. The Americans wanted General Weygand to take the place of the Vichy premier Laval, but Weygand refused to act against Petain. The Americans then contacted General Giraud, who had escaped from captivity in a German castle, and was burning to rejoin the fight and take over the French army in North Africa.

De Gaulle was keen to renew good relations with General Giraud. At a press conference in May 1942 de Gaulle had spoken of Giraud in glowing terms. In June and July de Gaulle's representatives had approached Giraud and told him of de Gaulle's wish that they should act in unison. In 1940 Giraud had been handed command of the French 9th Army when it was already in full retreat and being over-run by the Germans. It had not been possible to save that situation and Giraud himself had been captured while inspecting forward positions, unlike many of the generals whose headquarters were many kilometres behind their troops – out of sight and out of touch.

Taken prisoner, Giraud had managed to escape from imprisonment in a German castle by shinning down a rope made of the string from Red Cross parcels. When this, on test, had not been strong enough, a wire strengthening had been smuggled to Giraud inside a ham. After many adventures Giraud had reached the Vichy controlled area of France, where he was contacted by the Resistance. De Gaulle thought that Giraud could make a great contribution in bringing the French Forces in North Africa fully into the war on the Allied side. If he could do this he would take over the command of all French army units who would be taking part in the liberation of France. But there was only a deafening silence from Giraud. He had been overcome by the doubts about where his loyalty lay – to the Vichy government, which many considered to be the legal government – or to those who had kept the cause of an independent France alive.

If General Giraud had taken control of the army he would have treated Marshal Petain as an honoured old man who would still be placed on a pedestal. De Gaulle would have to take orders from Giraud. Thus the old hierarchical order would establish unity. Giraud's attitude caused de Gaulle great concern Certainly such an attitude would be completely unacceptable to the Free French forces who had rallied to de Gaulle's side in the earliest days. Giraud was viewed by these men as part of the decay and of France's downfall. He might be useful in some limited military position but leadership – no!

Giraud had the idea that he could turn the army under control of Vichy to the Allied cause after an Allied invasion. The doubt was how could troops who had been subject to the German yoke be trusted to remain loyal to the Allied side if there were reverses? And how could it be expected that such plans would not become known to the Germans and what harsh retribution would the Germans extract if such treachery became known to them? Any such action, with the fleet at Toulon still loyal to Petain and Darlan, could provoke them to cause havoc in the vulnerable areas of Gibraltar and Malta while an invasion of France was taking place.

If the Allies were going to invade North Africa, and they had in mind to use General Giraud, it would be essential for de Gaulle to tour his outposts to keep the loyalty of the Free French. It was also necessary to unify the Resistance within France. He named Andre Philip as Commander of the Interior. Jacques Soustelle was put in charge of Information. He forced the leaders of the three main French Resistance organisations – Combat, Liberation and Franc Tireurs – to unite their forces and organisations. To hasten the union he appointed General Delestraint as Commander of the Secret Army. Regular communications between the French and English part of the organisation were to be set up while de Gaulle was on his tour of Africa and the Orient. De Gaulle kept Churchill and Eden informed of these arrangements. As he left for Cairo de Gaulle travelled with the American ambassador, Averell Harriman. He seemed secretive and this confirmed de Gaulle's impression that there was some great and secret Allied action in preparation, but without the knowledge of the Free French.

The atmosphere in Cairo was as heavy as the weather. The 8th army had been driven back to El-Alamein, only a two hour armoured thrust from Alexandria. The British high command was not panicking about the situation, but beneath them there was confusion and disarray, not helped by the hostility of the local population. It showed itself in the Egyptians applauding only the Free French troops in the streets and in the cinemas.

If the British were depressed about the situation the Free French were not. At Bir Hakeim, between the 8th and 11th August, the French had made a heroic stand. At a review of the French 1st Light Division de Gaulle decorated General Koenig with the Cross of the Liberation. Other decorations were also awarded for this battle. After the battle Berlin radio's announcement that any French soldiers who had fought the Germans and had been captured would be shot, as they had broken the terms of the armistice, brought great anger amongst the troops. De Gaulle's announcement that in future any German soldiers captured by the Free French would be shot, provoking an immediate volte face by the Germans, had been very well received. De Gaulle also inspected the 2nd light division, finding them well equipped and eager for battle. There were also air force units and paratroops to inspect. He found the whole assembly well organised and making up a keen and powerful force - a sight to fill him with confidence and pride. He made useful contacts with the Egyptian press and government. And there, still at their posts, working quietly away keeping the Suez Canal open for the Allies during the war, French members of the Suez Canal Company were hard at work. There he saw the small room from which de Lesseps had masterminded and controlled the construction of the canal.

On the 7th August he met Churchill in Cairo. Churchill had told him that he had come to re-organise the military command. He also wanted to discuss Syria, while he was on his way to Moscow. These were difficult times. De Gaulle said the first, the British command, was entirely Churchill's affair. Free French troops would continue to fight under the British command. The second, Syria, was de Gaulle's business. The third matter, relationships with Stalin, would not be helped by the failure to open a Second Front on the mainland of Europe in that year, 1942. De Gaulle told him that he should let conscience be his guide. Churchill told de Gaulle that his conscience was like a good child, whom he always looked after.

De Gaulle was sure that Syria would show up Perfidious Albion in her true colours. The British were urging that elections should be held in Syria and Lebanon. De Gaulle informed him that the French National Committee had rejected this. No such elections could be held with Rommel and the Africa Korps at the gates of Alexandria. Were the British going to hold elections in Egypt, Irak, or Transjordan? Because of the French weakness after the fall of France Britain would have been quite content to see the French surrender their interests in the Levant, particularly Syria. But if this were the policy it would inflame xenophobia amongst the Arabs. It would produce increasing instability, which the British did not have the forces to control.

Field Marshal Smuts was also in Cairo at this time. This great man had started by opposing the British in the Boer war and had been a Boer government leader. He came with great strengths which were readily recognised by the British. He was made a member of the war cabinet in both the first and the second world wars. He was a man of particular influence with King George VIth. He was also a close friend of Churchill, who had been his prisoner for a few months during the Boer war. At a meeting Smuts told de Gaulle that if he had not managed to rally the French Equatorial countries to the Allied cause there would have been collapse in the Belgian Congo and thereby great difficulties for South Africa. There were voices raised in South Africa against joining the British cause and these could well have become irresistible. Indeed, South Africa could have joined the Axis powers, leading to German control from Algeria to the Cape of Good Hope. De Gaulle told Smuts that not all the Allies had the same appreciation of the importance of Free French control in the centre of Africa.

There was also going to be some Anglo-Saxon action in North Africa without Free French knowledge, approval, or participation. Smuts pointed out to him that it was the British bowing to the American point of view and indeed irresistible American pressure. It in no way meant that there was to be any lessening of support by the British for the Free French. Smuts reassured de Gaulle that the British wanted to displace the governor of Madagascar, who supported Vichy, and put the Free French in control.

On the 12th August de Gaulle left for Lebanon, intending to spend a whole month there, and in Syria renewing his contacts with the armed forces and the civil administration and population. In Lebanon he received a very warm welcome from groups of the population in many parts of the country. With General Catroux he reviewed the Druze camel squadrons. Going on to Syria he received an equally warm welcome, but it was also clear that the elite of Syria and Lebanon were seeking independence.

France could not grant such wishes immediately. If France surrendered her position in these countries the English would take her place for strategic reasons. In any case, de Gaulle did not consider that he had the right to make any such promises or decisions. The threat and the possibility of Rommel's troops gaining the territories meant that there could be no certainty that any elections would retain their validity for long. The French and British were in conflict over the supply of petroleum products to the region, from a refinery built at the Mediterranean end of the pipeline from Iraq.

Using the 1941 agreement about the funding of the Free French, the British wanted to offset these costs against the benefits from the oil supply in the Middle East. Because of the situation de Gaulle protested formally to Churchill on the 14th August about British interference in the French area of influence, contrary to established agreements. This was damaging the Allied standing in the area and was opening opportunities for unrest.

These difficulties were well known in the United States. The Secretary of State asked John Winant, the U.S. ambassador in London, to raise the matter with the British Foreign Secretary, Anthony Eden. Difficulties there could damage the war effort. The British and Americans continued with their preparations for the North African campaign, keeping them secret from the French. However this official silence did not contain the 'secret.'

In Cairo Churchill appointed General Montgomery to command the 8th army, after his first choice, General Gott, was killed in an aircraft crash on his way to take up the post. Further re-enforcements, particularly of armour, continued to arrive in the western desert. Preparations included the laying down of fuel and water dumps buried in the desert for concealment. The desert air force was greatly strengthened.

On the 27th August de Gaulle announced to the French delegation from London that the Americans had decided to make a landing in French North Africa. They would claim support from the Free French. There was no doubt that Marshal Petain would order the Vichy French forces to oppose the Allies. It was a diversion from the consideration of a direct invasion of France. Keeping de Gaulle out of the circle of knowledge was part of the continuing American attempt to woo the Vichy government. The Americans wanted to see which part of the French military, the Free French or the Vichyites, could best assist them in invading North Africa. The British Minister of State wanted de Gaulle to meet him in Cairo. De Gaulle insisted on Beirut, pointing out that on the two occasions that de Gaulle had been in Cairo the Minister of State had failed to arrange such a meeting.

Knowledge of these difficulties had reached London. On the 31st August Churchill telegraphed de Gaulle that he was aware of these serious difficulties and wanted to discuss them. He urged de Gaulle to hasten back to London for urgent discussions and asked on what date he expected to return. De Gaulle replied that the situation in the Levant was too serious for him to come away. Amongst these uncertainties de Gaulle spent much time and effort meeting the local political leaders. He assured them that France, as the power with the League of Nations mandate, would maintain stability and assist their forward progress. He saw the need to give these reassurances to avoid any cause for the fomentation of an insurrection. It was important to put the local services, such as the hospitals, in order. Those officials he met re-asserted their interest in continuing the contacts with Paris.

It was necessary to keep sufficient troops in Lebanon and Syria to bolster the local forces. Otherwise these countries could have provided a route for the Germans through to the oil fields of the Caucasus. The French and associated troops in this sector amounted to 25,000 men, but even this number was little enough to give a firm hold on these vast lands and 2,500 kilometres of frontier.

A visit from Roosevelt's envoy, Wendell Wilkie, to de Gaulle in Beirut gave the Americans the impression that the difficulties between the British and de Gaulle were the squabbles of old colonial powers. He regarded the French habit of wearing white uniforms as a relic of the days of Louis the XIVth. His report back to Roosevelt about his visit contained some element of malice.

On the 10th September 1942 the British invaded Madagascar. They had not been able by negotiation to obtain assurance that the island would not come under Japanese control. This seizure was in contrast with the taking of the main port, Diego Suarez, which was done with Free French knowledge and co-operation. When the British invaded Madagascar they announced that there would be an administration friendly to the United Nations. They told the Free French that they would be expected to produce this administration.

When de Gaulle returned to London it was to face the disagreement about the relationships in the Levant. It was agreed that the solution to these problems would be an amicable one. He then returned to the French equatorial territories. For the first time he was able to make one of his journeys in a French registered aircraft. From the French empire their airliners were resuming activity. Eight American aircraft had been obtained in exchange for the use of French bases in Africa. The most important of these was at Fort Lamy, in Chad, where there was an all-weather air strip. This allowed the direct flight of aircraft from the American factories across to the Azores and then on to Fort Lamy to gain quick access for these re-enforcements to the Middle East. Air France staff who had been stranded in Brazil and the Argentine when France collapsed were available as crew. After a 3,000 kilometre flight de Gaulle arrived at Fort Lamy where General Leclerc was able to invite him to inspect motorised troops ready for the assault into Libya. All the Free French troops were keen to move north into battle. He ordered General Leclerc to move north to link up with the British 8th army for the assault on Tunisia. It would be his task to prevent any Vichy forces opposing the Allied landings in North Africa. The African chiefs were entirely loyal and their people gave devoted service to the Free French cause. However they also had their eyes on the long-term goal of independence. These people, living in the wide expanses of grasslands, forests, and by rivers, raised their heads in the hope and expectation that the demands of war and their efforts would earn a great improvement in their conditions. De Gaulle fully recognised this. He arrived back in London on the 25th September. There were hot words with Churchill about the affair in the Levant, but the atmosphere cooled. Churchill thanked de Gaulle for returning to London and de Gaulle responded in an equally amiable fashion. Churchill wanted elections in Syria and the Lebanon, with which suggestion de Gaulle disagreed. Because of this disagreement Churchill would not co-operate with de Gaulle over Madagascar. The British would insert their own government, but this would be an attack on the rights of France!

Churchill was furious with de Gaulle. "You say you are France! You are not France! France, where is she? I am certain that General de Gaulle and those who follow him are an important and honourable part of the people. But one can also find others of equal value." De Gaulle interrupted "If, in your eyes, I am not the representative of France, why have you dealt with me concerning all her world wide affairs?" At this Churchill was silent.

Eden intervened and brought the discussion back to the affairs of the Levant. The two countries interests were intertwined. Churchill interrupted, charging de Gaulle with taking an Anglophobe attitude to increase his stature amongst the French.

De Gaulle considered that this attitude would be an excuse to keep the Free French out of the French North African territories. However, making this point would have been destructive, so he kept his own counsel and at that point they parted.

In the following weeks the atmosphere between the British and the Free French deteriorated. The Foreign Office threatened a formal break in relations. Communications between the Free French headquarters and offices around the world were interrupted by the British. De Gaulle could not see that any concessions were necessary on his side to re-establish good relations. However fierce the storm of disagreement may have been, calm soon returned. The interruption of French communications ceased very quickly. On the 23rd October Churchill sent a special message of congratulation concerning the action of the French submarine *Junon* against two large German naval vessels near the Norwegian coast. He also thanked de Gaulle for the part which French troops had played in the battle of El-Alamein. On the 30th October Field Marshal Smuts added to the reconciliation by stating that the Free French administration would take control in Madagascar.

Support for de Gaulle came from Czechoslovakia. President Benes declared the French National Committee, under the direction of General de Gaulle, as the legal government of France. He sought de Gaulle's recognition that the Munich agreement of 1938, whereby part of Czechoslovakia was given away to Hitler by Britain and France, was unlawful. De Gaulle made such a proclamation, recognising the pre-1938 frontier as the legal one. This proclamation was broadcast.

The Russians recognised that the Americans were dictating which French government would be in control and with whom they would deal. They recognised the Free French as the force in action for the people of France. Such American intervention would have stifled the growth of French resistance to the Germans.

In France, on the 22nd June, Laval had stated that he wanted the Germans to win the war. In July a legion of young Frenchmen was in action, under German command, against the Russians. In August Marshal Petain had dissolved the National Assembly. The President of the Senate and the leader of the Chamber of Deputies both wrote letters of protest to the Marshal. Mr. Heriot, the Leader of the Chamber of Deputies, returned the insignia of his Legion of Honour in protest at decorations being awarded to the legion fighting in Russia. This practice stopped. Persecution of the Jews in France increased, under the direction of a special 'Commissariat' set up to co-operate with the Germans. During this period the German occupation became more severe and in a three month period a thousand Frenchmen were shot.

There were still disputes and rivalries amongst the Resistance organisations in the unoccupied zone of France. De Gaulle formed a National Resistance Council around Jean Moulin. He informed the Americans of the deteriorating situation in France. It was a time at which many French leaders joined their support to de Gaulle's leadership.

On the 7th November 1942 the radio announced the operation 'Torch' landings on the west coast of North Africa. On the next morning de Gaulle went to Downing Street, where Churchill greeted him warmly. He explained that the invasion was an American operation and that the British only had a minor supporting role. The exclusion of the Free French was an American decision. There was no breach in the accord between Churchill and de Gaulle. With emotion Churchill declared "You have been with us since the worst times. We are certainly not going to abandon you now that the leaden skies are lifting to a brighter dawn!"

The British told him that there would be landings at several points in Morocco, at Oran and at Algiers. The operation had not gone unopposed. At Casablanca Vichy French troops had put up vigorous opposition. General Giraud had been embarked secretly on a British submarine which had brought him from the south coast of France to Gibraltar. The Americans were counting on him to take over command of the French troops in North Africa and bring them over to the Allied side. Churchill asked de Gaulle if he knew that Admiral Darlan was in Algiers. De Gaulle pointed out that the invasion had the possibility of recovering for the Allies both an army and a fleet which would be of great assistance for the liberation. He also pointed out that this part of the operation would have been much easier if he had been involved and had been in a position, as he would have wished, to co-operate. He had not been surprised that there had been some stiff resistance to the invasion. There were, in Morocco, many French elements which had opposed the Allies in Syria a year before. The British had allowed them to leave for North Africa, and now they were continuing their opposition. Allowing these forces to leave Syria had been in spite of de Gaulle's warnings. De Gaulle did not think that the opposition would be long lasting, but unless it was quickly overcome it would give the Germans time to bring up troops to oppose the landings.

De Gaulle expressed surprise that the landings had not included Bizerta, in Tunisia. This port could be used by the Germans and Italians to re-enforce their troops in North Africa and its exclusion from the assault would cost the Allies dearly in the overall campaign. De Gaulle also thought that the operation would have been more strongly mounted if General Koenig's division had been included. The British replied that the Americans had been in control of the expedition and their thoughts had been mainly on the difficulty of attempting any landings at all with troops who had sailed across the Atlantic to make landfall for their assault.

Churchill asked de Gaulle how he saw relations developing between the Free French and the French authorities in North Africa. De Gaulle replied that if the Free French were to exert any real influence it would be necessary to displace the Vichy appointed government from Algiers. If Admiral Darlan were in control for Vichy no agreement would be possible. "With him in charge there is no way of stopping the battle. For the rest, one will have to wait and see." What neither de Gaulle or Churchill knew at the time was how Admiral Darlan had used the Vichy French embassy in Washington as a base for agents to find out which British ships were being repaired at which American naval yards and when they would be sailing, making them easy U-boat targets. Darlan had passed this information to the Germans.

Information received at the Free French headquarters at Carlton Gardens indicated that everywhere the Americans were meeting serious resistance. De Gaulle had appealed over the radio to all

Frenchmen to come over to the Allied side. Many French officers tried to rally the troops to the Allied cause and some of the administrative buildings in Algiers were taken over, but there was fighting and Gaullist supporters Pillafort and Dreyfus were killed. It was clear that the message sent from Roosevelt to Petain, to allow the Allies to land unhindered, had been totally ignored.

By the 9th November the situation had worsened. Marshal Petain had given orders that the 'invaders' were to be opposed. General Giraud, seeing that the Allies were not able to give him command of the French troops, declined to go to North Africa. The worst fighting was in Morocco. In Tunis Admiral Platon was sent by Vichy to order Admiral Esteva and Admiral Derrien to give safe passage to German parachutists, who were then able to land without a shot being fired.

That evening there were long faces in London amongst the Allies. There was the prospect of a long struggle between Eisenhower's troops and the Vichy French. It was even possible that Spain would come into the war on the Axis side. However, in the end, good sense prevailed. General Juin, who had been commander in chief of the Vichy forces until the arrival of Admiral Darlan, prevailed in seeking a cease fire and this came into effect on the 10th November.

This fratricidal conflict had cost dear. The French had lost 3,000 dead or wounded, 1 cruiser, 10 lesser surface ships and 10 submarines, which had been destroyed or severely damaged, and 135 aeroplanes had been destroyed. On the Allied side 3,000 troops had been killed or wounded; the British lost two destroyers, *Broke* and *Malcolm* and some smaller ships. The Americans had the battleship *Massachussetts* badly damaged, other vessels also damaged, and lost 70 aircraft.

It was a terribly futile battle and gave Hitler great comfort. He was winning without fighting. De Gaulle met Admiral Stark, of the United States Navy. Eisenhower had been horrified at the nature of the battle and thanked de Gaulle for trying to prevent it. De Gaulle replied that he wanted to send a mission to Algiers and Admiral Stark promised to try to arrange it.

On the 11th November de Gaulle addressed a Free French rally at the Albert Hall, in London. The crowd was immense and most enthusiastic. But they were also very worried about the news from North Africa. It was close to civil war, with French troops fighting on both sides, though not yet against each other. America's continued dealings with the Vichy government had promoted the Vichy cause and there were still those in France who thought that France's salvation could come sooner and at a lower price if Roosevelt still had influence with Hitler.

However this was not the mood of the rally. One retired general, from high up in a gallery, shouted for de Gaulle to give way to General Giraud. He was unceremoniously removed from the hall. What the intervention did show was that among the senior French military – a genuine 'Old Guard' - there was bitter resentment at such a junior general as de Gaulle stepping from his low place on the ladder of the military hierarchy to lead the nation. They had not understood that he had held no field command since the fall of France. He had taken over the political leadership in the vacuum after the disaster of 1940 and had been recognised as leader by the British only 11 days later. Only he, standing for France, had been able to stop British rampages through the French governed territories of the Levant.

In his oration to the meeting de Gaulle reviewed the Free French progress in the war. He kept open the opportunity for all French people to join the Free French. He reminded the audience that whatever the difficulties of the last few days in North Africa, the balance of forces on the side of liberty was now decisive. Only this would bring about the eventual liberation of France. He reminded them that their purpose was a France united as a nation, united with all its territories, and with a single system of law. He ended with the call "A united struggle for a united country!" The ovation nearly brought the house down. The doubts were gone, the duty clear.

The unity of the French was clear in London, but Eisenhower was trying to end the battle in North Africa. On the 10th November General Clark had received the order to cease fire, to try to reach a negotiated settlement with Admiral Darlan, the arch Vichyite. Admiral Darlan would have none of it and he took a stand, supported by the generals in North Africa, that they had won a victory in the name of the Vichy government.

They certainly had the appearance of legality. The Americans might have thought that they had initiated a cease fire to allow the French in North Africa to come over to the Allied side. Laval took the attitude that the Americans should be invited to surrender as it was clear that they had no stomach for any further conflict. If there was dithering in the Vichy military in North Africa he would take over command. On the 1st December Admiral Platon spoke on the radio to the French in North Africa. He reminded the people, on behalf of Marshal Petain and the Vichy government, that it was illegal to treat with these invaders and that they should soon reconquer North Africa.

On the 16th November de Gaulle had met with Churchill and Eden. Churchill seemed in a very good humour, but Eden seemed troubled. Churchill fully understood de Gaulle's feelings, but they must not lose sight of the objective of kicking the Axis out of Tunisia. All undertakings to the Free French remained valid. All Eisenhower's actions were of temporary effect and would not affect long-standing obligations. Churchill then showed de Gaulle a telegram which he had sent to Roosevelt. It made two points:

1.   All Eisenhower's actions were for temporary expediency.

2.   Churchill gave approval for Eisenhower's actions on condition that they were only a temporary expedient.

De Gaulle stated that he would support Churchill's action but that it held echoes of the 18th century, when Frederick the Great paid the Court in Vienna to keep quiet about his appropriating Silesia. It was not in keeping with the traditions of the Renaissance. It certainly was not in keeping with the traditions of the cause of freedom, for which so much blood was being spilt. He asked them what the consequences would be if the main result of the Allied action were to saddle them with Admiral Darlan as leader.

Churchill repeated that current events were not a signpost for the future. De Gaulle repeated that France would not accept the arrangements indicated. The National Committee had prepared a communiqué and he wanted permission to broadcast it on the

B.B.C. Churchill replied that he fully understood de Gaulle's position, but asked him to wait a little before broadcasting the communiqué. De Gaulle would be allowed to make the broadcast and Churchill would telegraph Roosevelt telling him of de Gaulle's need to make his position clear. De Gaulle pointed out that it was essential to avoid giving a fraudulent impression that Darlan and the Free French were one and the same thing. American radio stations had transmitted Admiral Darlan's broadcasts with the prefix 'Honour and Country,' taking the Free French symbol. The B.B.C. had compounded the fraud by retransmitting the broadcast. De Gaulle turned to Eden and expressed his total lack of comprehension as to how the B.B.C. had taken part in this deception.

Before they went in to luncheon Eden took de Gaulle aside and expressed his disquiet about the whole affair. De Gaulle expressed regret that Eden had allowed himself to get involved in such trickery. In such an atmosphere the luncheon was strained, and even the ladies could not lighten the mood.

After lunch Churchill and de Gaulle went into private conversation. Churchill told de Gaulle that his position was secure and that Darlan had no future. Giraud was politically bankrupt. "You hold the honour. You have the correct path. You will stay at the head. Do not take a collision course with the Americans. It is useless and you will gain nothing. Be patient and you will succeed. There is no alternative." Then Churchill expressed his disgust at Darlan. Of course it had been Darlan who, in 1940, by his refusal to organise the French fleet out of Axis hands, had brought about the tragedy at Oran. Churchill would never forgive him.

De Gaulle expressed his surprise to Churchill that the British Government was trailing in the control of events behind the Americans. "I do not understand you" de Gaulle said. "You have been in the war since the first day. One could say, in truth, that you are the war. Your armies are victorious in Libya and yet you follow behind the Americans, whose soldiers have never seen a German. You have the moral control of this war. The whole of public opinion is behind you."

Churchill reminded him how, a few days earlier at the

Guildhall, he had spoken a eulogy about General de Gaulle and the Free French. In contrast General Giraud had always avoided the tough decisions or action. De Gaulle replied that to keep Giraud on their side he should be offered some sort of official position without delay.

In a speech at the Mansion House, given by the Lord Mayor of London on the 10th November 1942 to celebrate the victory at El-Alamein, Churchill had said "At this time our thoughts turn towards France, groaning under the bondage of the German heel. Many ask themselves the question: Is France finished? Is that long and famous history, adorned by so many manifestations of genius and valour, bearing with it so much that is precious to culture and civilisation, and above all to the liberties of mankind – is all that now to sink forever into the ocean of the past, or will France rise again and resume her rightful place in the structure of what may one day be again the family of Europe? I declare to you here, on this considerable occasion, even now when misguided or suborned Frenchmen are firing upon their rescuers, I declare to you my faith that France will rise again. While there are men like General de Gaulle and all those who follow him – and they are legion throughout France – and men like General Giraud, that gallant warrior whom no prison can hold, while there are men like those to stand forward in the name and in the cause of France, my confidence in the future of France is sure."

It was not only Churchill who had paid tribute and acknowledgment to de Gaulle. In a speech at the Mansion House on May 29th 1941 Anthony Eden, the Foreign Secretary, had said " All honour, too, to those Frenchmen who refused to accept what they considered a dishonourable armistice and left their hearths and homes in order to maintain the struggle at our side under their gallant leader, General de Gaulle."

These were only two of many examples of public support for the Free French. There was no difficulty with British support; it was only American doubts which plagued the prospects of Allied unity, and this was only, in the main, the result of Nazi propaganda against the Free French in the eighteen months between the fall of France and Hitler's declaration of war on the United States.

The Americans were in full discussion with Vichy and Vichy was changing its stance by the hour to suit the immediate circumstances. Vichy represented so much that was against the principles of the British. These American actions would delay and impede the overall growth of the Allied forces and undermine the Allied cause.

Churchill understood de Gaulle's anxiety and asked him to stay in close touch and to come and see him as often as he wished. Throughout de Gaulle understood that Churchill would be steadfast in his support for the Free French National Committee. Churchill had expressed confidence that Fighting France would emerge stronger and more necessary than ever.

On the 22nd November General Clark resumed negotiations with Admiral Darlan. He was prepared to give the Admiral full authority, treating him as an ally. After Free French protests Eisenhower exclaimed "I will recognise Darlan if he gives me Algiers and I will recognise Laval if he gives me Paris!" Darlan used the advantage of his position to, by the 7th December, have the Americans declare him Chief of State of the French territories in North Africa and Commander in Chief of all the French forces.

The Germans, learning of these arrangements, occupied the southern part of France. The Vichy army in France was forced to lay down their arms. General de Lattre de Tassigny was dismissed and imprisoned. But in Africa all the French officials, in order to keep their positions, submitted to Admiral Darlan's rule, put into effect by an 'Imperial Council.' In France General Weygand was arrested by the Germans and deported to Germany. And so the fiction of the independence of the Vichy government was exposed and its power uprooted. Finally, the only remnant of Vichy sovereignty rested with the fleet at Toulon. But Hitler had no use for surface fleets. The loss of so many of his vaunted capital ships, such as the Graf Spee and the *Bismark*, caused him to lose interest. The later loss of the *Scharnhorst*, *Tirpitz* and *Lutzow* would complete his surface ship disenchantment.

When the Germans occupied southern France the French ships, which had been disarmed under the terms of the armistice, suddenly came under the control of the Germans. Marshal Petain had neglected to send them to North Africa, out of the clutches of the Germans. When de Gaulle sent a secret emissary to Admiral Laborde to remind him of his duty to keep the French ships out of German hands the emissary, Colonel Fourcault, was threatened. From the 26th November the ships of the French fleet came under German control. The Germans, in their advance, put artillery on the heights above the fleet anchorage and mined the harbour and its entry. They had the French fleet at their mercy. Marshal Petain and his naval command, paralysed by the consequences of their inaction, ordered that the ships should be scuttled.

Three battleships, the *Dunquerque*, *Strasbourg* and *Provence*, 8 cruisers, 33 destroyers and frigates, 16 submarines and more than 40 other vessels went to the bottom. Two of the medium sized warships and 5 tankers were seized and used by the Germans. But 5 submarines, by the heroic action of their commanders, sought to escape. Three reached Algiers, one took refuge in a Spanish port and one was sunk en route. De Gaulle was overcome with grief at the loss of so much of the French fleet by Petain's stupid inaction. At this further time of French tragedy he was comforted by a telephone call from Churchill expressing his sympathy and condolences.

The disaster at Toulon did much to rally the French people to de Gaulle. The completion of the German occupation of France showed the fallacy of the pretence of some residual independence. There was now no other course open to freedom loving French people than resistance.

The recognition of Darlan as the man in charge in North Africa by the Americans provoked general indignation. On this there was complete unanimity amongst all the French. When all the French saw the Allies treating with de Gaulle's opponents people felt frustrated and the American actions were despised.

The B.B.C. broadcast a statement that General de Gaulle and the National Committee would in no way recognise the negotiations taking place in Algiers for these negotiations were intended to maintain Vichy control in North Africa and they would be completely repudiated by the Free French forces. "The union of all French overseas territories in the fight for liberation is only possible if the conditions conform to the wishes and the dignity of the French people."

The British continued to give the Free French every support, but this carried little weight with the Americans, and the British had little effective influence on the Americans. Three days later de Gaulle was stopped from broadcasting on the B.B.C. a declaration of support for French Resistance organisations in France, which stated that General de Gaulle is the undoubted leader of French Resistance and, more than ever, we are all behind him. "We demand that all French territories in North Africa which have been liberated shall be placed immediately under the control of General de Gaulle." The censors from Washington put their veto on the publication of this document.

On the 21st November de Gaulle himself met censorship. In a speech for a broadcast to the French people, which had already been recorded by the B.B.C., de Gaulle asked, "Is our national liberation to be dishonoured?" Then he continued "Non!" Shortly before the broadcast he was told that the Allies had decided that there should be no broadcasts concerning North Africa, on the insistence of the Americans, and this decision was with the agreement of the British Government. This was a stupid restriction, for de Gaulle immediately used the Free French radio stations at Brazzaville, Douala and Beirut.

There were other disagreements, over the Indian Ocean French colonies of Reunion and Madagascar. But by the 14th December de Gaulle and Eden signed an agreement bringing these colonies into the war on the side of the old ally, England. British army and naval officers would help with organising the military activities. By this means many of the troops who had been taking orders from Vichy were brought over to the Allied side.

In French Somalia it was also intended that Gaullists should take over. This was opposed by Washington, who sent the American consul from Aden to put American policy into place. Fighting France, with British support, took over the colony and brought it in on the Allied side. The winning over of French Somalia to the Allies completed the list of French colonies in the Indian Ocean now lost to Vichy control. In French Somalia there were 200 officers and 8,000 men who were freed to fight in Libya. The French were coming together to fight on the same side. British, French, and Americans were joining together to fight the Germans and Italians. The final battles to drive the Axis forces out of Africa were imminent.

But Vichy had not yet finished damaging the Allied cause. At Bizerta Admiral Derrien had followed Vichy's orders and allowed the Germans to take over 4 surface vessels, 2 patrol boats and 9 submarines, all obtained intact in the port. This further loss of French ships to the Germans was another episode in a long and shameful series. If anything it underlined the validity of de Gaulle's harsh criticism of the Vichy government and the justification he had given in July 1940 for the British action in disabling the French fleet by the attack on Oran.

These delays had helped Eisenhower train his troops. Those who had come to the landings in Morocco directly from the United States were completely inexperienced, until the bloody encounter with the German armour at the battle of the Kasserine Pass. The difficulties of the invading Allied forces were made much worse by the German submarine attacks on the Atlantic convoys. The shipping losses in the first few months of 1943 were the worst in the whole Battle of the Atlantic, and the Atlantic lifeline was nearly severed. Anything that the Fighting French could bring across Africa to the Allied cause was especially valuable at this pivotal time. Defeat for the American invasion force on the West African coast would have prevented any early prospect of carrying the campaign of liberation on to mainland Europe.

The value of French troops had been shown at the battle of El Alamein by General Koenig's 1st Light Division on the southern Allied flank. Later the 2nd Light Division had taken part in the rout of the Africa Korps as it retreated westwards. These troops, joined with the French troops further west, could play a vital part in the final expulsion of Axis forces from Africa. With artillery elements brought in from French Somalia a fully equipped Free French division could be assembled at the western end of North Africa. Other French troops could join from Chad, where General Leclerc had been preparing since 1940. He was ordered to co-operate with General Alexander.

When General Leclerc was coming up from the south General Alexander advised him that as he captured the Fezzan it would come under British control and the use of Francs as the currency would not be allowed. General de Gaulle countermanded this order. Charles Peake was sent from London with the disagreeable message that General Alexander's words were the British Government's decision. De Gaulle was adamant. Leclerc was to have no British interference whatever in the French territory. On the 12th January the French forces coming up from the south had overcome the enemy and were striking towards Tripoli. On the way Leclerc's troops took forty officers and nearly a thousand other ranks prisoner.

This was a military victory but the political atmosphere was still cloudy. Not all those in Morocco and Algeria who stated that they were Gaullists were pressing on for the cause. Some were helping themselves to advantages. Many did not like Darlan remaining in charge and others who supported Giraud were disappointed in the lack of success for their support. It was the French political scene of the 1930's under a Fez and with palm trees. General Noguès had three officers arrested in Morocco and ordered them shot. They were saved only when Eisenhower shipped them out to Gibraltar. Darlan appeared to change sides to join with the Allies and was intent on making a profit from his courage.

De Gaulle had to rush to take control in Algeria. Algeria was to trouble him for the rest of his life. The urgency of the situation in Algeria did not trouble Washington or London and they offered a thousand excuses to delay him. Only Eisenhower seemed to understand, as he did on many later occasions. Eisenhower had been surprised by the strength of the opposition the landings had provoked. He was disconcerted by the confused machinations of the French body politique and worried that it would divert, delay, or even destroy the Allied effort. There was a community of urgent interest with de Gaulle and Eisenhower knew it.

When de Gaulle's representative, General d'Astier, arrived in Algeria on the 20th December he found an acute crisis. On the

155

surface all seemed quiet but it was boiling underneath. Giraud was vexed, having been denied command of the Allied forces. He had been humiliated by being treated as a subordinate to Darlan. Because of these slights Giraud was ready to accept de Gaulle's offer of co-operation in rallying the troops. It was clear that Admiral Darlan had to be removed. Then all the French troops of good will could be rallied.

Local political officials wrote to Admiral Darlan that as the Vichy government was no longer independent he had no legal authority in North Africa. The Americans informed Darlan that they wanted to deal directly with de Gaulle. If the political turmoil were not sorted out quickly there could be bloodshed.

Admiral Darlan took a stiff attitude with General d'Astier. He stated that he, and he alone, was the only suitable leader and rallying point for the different French interests in North Africa. There was then an argument between Darlan and Giraud. When d'Astier returned to London he had gained the impression that Darlan would not long remain in power. That afternoon de Gaulle learned that Darlan had been assassinated by Fernand Bonnier de la Chapelle. It appeared that the act had been done by those who were angry at the disunity of the French but behind it seemed to be the interests of those who had exhausted Darlan's usefulness as a 'temporary expedient.' Before his execution the young man stated that he had done it to rid France of the dissenting voice which was a barrier to French unity.

Whatever the rights or wrongs of Darlan's assassination it freed the scene of a major impediment. The execution of the assassin was carried out after a hasty court martial in the dead of the night. It was never known who might ultimately have been behind the deed itself. To de Gaulle the errors which had caused so much damage to the French fleet were a symptom of the rotten core of the French State.

INTRIGUE

Darlan's death had major consequences. De Gaulle telegraphed Giraud on the 25th December 1942 that it was more than ever necessary to unify the functions of the State. De Gaulle proposed an urgent meeting with Giraud to centralise and unify all French forces fighting for the liberation. Darlan's death had given the Americans a clear field to install in Algeria whichever French leader they chose. On the 26th December Giraud replied that the recent assassination made the atmosphere in North Africa unsuitable for a meeting. It was in every way an unsatisfactory response. De Gaulle urged the need for a unified French nation, in military and civilian organisation, to speed the liberation. Divisions would fail France. The dissentions would become known to the British and Americans and would undermine France's position, perhaps for years to come. For this reason de Gaulle made his call for unity public on the 2nd January1943.

An incident the previous evening made the call for unity more urgent. General Giraud, as civil and military governor, had arrested several dozen people who had aided the Americans when they had first landed. They were accused of complicity with the Americans in trying to take control. The American influence delayed any acceptance of a meeting between Giraud and de Gaulle. De Gaulle knew the urgency to unite the French forces. The Americans were at odds in Washington between their military and their political aims. They regarded French divisions as an opportunity to impose their will.

Roosevelt had wanted de Gaulle to visit Washington soon after the North African landings but now the invitation was postponed. Linked with this Giraud sent a note to de Gaulle from Algiers agreeing to a meeting but citing pressure of essential duties as a reason for his unavailability before the end of January.

Churchill could see there were serious problems in the French camp. On the 17th January he asked de Gaulle to meet with him discreetly, and to arrange a meeting between de Gaulle and Giraud. De Gaulle declined this suggestion. There would be a conference between Roosevelt and Churchill at Casablanca. What part would there be for France in the discussions? Instead he renewed his appeal for a meeting with Giraud, on French territory and whenever Giraud wished.

Two days later Churchill sent de Gaulle a telegram. Churchill was very upset with de Gaulle's refusal to meet Giraud under Churchill's auspices. It had damaged his relationship with Roosevelt. Churchill would do no more to aid the Fighting French with the Americans until the leadership of the Free French was clear. However the message was softened by a direct invitation to attend the Casablanca conference. De Gaulle replied that the war situation demanded that they should all meet and all other considerations and disputes must be put aside.

The French National Committee gave de Gaulle its approval for this stand. De Gaulle included General Catroux and Admiral Argenlieu in his party and they arrived in Morocco on the 22nd January. De Gaulle was met, on behalf of Roosevelt, by General Wilbur, an old acquaintance from senior military training. Churchill's and Giraud's representatives also welcomed de Gaulle. The windows of their vehicles were blacked out to conceal de Gaulle's arrival. The meeting was secluded and under American guard – almost like being imprisoned – and on French territory.

In discussions with Giraud it was clear that although Giraud had escaped from German captivity he was not hostile to the regime in Vichy. He gave support to the position of those who had opposed de Gaulle's attempt to land at Dakar in September 1940. The impression was that in some ways Giraud was equivocal to the Allied cause and lacked resolution in uniting the French forces, even though he was keen to fight the Germans.

During the conference de Gaulle was visited by Mr. MacMillan, British Minister of State, at Churchill's behest to try and bring about an agreement between de Gaulle and Giraud. De Gaulle insisted that any such agreement had to be between the French but he went, as requested, to see Churchill.

De Gaulle expressed with some force that he would not have come to the meeting if he had known that, on French territory, he would have been surrounded by American bayonets. "We are in an occupied country," Churchill cried. Churchill explained that he was trying to work out a solution for the French empire with President Roosevelt. They wanted Giraud to be the military commander, with de Gaulle and Giraud in joint overall command. They envisaged General Georges as the third joint president. Those who had been Vichy collaborators, such as Noguès and Boisson, would remain in their posts. It was an American idea and de Gaulle should have confidence in it.

De Gaulle replied that it would suit well American N.C.O.s, but surely they did not expect him to take it seriously. De Gaulle had the highest regard for Churchill and Roosevelt, but they had no authority to meddle in totally French affairs. They had already meddled in Algeria, with dire results and severe damage to the cohesion of the Allied cause. They had given no proper thought to the position of Fighting France. Churchill pointed out that in forming his government it had been necessary, for political reasons, to include some of those who had supported the Munich agreement. They had rallied as well as any others. De Gaulle explained that he had not come from a political background, stained with all the efforts of winning and retaining power. Churchill explained that he and Roosevelt were united in their view. The politics had to be organised. It was arranged that de Gaulle and Roosevelt should meet, late in the evening. De Gaulle was accompanied only by his interpreter. Behind the curtains of the room de Gaulle noted that many shadowy figures were lurking, including the President's aide, Harry Hopkins.

De Gaulle was impressed by Roosevelt's high ideals. He was well served by his knowledge, his bravery and his intelligence. His powerful country could and would provide the tools for victory. The American tendency had been for a long time towards isolationism, but now they had enrolled in the cause of freedom they had adopted the cause with messianic zeal. Americans wanted to adopt the whole world, to assist the oppressed peoples everywhere, and to serve the cause of liberty and freedom by placing into service their vast industrial power, and with it their control.

If it were to be an American led war, it would be an American led peace. France, if she were to be saved by American blood, would have to adopt American ideals. De Gaulle's idea of a totally independent and sovereign France was not part of Roosevelt's vision. It was not as though Roosevelt had total control, for he had twice to seek re-election. Between elections he had to suffer continuous harassment by all the arms of the media. He had to struggle continuously against his own ill health. Underneath the posturings of the politics de Gaulle felt that Roosevelt had a warm sympathy for him.

Roosevelt was insistent on his style of solution to the French problem. De Gaulle was certain that, in the end, the only solution that would work was one which would emerge by a true decision of the French people.

The next day de Gaulle met General Giraud. "What do you propose?" de Gaulle asked. Giraud put forward the plan of Roosevelt and Churchill: Giraud first, de Gaulle second, and Georges third, as a triumvirate to rule. All the old functionaries would remain in place. This was unacceptable to de Gaulle. He questioned Giraud's right to assume such powers, without any election. In France any Vichy supporters were viewed with distaste, and Giraud had intended to keep many of those in North Africa in place. If Giraud were in control it would be seen as power held in the name of Marshal Petain and it would be total anathema to the Free French.

Giraud repeated that this was a political and not a military matter. He had agreed with Roosevelt that the Americans would equip all the necessary French army units. By this means he hoped in six months to create twelve new divisions. He challenged de Gaulle to produce, in the same time, even half that number. And if he did try, from where would de Gaulle get the necessary arms?

De Gaulle replied that the troops in North Africa belonged to France, and they were not Giraud's personal possession. The most important task was to unify the French forces. The Fighting France forces symbolised the spirit of resistance to the enemy and had actually fought hard on the Allied side. They would be the ones whom the people of France would trust to spearhead the liberation. Those in North Africa who had submitted to German control through the Vichy government would not be accepted or trusted; it would not be just a matter of numbers and armament.

De Gaulle proposed that the best solution was to form a French temporary government in Algeria, which, with liberation would become the Government of the Republic. Giraud would receive, from this government, command of the Army of Liberation. There would have to be a repudiation of the armistice signed by the Vichy government with the Germans and France would be recognised as an independent country by the whole world.

Giraud would take time to come round to agreeing to this solution. The need to rally all the countries of the French empire, from Indo China to the Antilles, was urgent. Local issues in North Africa could not be allowed to delay and lose opportunities. One insect could not be allowed to remain and ruin the whole bag of flour. The difficulty was that the Americans kept their insistence on their proposal and the French dining together that night were in melancholy mood. The Americans told de Gaulle that in North Africa only one in ten of the French population were Gaullists.

Then Roosevelt and Churchill insisted on holding to their agreement with Giraud to provide the arms as they had agreed. The Americans and the British issued a statement that in the interests of the people of France, the President of the United States and the British Prime Minister recognised as Commander in Chief General Giraud. They recognised Algiers as his headquarters and would give every assistance.

Churchill had been in discussion with Giraud and had written down on a corner of the table that the pound sterling would exchange at 250 francs to the pound. The agreement reached with de Gaulle in London had been that it would be at the rate of 176 francs to the pound. Roosevelt had discussions with the Sultan of Morocco to establish Giraud's control and give him something to direct immediately.

That evening Harold MacMillan visited de Gaulle and expressed concern as to how this statement would be seen by the Fighting French, He wanted de Gaulle to keep quiet about the arrangements that had been made only twenty-four hours before the end of the conference.

Early the nest morning MacMillan and Murphy came to see de Gaulle with a communiqué which Roosevelt and Churchill had prepared during the night. They wanted Giraud and de Gaulle to publicly agree on it. Giraud had already accepted it. It was too vague to have any real meaning, that "on behalf of the French empire the two generals accepted the principles of the United Nations." The two generals would form a united committee for the war effort.

De Gaulle held discussions with his advisors. Their conclusion was entirely negative. The messengers were told that no unified increase in France's power in the war effort could result from such a foreign intervention. De Gaulle would see the two leaders again during the day. With Churchill it was the most ill tempered meeting of the whole war. De Gaulle judged that Churchill was holding to his position with some embarrassment. On returning to London he would publicly announce that de Gaulle was the sole cause of the discord. De Gaulle replied that his regard for the Prime Minister and his faith in the Anglo-French alliance led him to deplore Churchill's current attitude. To preserve his alliance with the Americans he had taken a position which was unacceptable for France, unsettling for Europe, and regrettable for England.

Then de Gaulle went to see Roosevelt. Roosevelt expressed his unhappiness that agreement had not been reached. "In human affairs" he told de Gaulle, "you must offer some drama to the public. Your meeting with General Giraud is well known. Some form of joint communiqué needs to emerge from such a meeting and its effect will be dramatic. That is why Churchill and I believe that agreement needs to be sought." "Leave it to me," de Gaulle told him. "There will be a communiqué so it is better not to press yours."

De Gaulle presented the other members of his delegation to the President. Roosevelt; Giraud, and his team, then came in. In a loud voice Churchill then repeated his diatribe against de Gaulle. President Roosevelt then, in a quieter tone, presented his final demands. It was that he, Churchill, Giraud and de Gaulle should all be photographed together. "Certainly," agreed de Gaulle, "for I have the greatest regard for this fine soldier." "All I want is that you should shake hands in our presence" the President continued. "I will do that for you," replied de Gaulle.

Four chairs were taken out into the garden. Handshakes were exchanged. The cameras clicked. All was well! Smiles were exchanged and the impression of French unity was displayed before the world.

Before leaving the conference de Gaulle and Giraud discussed a joint communiqué. They re-affirmed their faith in a French victory and in the triumph of human liberty. This had been changed from 'democratic principles' at Giraud's request.

The question of why the Americans and British were so insistent that the Free French should come to an accommodation with the former Vichyites has puzzled many. Sir William Stephenson – known as INTREPID – had been charged by Churchill with setting up the British Security Commission in Washington. After the fall of France in 1940 the French embassy in Washington had been a Vichy stronghold and did much to discourage Americans from having any faith that Britain could resist invasion. The rumour was spread that in ten weeks Britain would be defeated. It was therefore a waste of time supporting Britain with arms. Initially it did not matter that Britain might be defeated if the arms supplied were paid for with 'cash on the barrel head.'

When Britain's credit became more stretched, on German instructions, the French embassy in Washington tried to enter into negotiations with American companies to refuse to supply Britain at all. They were told that France was co-operating with Germany and that all Europe would be united under the Nazi flag. There would be great opportunities for American companies and those who had supported or supplied Britain risked being excluded from lucrative contracts. Many companies in the United States either were, or had dealings with, American subsidiaries of German companies.

The impression of Britain's weakness was greatly increased by the reports of the new American ambassador to Britain, Joseph Kennedy. Not only did he endorse the view that Britain would soon be defeated. He tried to take advantage of the situation by

163

demanding for himself special pecuniary advantages in the distribution of whisky and gin to the United States, for two brands of which he held the sole distribution rights. The situation at the American embassy in London was even worse. A cryptographer at the embassy had been passing the texts of messages passing between the British and American governments. Tyler Kent was eventually arrested and in his flat were found 1,500 texts of messages between the two countries. He had passed them through Anna Wolkoff to the Italian embassy in London. From there they were sent to Rome and handed to the Germans. When the German embassy in Rome transmitted the texts to Berlin the radio traffic was heard and the code deciphered at Bletchley Park. It was from there that the leak was detected.

Hitler was able to read these most secret communications, including those between Churchill and Roosevelt, within a few hours. What it did give away was the Chamberlain government's wish to go to almost any lengths to appease Hitler, even after the declaration of war. These messages could have destroyed President Roosevelt's efforts to give Britain support during early 1941, while America was still neutral. Many of them were from 'former naval person' to POTUS, i.e. from Churchill to the President of the United States. Had these become public knowledge Roosevelt might have been impeached.

The co-operation between Britain and America had seen a one-way traffic of goods and material between the countries. In August 1940 Sir Henry Tizard had taken what the Americans called "The most valuable cargo ever brought to our shores" across the Atlantic. German agents nearly hijacked the cargo in Washington. Perhaps the most valuable item was the cavity magnetron valve, invented by Randall and Boot in Birmingham. It allowed the construction of centimetric radar sets that were small enough to fit into aircraft and would greatly increase the effectiveness of night air defence. Other 'gifts' to cross the Atlantic were details of atom splitting work done at British universities such as Cambridge and Liverpool, with details of how this primary research could be converted into a weapon. The British were leaders in this field at that time, but the Germans also were in the race and their interest in heavy water production at the Norsk Hydro plant showed where their intentions lay. It was a race for the atomic bomb.

The other main leak of information between the United States and Britain occurred at the French Islands of St. Pierre and Miquelon. The transatlantic cable ran through these two islands in the mouth of the St. Lawrence rive, off the south coast of Newfoundland. The Nazis bribed a technician to splice into the cable so that the traffic could be read. When the Free French took over the islands the British and Americans were furious. They had not dared to take over the islands for fear of angering Hitler and giving him an excuse to invade other French colonies. They had also not wanted to give French Canadians the excuse that they were fighting only to surrender French possessions to the Anglo-Saxons. Eventually the British and Americans saw the sense of the action, and there was the advantage of removing the islands from the Axis information source, which had given details of forthcoming transatlantic convoys.

The assessment of the British and American intelligence services was that keeping lines of communication open through Vichy sources in the United States could be a useful route for passing disinformation to the Germans. The view was that "We can unite patriotic Frenchmen everywhere, once we're in French North Africa. Then France itself will revolt and the corrosion will spread."

This view showed a tragically simple misunderstanding of the feelings of the French. The British and Americans had not understood anything of the tragedy of the French situation, where in Syria Allied blunders had led to Frenchman firing on Frenchman. The conduit from Admiral Darlan to the Germans had been unforgivable in the eyes of the Free French.

The idea that a quick melding of all French forces in North Africa could be achieved was naïve folly in the extreme, and de Gaulle would have none of it. The British and Americans had forgotten that de Gaulle had been court martialled by the Vichy authorities, sentenced to death, and deprived of his nationality. His status with the Vichy authorities was nil. It had been Churchill and the British government which had recognised him as the leader of a new France, the Free French. In rank he was junior to every other French general. There were those in the French secret service, the Deuxieme Bureau, who did not follow the standardised loyalty to Vichy and to whom co-operation with the Germans was absolutely abhorrent. Many worked secretly for the Resistance. France was split and the Allied policy was untenable.

And so de Gaulle, knowing so well the mind of the Free French, for he had given his orations at the Albert Hall meetings in London and reviewed the Free French troops on Bastille Day, in London, could not accept the Allied plan for French integration. Somehow the troops who had been loyal to Vichy had to be won over to the Free French cause by their own individual decisions. In the end the Germans helped. A few days after the Allied landings in North Africa they occupied the southern, Unoccupied Zone, of France. The Vichy government became a total puppet of the Germans. The troops saw the reality and gradually gave their support to the Free French cause. When the French 1st Army landed in the south of France in August 1944 it was a force of 80,000 men.

It would be a tough battle for de Gaulle. The Allies would not let him go to review the French troops fighting in Libya. He was taken back to London by a British 'plane on the 26th January 1943. On the 9th February de Gaulle gave a news conference about the Casablanca conference. Following this news conference de Gaulle was forbidden by the British Government, and notified in writing, to return to the Middle East. The American and British press were primed to support French unification around Giraud. De Gaulle was accused of being proud and ambitious and quite unsuitable to continue leading the Free French. He was pictured as being a dictator. But many of the French strongly supported de Gaulle for his unswerving opposition to any surrender to the Germans and for being steadfast in upholding the honour of France. They would not follow any other leader and in attempting to unite the French the Allies had managed to divide them.

In the French Navy and the Merchant Marine the support for de Gaulle was firm and this showed in the crews of the ships in the United States and the United Kingdom refusing duty. The Americans became exasperated, but they did realise that their policy had been deeply damaging to the Allied cause. While de Gaulle was accused of hindering the Allied cause he actually ordered those sailors who had come over to his side to go back aboard their ships and resume their duties. In North Africa the troops demonstrated their support for de Gaulle, for the first time. Throughout the war years there were many occasions when de Gaulle was on board French ships, inspecting and encouraging their crews. With him were admirals such as Muselier, all taking a subordinate role to de Gaulle himself. It was as though by stripping him of his Nationality the Vichy government had cleansed him of any contagion of defeat, so that he could move freely outside any regime of the previous political or military hierarchy. Those who heard his London orations and his broadcasts knew, by patriotic instinct, that he was their one leader for their liberation.

De Gaulle recalls that at the same time the Americans offered him 'honey and vinegar.' He was invited to Washington, but any detail of time or occasion or itinerary was left deliberately vague and unsuitable for the formation of any definite plan.

Meantime, in France, the situation was deteriorating. Laval had taken authority to promulgate laws with his signature alone. Petain did not count. In February 1943 laws against Jews and laws to impose forced labour were introduced. The priests and the people protested, but they were crushed by the jackboot.

In England de Gaulle received definite support from many sources. Well known parliamentarians declared, on the radio, that de Gaulle was the undoubted head of the Free French. The Resistance in France was becoming more organised, but with larger groupings came more danger of discovery, arrest, torture, and death. Jean Moulin came to London for discussions. He knew that his days of being able to evade capture were numbered and yet he stuck to his task for the Resistance. He was determined to build the Resistance into the strong and determined force which would take part in the liberation of France. Recognising Moulin's destiny, de Gaulle invested him with the Croix de la Liberation at a private and most moving ceremony. Moulin was eventually captured by the Gestapo and suffered the most horrendous tortures, which led to his death. He gave away no secrets. Eisenhower was to say that the Resistance was worth five divisions in the battle for France.

Political intrigue now dominated events. General Giraud declared on radio that France did not have any policies of racial prejudice. A few days later he had to withdraw copies of an official journal which promulgated Marshal Petain's decrees which were absolutely to the contrary. He then signed a set of decrees abolishing Vichy's laws in Algeria. Churchill and Cordell Hull supported Giraud in this. If there was progress on this front then de Gaulle could go to a good reception in Algeria, where Eisenhower offered to welcome him.

This offer did not suit the British and American governments and he was threatened with abandonment. Archbishop Spellman came from New York with a message from the President of the United States. They expected de Gaulle to follow the policies of Liberty, Equality and Charity. Liberty meant not imposing conditions for joining the Fighting French to Giraud. Equality meant becoming part of the triumvirate suggested at Casablanca. Charity meant pardoning and working with all those French who had for years opposed de Gaulle and been loyal Vichy supporters. De Gaulle was faced with the possibility of being kept in England, out of the action. Monsignor Spellman asked de Gaulle how he would tolerate being kept out of the action when France was being liberated.

De Gaulle replied that it would not be liberation but would be an authority imposed on France by the Anglo-Saxons and leaving in power those who had worked under the authority of the Germans. Such an arrangement would be against the will of the French people. In this way de Gaulle made a significant impression on the cleric.

On the 2nd April 1943 Churchill asked to see de Gaulle. Churchill said that de Gaulle's arrival in Algeria would be divisive unless there was a strong accord with Giraud. De Gaulle would not accept the imposed conditions and so Eisenhower wanted de Gaulle's visit postponed. Two days later Eden and Winant, on returning from Washington, told de Gaulle of American anger at this stubbornness. All would be well if he would put the Fighting

French under Giraud's command. De Gaulle replied that all would be well if Giraud had stayed loyal to the principles of French freedom in 1940 and had opposed Weygand and Petain at that time. Then the position could be different. What the Allies demanded would provide an administration but without a national rallying purpose and would lead to later disorder. It would lead to the legal imposition of old laws, dating from 1872, which would make the re-establishment of democracy very difficult. The Allies could be creating a civil war.

The National Committee in London stood firmly behind de Gaulle. National unity was paramount and a united front to the press was essential. The matter was most urgent. In Algeria there was a swelling of support for de Gaulle. Giraud was met with cries of "Vive de Gaulle!" and on the 1st May the workers parade demanded de Gaulle. Churchill recognised the swell of support for de Gaulle because it fitted so well with his own long felt call "Trust the people!" He met de Gaulle and read out to him reports from Harold MacMillan about the support for de Gaulle in Algeria.

There was still severe fighting in North Africa, with Rommel's skilful control exacting a high price for the ground won. One French general was killed in this fighting and the poorly equipped French troops in some areas were struggling to repel the Germans. But in the middle of March the 8th Army, under Montgomery and with Generals Lerclerc and Larminat leading the French troops in the battle, broke through the Mareth line. Trapped between the 8th Army and the Americans advancing from the west General von Armin surrendered 250,000 Axis troops to the Allies. In North Africa, amongst the rejoicing at the Allied victory, everywhere were heard cries of "Vive de Gaulle" from the population. Even the American press reported this outpouring of enthusiasm and emotion. Suddenly many units of North African troops declared for de Gaulle and on the 27th April General Giraud surrendered his pre-eminence. On the 15th May the National Committee reinforced its support for de Gaulle by stating that he was the singular head of the Resistance and the only person entitled to undertake negotiations for France. This support came direct from the Resistance in Paris. It was widely broadcast, even by the

British and Americans, and was decisive in establishing de Gaulle in an unassailable position.

On the 17th May General Giraud sent a message insisting that de Gaulle should come to Algiers to form a new French government. On the 25th May de Gaulle replied that he would come within the week and was happy to work with Giraud in the service of France.

Before he left England de Gaulle wrote to King George VIth recalling how he had been welcomed by the King himself, his family, his government, and the people in the tragic days of 1940. He expressed thanks for the hospitality which thereafter had been accorded to the Free French and its leader. De Gaulle would have liked to express his personal thanks to Churchill, but Churchill was away abroad on another of his secret missions. Instead, he saw Eden at a friendly meeting. "What do you think of us?" Eden asked." "Nothing is more kindly than your people. But I do not think as kindly of your politics" he replied. Eden told him "Do you know that you have caused us more difficulties than all our other allies in Europe?" "I do not doubt it" de Gaulle replied, smiling. "France is a great power."

ALGERIA

On the 30th May 1943 a plane landed in North Africa carrying de Gaulle and the senior members of the Fighting French. Generals Giraud and Catroux welcomed them. It was a French occasion, with the Marseillaise, a guard of honour, and a convoy of vehicles of French make. The French cause was making progress.

Their arrival was unannounced, but in some quarters their arrival had become known and there were cries of "Vive de Gaulle!" Giraud and de Gaulle were seated opposite one another at a grand dinner that evening. However nothing could disguise the deep divisions amongst the French which the Allies had fostered. In North Africa de Gaulle lacked all the background support for power.

Outside the upper realms of the French hierarchy, amongst the people, the support for de Gaulle was solid. When he laid a wreath at the memorial a crowd, which had suddenly assembled, greeted him. General Vuillemin, who had been Commander in Chief of the French air force at the time of the collapse of France in 1940, asked for employment as a squadron commander. He was keen to do anything to help the recovery of France.

There was agreement about the procedure for governing the French effort. There would be disagreements about the details of individual courses of action. Until the French people had the free choice of members of a government the group in Algeria would have to exercise all the powers of the French State. Algeria was a part of metropolitan France, so that it was a French Government on French soil. The military commander, out of necessity, would have to have undue authority compared with the normal civil situation. De Gaulle could not allow the National Committee in London to be replaced by any other authority, for it combined senior civil and military figures. Flanked by General Georges and Jean Monnet the group around de Gaulle numbered nearly 40. De Gaulle issued a statement, which was widely reported, that the provisional government in Algeria would undertake all the functions of government until the re-establishment of a properly elected government in a liberated France.

Mr. Peyrouton, who had been Governor General in Algeria, wrote to de Gaulle and offered to surrender his position and serve in the army. This offer was readily accepted and it made it much easier to centralise power. The news was reported world wide next day. It led to a massive surge of volunteers to join the Free French troops. The Free French troops had been sent from Algeria to Libya by General Giraud, with Eisenhower's agreements. In their new camps they could not absorb thousands of young soldiers from Algeria.

De Gaulle was then accused of setting up his own dictatorship. The guard at his residence was reduced to only ten Spahis, from North Africa. De Gaulle sent a letter to Giraud, accusing him of a late night 'putsch,' but necessity and the support for de Gaulle brought about a sort of unity. The two generals were to head a new committee, which would exercise all the powers and duty of the state. General Catroux would be Governor General of Algeria. Although de Gaulle knew how some, like Boisson, had opposed him, he was prepared to accept them into some of the responsible positions for the purpose of unity.

De Gaulle was reassured that his overall leadership of the Free French was untouched. He eventually won Giraud's support. It enabled de Gaulle to announce on the radio, to the people of France, that there was a full French government functioning in Algeria and it was ready, at the earliest opportunity, to move to Paris. These developments brought severe Allied opposition and the British and Americans restricted the broadcasting of the news. There were British delays in letting those who had been chosen for the government leave London for Algeria. On the 30th May Churchill and Eden flew secretly to North Africa. On the 6th June they invited de Gaulle and Giraud to a working dinner. Churchill stated that he did not wish to meddle in French affairs but it was necessary for His Majesty's Government to take account of what was happening in such a vital area for the Allied campaign.

De Gaulle reassured them that he wanted everyone to combine and he hoped to be able to include a fully enthusiastic General Giraud in the French and thereby the Allied ranks. However

Giraud would have to confine his efforts and activities to a military role, under overall French legal authority. There was a difficulty for the French. They did not have sufficient fully trained and equipped units to provide the Allies with a complete army, so they could not be worthy of providing a Commander in Chief. They had men enough, but they were untrained, were short of any heavy armament, and lacked the specialised additional units, such as signals. There was great potential, with 500,000 men available. There was gold to buy armaments in the United States. Much time and opportunity had been wasted in the previous two years. Thirty thousand troops had been lost to the Middle Eastern battle when they were transported out of Syria instead of being given the opportunity to join the Allied cause. De Gaulle abhorred these wasted opportunities.

If circumstances did not provide General Giraud with a strong and viable command opportunity, he could still give great service. He could become Minister of War, but if he declined such an administrative post he could become Inspector General and also serve as senior liaison with the Allies. De Gaulle put both propositions to Giraud, but he refused both. Allied support and influence had persuaded him to hold out for the position of Commander in Chief with the additional authority to block decisions of the National Committee. It was not de Gaulle but Giraud who would become the virtual dictator.

By taking such a stand Giraud found himself gradually isolated and rejected. The Allies put the decline in his status down to de Gaulle suppressing him, whereas the problem arose from Giraud's ambition to have overwhelming control and command. When he did not win Giraud went into retreat. De Gaulle regretted the decision, but the cause of the general good made any alternative impossible. However it was later found possible for Giraud to give important service because De Gaulle would be Minister of Defence and Giraud would command the troops. De Gaulle would also deal with the Allied High Command in the preparation of combined operations.

Giraud then called a meeting behind de Gaulle's back, but all present stated that they would not take any valid decision without de Gaulle. Army and Air Force generals rallied to de Gaulle's side in the dispute. Eisenhower warned of his intention to launch an attack on Europe through Italy, an attack which would lead to the liberation of France. He required absolute assurances that his rear would be defended and that no French action or disputes in North Africa would endanger the smooth flow of supplies. Eisenhower wanted Giraud to be the total French commander in North Africa and the only channel for the Allies to the French. He also stated that the continuation of supplies to the French depended on this condition being met.

De Gaulle replied that he could not accept any such conditions. The French organisation depended on the decisions of the French Government. He pointed out that the Allied countries expected their commanders to obey the orders of their governments. Eisenhower was unmoved. De Gaulle replied that Eisenhower had acted on the orders of the American and British governments. Did he expect that the French could do anything different? Could he expect the French to take orders about their organisation from any external power? The Vichy government had had to do so from the Germans. De Gaulle asked Eisenhower if he would take orders from a foreign government? Eisenhower replied that he understood de Gaulle's position, but his concerns were for the immediate battle. De Gaulle replied that he fully understood the urgency of combining all the elements of the French troops. He reminded Eisenhower that in the previous war it had been France which had provided the arms to the Allied countries, such as Russia and Serbia and Belgium. The French had not sought to impose such conditions on their allies. To this Eisenhower was silent.

Eventually the Allied High Command sent de Gaulle a note stating that in all French territories the sovereignty of France would be respected and upheld. It had embroiled Eisenhower, the long term and faithfully military man, in complex politics alien to his nature, training, and inclination. He had been brave enough to hurl onto the African shore an army which he had brought across the ocean. In all the battles which were to follow he was to show the same courage and tenacity to achieve the final goal – victory. De Gaulle would always honour him as the man who commanded the Liberation of France.

The French National Committee would not accept Giraud as its overall head and threatened him with loss of command if he did not declare himself subordinate to the Committee. He could become a senior member, under de Gaulle's presidency, of the Military Committee. It was not a solution which de Gaulle would have liked. And then Giraud announced that President Roosevelt had invited him to Washington to discuss the supply of arms. He wanted any further discussion postponed until his return, at which point Giraud then left for Washington. It was a decision of the United States that they would not recognise that France had a government.

Churchill publicised the view that the problems were those caused by de Gaulle. It was taken up with enthusiasm by the American press. In the event Giraud's stay in the United States was not treated as a matter of any significance. The idea of arming several French divisions did not arouse any enthusiasm. The way in which Giraud was treated as a subordinate by the White House did not attract general approval in America. Giraud was received by Roosevelt as a French soldier fighting for the Allied cause, when for the moment France did not exist. The ambassador of the Free French was not invited to the White House dinner. France's national day, the 14th July, was totally ignored by the Americans in respect of their guest.

During Giraud's trip he told the Canadian press that his only task was to create a powerful French army. Landing in England he told the press that no-one had the right to speak in the name of France. He had made clear, and it was well understood, that Giraud's role in French affairs was only secondary.

In Algeria the National Committee held two meetings a week, to get on with the work. Politics were put aside to prepare all the arrangements necessary for a proper legal framework in a newly liberated France. The abuses committed by the government in Vichy would have to be marked and punished. These decisions, taken in unity, did much to focus on de Gaulle's leadership.

All was not well in neighbouring Tunisia. When de Gaulle went there on the 26th June 1943 he found that many there had

175

supported the Germans and Italians. Many French citizens had had their goods pillaged and some had been imprisoned. General Mast had started to correct the situation and he had prevented the storm of vengeance that might have broken out. It was essential to mobilise Tunisia on the Allied side. Problems of native insurrection seeking independence were overcome and then Tunisian forces had to be incorporated into the overall French effort.

De Gaulle went to see the Tunisian ruler, Sidi-Lamine, at Carthage. It was clear that the ruler's purpose was for the benefit of his country and he won de Gaulle's respect. In an address to a mixed French and Tunisian audience de Gaulle emphasised the importance of the necessary military effort to beat the enemy. He reassured the crowd that after victory was won de Gaulle had no purpose for his own power. This was on the 27th June, and if it had been received and understood by Roosevelt, might have done much to calm American fears about de Gaulle's intentions.

He had told the crowd that his only purpose was to serve France. The enemy had to be beaten, traitors dealt with, friendships that had been formed in the struggle preserved, and those who had been released from bondage helped to march forward to freedom. The day of victory would allow an open-armed embrace to all those who would be weeping with joy. There would be a benediction from those who had died fighting for their freedom. In French this was the dramatic type of declaration which had, throughout the war, swept up in emotion those who despaired for the France they had known. It was the light in their darkness. It was the type of appeal that could never have moved an English or an American audience.

In Algiers, on the 14th July, there was a patriotic celebration of the renaissance of the French state. It was also a celebration of national unity. There was a sense of urgency to take part in the next battle. De Gaulle told the crowd that it was a united France which was recovering. France's troops had more need, more urgency, more desire, to fight. The suffering of her people was the spur to this effort. France was not a Sleeping Beauty, waiting for an awakening kiss. France was a tortured captive, suffering under the blows of a tyrant.

He told the crowd "France has chosen a new path. French men and women, for fifteen centuries France has suffered grief and glory. Our present trials are not yet ended. But it is the end of the worst drama in our history. Raise your heads. Let us march together in the struggle, and, with our victory, go forward to our new destiny!" It was a speech that produced a wild burst of patriotic emotion. It was a true echo of Churchill's speech at the Mansion House in London after the victory at El-Alamein, where he had said "This is not the beginning of the end, but it is perhaps the end of the beginning!" Two men, one goal, one shared emotion.

The consequence of de Gaulle's speech was to end the intrigues which had divided the political elements. De Gaulle was the only man who could galvanise the French nation for the struggle to come. After this, no Frenchman could oppose him. The American representative present, Mr. Murphy, was impressed and expressed his congratulations.

De Gaulle's reception was repeated at Rabat, in Morocco, on the 6th August. There had been those who had kept quiet in the shadows and those who had vilified the Free French. Now it was all sunshine and de Gaulle received universal acclaim. The King of Morocco, Mohammed-ben-Youssef, had face-to-face talks with de Gaulle. He was ready to give support, but made it clear that he expected independence from France to be granted in return. Before the Casablanca conference he had been poisoned in his attitude to France by Roosevelt, but still he remained faithful to the French cause. In return for his support, and recognising that the king's ambitions for his country were no different to de Gaulle's for France, they established a personal friendship which was to bring Morocco forwards to peaceful independence within a few years.

When de Gaulle entered Casablanca on the 8th August the walls were covered with French flags. Six months earlier de Gaulle had been billeted in the suburbs, in secret, and surrounded by barbed wire and American guards. Now he took the salute at a grand parade and addressed a human tide and enormous crowd of enthusiastic people. On the 10th August he received a wonderful reception from the Berber tribesman and their chiefs.

At this point the French West Indies rallied whole-heartedly to de Gaulle. Since 1940 Admiral Robert had under his command and under Marshal Petain's orders two cruisers, an aircraft carrier, and many lesser ships. By maintaining strict neutrality he had obtained supplies from the Americans. After 1941 de Gaulle's representatives, based in British West Indies headquarters, had managed to enrol 2000 volunteers for the Free French. At the start of 1943 there was a surge of support for de Gaulle. In March French Guiana declared for de Gaulle and on the 16th the Vichy governor was deposed and the Cross of Lorraine emblem erected. Again the Americans interfered, putting in place Giraud's rather than de Gaulle's envoy and threatening supplies to the colony to support their choice. The later unity of the French in Algeria solved the problem.

In June 1943 Martinique took the same decision. In April de Gaulle's representative had offered Admiral Robert, at Fort de France, suitable terms. The admiral wobbled, but the local political leaders pushed and on the third anniversary of de Gaulle's 'Appel' from London, the 18th of June, a Cross of Lorraine was placed at the war memorial and in three weeks Martinique was in de Gaulle's camp. The same happened in Guadeloupe. The essential win was to gain control, officially, for the Free French of all the gold reserves of the Bank of France which were in the old fort on Martinique. The Battalion of the Antilles was brought to Europe and took an effective part in driving the Germans out of western France, but with the loss of their colonel.

Apart from Indo-China, which the Japanese were occupying, the whole of the French empire was now firmly on the march for the liberation of France. It was the same as when Churchill had spoken defiantly of "The old lion, with her Lion Cubs at her side," resisting German invasion after the fall of France.

The French fleet at Alexandria, which had remained neutralised under Admiral Godfroy's command since 1940, but on the best of terms with their British 'hosts,' declared for de Gaulle in June 1943. One battleship, four cruisers, and many other ships were added to the Allied fleet. Combined with the French ships from the West Indies it made a formidable fleet, which would take part in the bombardment supporting the landings on D-day.

With the prospect of the invasion of Italy the Allies needed the help of the Free French troops and ships. On the 10th July British and American troops landed on Sicily. The French were not involved in this campaign. It took six weeks to drive the Germans off the island. Mussolini was overthrown and the Italian government, under Marshal Badoglio, came to terms with the Allies. German troops came south down the Italian peninsula in large numbers to oppose the next stage in the Allied campaign. De Gaulle spoke on the radio of the fall of Mussolini as being a certain sign of the defeat of the Axis powers and was, for France, the first just revenge. There would need to be a reconciliation rather than a savage revenge. De Gaulle mirrored Churchill's thoughts of the need for magnanimity in victory, to avoid the possibility of renewed conflict which the harsh terms imposed after the First World War had made nearly inevitable.

When Giraud returned to Algeria from abroad on the 31st July the National Committee decided that there should be no division at the head of France's efforts and that de Gaulle was to be the sole leader. All the French forces were to be united. Giraud would be Commander in Chief of the French forces. General le Gentilhomme, recalled from Madagascar, would be Minister of National Defence. General Juin was appointed head of the French troops to invade the Italian mainland.

The Committee for National Liberation was growing in authority and power. They issued a statement, that the Vichy government and those who supported them had collaborated with the enemy, had sent French workers to be slave labour in Germany and that those who had fought against the Allies would be held to account for their actions. All the French missions in Allied countries were brought under central control. Arrangements were put in place to ensure smooth relationships between the Allied invasion force, which would enter France, and the French Government and people. The French also demanded to take part in the negotiations of the formal Italian armistice. The Italians had invaded some of south eastern France and the restoration of this territory had to be ensured.

179

General Giraud was pleased with his appointment as Commander in Chief of the Free French forces. General Leclerc and his column would control Morocco, with General Larminat in Tunisia. Naval and air force units were sent from North Africa to Great Britain to operate from English bases and add to the Allied strength. With the new collaboration between de Gaulle and Giraud they sent a joint memorandum on the 18th September to Churchill, Roosevelt, and Stalin.

Whatever happened in Italy there would be a Free French preparation for the invasion of metropolitan France from the south. Some Free French forces would also enter France from the north as part of the Allied cross-channel invasion. It would take at least a full armoured division to ensure the liberation of Paris. Parachutists, commandos, ships and several squadrons of aircraft would be needed to support the cross-channel invasion. After victory in Europe forces would have to be transferred to the Far East to liberate the French territories there.

On the 3rd September the Italians capitulated and the Americans landed at Salerno. The British arranged that France's interests were protected in the negotiations for the Italian surrender and General Eisenhower was accorded the power to sign for all the Allies, with the French sending a representative to the ceremony. However when it came to the actual event France was not mentioned as a signatory power. There was severe discontent amongst the French. The British and Americans stated that General Giraud had been kept informed, but this undermined all that had been agreed with the National Committee.

Whatever French feelings, the removal of Italy from the Axis side was satisfactory, and the French published a statement of approval of the fact. Giraud denied that he had been informed of the armistice negotiations, but this statement was refuted by the British and Americans. Whatever the truth of this dispute de Gaulle announced to a crowd in Oran that it would be the French purpose to hasten the defeat of the enemy and to join with all countries of goodwill to rebuild the world. Whatever de Gaulle's intentions, France was still not a strong force on the Allied side.

The next target was the liberation of Corsica. It was not a vital target in the overall prosecution of the war, but it was the first part of metropolitan France which could be liberated and its liberation would be a great boost to French morale and stature in the world. Preparations had been made by the Free French since 1942, but sadly their chief organiser was captured by the Italians and tortured to death just before the landings of the Allies in North Africa.

On the 12th September Corsica was invaded, by a smaller force than intended due to a shortage of transport. The use of mountain troops was effective in dislodging the Germans from the centre of the island. By the 4th October the French troops had reached Bastia. The Germans withdrew, leaving behind a large amount of equipment. The first part of France had been liberated. It had been a difficult task, to force a landing and fight a successful battle 900 kilometres from the North African bases.

Unfortunately Giraud played politics with the situation and had to be restrained. He had become too embroiled with the American attitude to the Mediterranean situation and it would interfere with the development of the political system which the National Committee had deemed necessary for the successful re-establishment of proper law and order in the months to come. He also suffered the disaster of his family being seized by the Germans.

De Gaulle recalled Pierre Mendes-France to take the financial portfolio. Other appointments and re-arrangements strengthened the provisional Government. With these tasks completed de Gaulle went to Corsica on the 8th October. He spent three marvellous days there. He told a crowd in Ajaccio that a wonderful tide of national enthusiasm was rising. He also spoke of Italy, ruling out any long term hostility to the Italians, echoing Churchill's words to the Italians of 1940, about the Italian people never being the natural foes of the British. In every town and village he received a marvellous welcome. Even the Italian prisoners of war showed signs of friendship.

With the first part of France liberated it was time for the National Committee to transform into a consultative assembly. Support for de Gaulle increased and ideas for the future of the nation burst forth. The autumn of 1943 was springtime for the new

France. It was decided that the French must help the Allies in the Italian campaign. On the 9th October the decision was taken that the common task was for all and that the Allied victory would have a strong French component.

POLITICS 1943

In the development of the French organisation in Algeria de Gaulle was faced with the problem of the communists. In 1940, because of the Russian-German treaty, they were actually on the side of the Germans. All this changed overnight with Hitler's attack on Russia in June 1941, but they were hostile to the leaders of the old French political system who had formed the National Committee and to de Gaulle because of his powerful position.

De Gaulle wanted to unite all the forces of the resistance, at least for the duration of the war, and offered to include two communists in the National Committee. They demanded specific portfolios and demanded to know the full programme for the future. The future was still uncertain and de Gaulle could not delay his duties to attend to the detail of such political matters, so the discussions were broken off.

Some of the communists wanted all out insurrection in which they would seize power. Others, such as Maurice Thorez, who was repeatedly travelling to Moscow for instructions, wanted to join the administration and undermine it for the communists to take over from within.

By November 1943 some reasonable agreement had been reached and the combined government could function in Algeria on behalf of the French nation. There would be strong representation from the Resistance in France, some from the political parties, and some from those members of parliament who had not voted in support of Petain in 1940. And so a Consultative Assembly was formed. The Americans and British knew little and cared less about de Gaulle's difficulties in welding all the French elements into a force which could give the Allied cause the maximum support. Roosevelt's support for Giraud had impeded de Gaulle in his task and delayed the French unity and power of arms.

There were shortages of arms, money, and the means of distributing information. Some were keener on identifying traitors and planning methods of punishment. Above all, they had a special regard for de Gaulle. His treatment by Vichy – the death sentence, deprivation of citizenship and confiscation of his property – had aroused great sympathy. He also knew the suffering imposed by the Vichy regime. By his example of keeping them focussed on restoring the power of the State and French sovereignty under the rule of law no one could challenge the leadership of a man who had been so badly treated. This was leadership and his example was virtuous and not vainglorious.

If France were to be restored to her position amongst the great nations of the world she would have to use all her energies. It would not be a position granted by Roosevelt and Churchill as an automatic right, it would have to be earned, and de Gaulle well understood this. Elsewhere there were French politicians whose woolly thinking was unsuited to the urgent pressure of the challenge of liberation. With the invasion of France scheduled for less than a year away the need to accelerate the build up of French forces and to avoid any internal dissentions or splits was paramount.

The opening of the Consultative Assembly on the 3rd November 1943 was a very moving event. It would express the national will and would pay as much attention to moral rejuvenation as to reconstruction. It would re-establish France as a great power. Everything would have to be rebuilt under the umbrella of justice and with the repatriation of prisoners of war and slave labourers needing special care in their re-integration into French society.

By the D-day landings in June 1944 the Assembly had met more than 50 times, with de Gaulle present for more than 20 of them. The most difficult decision was how to deal with those who had actively supported the Vichy government. It would be essential to act justly and avoid vengeance. It was a problem happily beyond the experience and outside the need for consideration in Britain and America.

De Gaulle received strong support for the way in which he had negotiated France's position with the other Allies. In dealing with other questions of policy of a less immediate nature it was difficult for de Gaulle to obtain adequate focus and clarity for an agreed policy. He alone had to formulate policy in the early days of the Free French organisation and there was no general will to address these matters anew. A liberated France would have a government which could deal with all these comparatively minor matters. There was little thought that at the moment of victory there would need to be in place a policy to ensure that the terms of the armistice were suited to France's long term interests. Perhaps there was a fear that any discussion must illuminate differences of opinion which could appear divisive at the very time when all the efforts to achieve unity had borne fruit. Any divisions would sully the combined efforts for the liberation. This was certainly the view of those French in London who had been with de Gaulle at the founding of the Free French movement in 1940 and 1941.

This reticence left it to de Gaulle alone to represent France's worldwide interests in the manner and on the terms which he had used in earlier years. To the Allies it seemed that he alone was the voice of France and that, in contrast to Britain and America, the approach appeared to be much less democratic in its process. Here it is certain that Anthony Eden's duties in meeting with de Gaulle at some of the most difficult times in dealing with contentious issues, as Churchill's representative and on behalf of the War Cabinet, was a division of some of these hard political tasks which de Gaulle could not delegate on France's behalf. With a political entity discredited by the armistice and old generals, whom the French Prime Minister had described as being unwilling to fight when France was being overrun, de Gaulle was alone in promoting France's cause. From the first, Churchill had recognised this and he had allowed de Gaulle a degree of latitude which he would not have bestowed on others. Whatever the difficulties the British might have had in their dealings with him, to his own office staff General de Gaulle was known as 'General Nuisance' because of his demands, his changes of mind, and his appalling handwriting. Yet the burdens he faced, and with so little support, were overcome and his staff were totally devoted to him, for he so clearly embodied the spirit and the honour of France. Perhaps it was not Stalin who should have been named 'The Man of Steel,' but de Gaulle who merited the title.

BATTLESHIP *RICHELIEU* AT ORAN IN 1943 AS PART OF THE ALLIED FLEET

TEMPORARY IDENTITY CARD
ISSUED BY AUTHORITY OF THE
COMMANDER-IN-CHIEF, HOME FLEET

(Valid only if bearing date stamp of
Commander-in-Chief, Home Fleet)

FRENCH NAVAL RATING

Name. SAUZAY Jean
(In full)

Official No. I22.L. 35

Rating. Electricien

Signature

(Validity of this card expires on 1st June, 1944)

IDENTITY CARD OF JEAN SAUZAY, ELECTRICIAN ON BOARD THE *RICHELIEU*. FOR MORE THAN 60 YEARS HE PROUDLY CARRIED THE IDENTITY CARD IN HIS WALLET. THE BACK WAS STAMPED BY BOTH THE FRENCH MARINE AND THE HOME FLEET

De Gaulle was not a man of any ruthlessness. At no time was he uncivil in any crude manner and his behaviour was always that of a gentleman. After an unfortunate outburst at luncheon Clementine Churchill received, the next day, a swamping with flowers of apology. Because of the creation of the French Consultative Assembly in Algeria it was clear to the Germans that the Vichy government had no ability to control French affairs in North Africa. This contravened the terms of the armistice, by which all French troops, both in metropolitan France and the French empire, were to cease all hostilities against the Axis. The Germans took full control in metropolitan France and the Vichy controlled area was occupied by German troops. The delay for two and a half years, after the defeat in 1940, in the completion of the German occupation of France was to benefit the Allies when the landings took place in the south of France in August, 1944. The German preparations in that southern region were much inferior to those on the Atlantic wall, so that the Allied advance from the south was much faster than the Allies had expected or planned for.

In the Vichy government Petain transferred all powers to Laval, with Petain withdrawing from control of the government. Laval, after returning from a visit to Hitler, re-formed the composition of the government and co-operated much more closely with the invader. The Germans had a controller in the government in the person of Herr Renth-Fink. He reported directly to Hitler and henceforth all French laws would be dictated by the occupiers. Henriot and Paquis used all their skills of mass deception to try and fool the masses that the Vichy government was still in control. Many were deceived into supporting this puppet government. There were attempts to declare the National Assembly of 1940 as the continuing legal government of France. Hitler, in a letter from von Ribbentrop, informed Marshal Petain that the Wehrmacht was the controller of public order in the whole of France.

When the Allies realised that Giraud was not able to balance and share control with de Gaulle they sought another solution. They wanted President Lebrun to be the head of the government, but he had been displaced from Vichy and had retired. Could he be brought to North Africa to become the titular head of the National

Committee? He would then be able to name the ministers of the government. He had never fully succumbed to the power of the invaders. It would rid Washington and London of the intransigent influence of the damned General de Gaulle!

At the same time Marshal Badoglio, as head of the Italian government, entered into secret negotiations with the British and Americans to surrender Italy. It so happened that President Lebrun had retired to Vizille, which was in the south eastern area of France which was under Italian occupation. The Italians proposed to Lebrun that he should become a member of their government. The Allies had a secret agreement with Badoglio that after landing at Naples they would rush to Rome and re-install King Victor-Emmanual as head of state. From Italy Lebrun could go wherever he wished. Lebrun refused this proposition most forcefully. He informed the Italians that Italy and France were in a state of war, and that for him the Italians were the enemy. The Germans came to know of these approaches and the Gestapo transferred President Lebrun to Germany.

If these intrigues were a fascination, the realities were terrible. On the 9th June 1943, a few days after de Gaulle's arrival in Algeria. General Delestraint, head of the Secret Army, had been arrested in Paris. On the 21st June, in a Gestapo operation, Jean Moulin was arrested. Several weeks later he had died as a result of Gestapo torture. He never revealed any secrets.

Jean Moulin had been one of those who was genuinely irreplaceable. If his loss was a severe blow to the running of the Resistance, it was also to have political consequences. The loss of such a dynamic, central, and well known figure left a collection of almost anonymous leaders to replace him. None had the stature to inspire the dangerous work. It had been known that he was de Gaulle's personal delegate and so the whole Resistance movement looked again to de Gaulle personally. It was clear that the time for action to support the liberation of France was approaching and the need for effective leadership was ever more urgent.

It left the communists in a stronger position. It was not until September 1943 that de Gaulle named Emile Bollaert as his personal delegate to the Resistance forces. He had the misfortune to be quickly arrested on the Brittany coast and sent to Buchenwald. Pierre Brossolette also fell into the Gestapo's hands and died after trying to escape. In March 1944 Alexandre Parodi, whose brother had died for the Resistance, was given the leadership. The National Resistance Council came under the leadership of Georges Bidault, a Christian Democrat who later became Prime Minister.

During these months at the end of 1943 and the start of 1944 de Gaulle was able to broadcast from Algeria to the French people. It was different from the broadcasts which had lightened their darkest hours soon after the armistice, when all the broadcasts on the BBC had been introduced "Ici Londres, Francais parlent aux Francais." Algeria was part of France - symbolically it had become a Home Service broadcast. The BBC remained the avenue by which many messages to the Resistance were broadcast. After the introduction "Ici Londres" the messages were all in code. They were innocuous little pieces of news about rabbits, flowers and auntie's hats. Each had a special destination and some had none, being merely false trails. It was part of the great subterfuge by which important messages for the Resistance were cloaked in nonsense or riddles, having meaning only for the special group for whom they were intended. Later there would be special messages to the whole Resistance movement, indicating that invasion was near or had taken place – a general call to arms.

For the dispatch of agents, to land in small fields in the centre of France, England remained the base. It was close and within range of Westland Lysander single engined aircraft which were the most suitable for the job. Other missions, with larger cargoes to be dropped by parachute, were undertaken by larger RAF aircraft from squadrons such as number 318.

Giraud faded from the scene in April 1944. After several incidents his conduct could not be ignored. De Gaulle removed him from the Commander in Chief's position and offered him the post of Inspector General. Giraud declined, and retired.

These were the hardest times for the people of occupied France. The rations were reduced to a daily 1,000 Calories. One and a half million French prisoners of war were in enemy camps. One hundred thousand had been repatriated, but one million French forced labourers had been taken for the Reich. The Germans had taken 65 per cent of the railway engines, 50 per cent of the wagons and 60 per cent of the lorries.

It was the price of the armistice, and worse was to follow, for the soil, the towns, and the cities of France would take a terrible punishment as the cost of liberation. Major centres of transport would need to be bombed to prevent the movement of German reinforcements. Coastal bases where the U-boats lurked in their concrete pens were under aerial bombardment. The thickness of the concrete, poured by French slave labour, required the heaviest bombs such as the 'Tallboy,' which went supersonic in its descent and penetrated deeply before exploding, causing underground shockwaves and doing immense surrounding damage. These attacks killed 30,000 French civilians before D-day, despite the best efforts to avoid French civilian casualties. Before an attack on the Michelin tyre works at Clermond-Ferrand the RAF swooped low to allow the workers time to escape. The RAF received a special message of thanks from the workers for the warning. The Germans suppressed the civilian population by the taking of hostages, their execution, and by torture.

In these times of the greatest hardship, the darkest hours before the dawn of liberation, the oppressed and afflicted held de Gaulle's name before them. In many prison cells those about to die had inscribed de Gaulle's name on their cell walls, with the hope that their sacrifice and torment would be remembered at the hour of liberation. Their last letters often mentioned de Gaulle. Their last cry before extinction by the bullet was often "Vive la France! Vive de Gaulle!" This news, smuggled out of France, with photographs of some of the prison cell walls, brought to de Gaulle the same anguish which Churchill suffered when he had heard of the losses in the Dardanelles in the First World War.

Perhaps it was these strains which caused de Gaulle's illness at the start of 1944. With good medical care he recovered. The strains of leading the Free French for more than two years, against a background of intrigues and deceptions, had taken their toll. Palewski, Billotte and Soustelle were his closest advisors at this time, ensuring that he was troubled by only the most important and urgent decisions. De Gaulle had always found it best to visit outposts to see for himself the situation and to be seen by those with the responsibilities. He had no pre-war reputation. Indeed, to have held senior position in the failed hierarchy of French government which had brought about the disaster of 1940 would have been a disabling burden. It was only when he had addressed the large gatherings in the Albert Hall in London that he had become well known to the French. He was as inspiring to the French as was Churchill to the British and in those deadly times neither nation could have done without their leader.

His family life in Algeria was simple. His wife and daughters joined him. His son Philippe was serving in the French Navy in the Channel and in the Atlantic. At his villa, in the evening, he would work alone on his numerous speeches. They would have many guests to dinner, a simple meal, entertaining both French and foreigners. Sundays would be spent away, at a little house in the country.

As for so many French families, there were the sad trials of occupation and repression. A niece was deported to Ravensbruck concentration camp. His sister was arrested by the Gestapo and imprisoned for a year in France, while her husband, aged sixty-seven, was sent to Buchenwald concentration camp. One of their sons had been killed in the battle for France while three others had escaped to join the Free French forces. In 1943 de Gaulle's brother was arrested by the Germans and deported to the camp at Eisenberg. His wife and their five children crossed the Pyrenees on foot and eventually reached Morocco.

In Algeria de Gaulle headed the twice-weekly meetings of the National Council. Through the latter half of 1943 and the early part of 1944 preparations were made for the restoration of law and order in a liberated France. Eighteen Commissioners were appointed to head the government in the regions. Their specific task was to safeguard the French and Allied troops and establish a full and proper legal framework for the French Republic. They would be responsible for caring for the needs of the people in the early and chaotic months after the liberation. Local Resistance organisation would have an advisory and not a controlling role.

There would be difficulty in keeping law and order. Tens of thousands of French citizens had been shot and retribution on those who had collaborated with the invaders and their local accomplices was certain. The supremacy of law under the rule of the State had to be established quickly. The legal criteria were complicated by the actions of the Vichy government. How legal were their pronouncements? Would obedience to their laws be a defence when pre-war laws against damaging France had been broken? These offences were exceptional and special tribunals would need to be set up to try the cases. In the end more than 7,000 death sentences were passed, of which de Gaulle commuted more than 6,000.

In Africa de Gaulle arranged with the National Committee that there should be greater autonomy for all the French territories which had done so much to aid the Free French cause. For France itself there would be great problems of shortages and inflation. Those who had profited from the occupation would need to make a special contribution. If the hopes of the people were not to dissolve in despair and then anger brought about by on-going difficulties there would have to be special controls and nationalisation of the essential services. Failure to improve the lot of the people quickly would threaten a communist takeover.

DIPLOMACY

The Russian failure to support the Warsaw uprising, and the refusal to allow British aircraft the use of bases in Russian controlled areas to the east to supply the Polish Army of the Interior in its struggle, allowed the Germans to destroy Polish resistance. The Russians then imposed their agreement with the Polish Committee for National Liberation, their puppet organisation supported from Moscow. The Polish government in exile, in London, was excluded.

The French were in no better position to help the Poles than the British. Russia took Poland's eastern territories, which had been regained in 1920, and gave Poland in exchange territories in Silesia and Prussia. America did not care sufficiently about Poland to threaten disagreement with the Russians. Their whole policy was to get Russia to enter the war against Japan. Britain had no power in the matter, separate from America and France had no place in the discussions at all. De Gaulle offered support when France had the means, but it would be far too late; except for the Polish gold, which had been deposited with the Bank of France. De Gaulle reminded the Russians that the Polish government in London was recognised by all the Allies and was in command of the Polish troops fighting in the United Nations forces. The gold was theirs to command. The Russians took this rebuff with very ill humour.

The stand on behalf of the small states of Europe earned gratitude for France. An agreement with Spain allowed Frenchmen who were able to cross the Pyrenees to reach the French North African territories. As far as Britain was concerned, the appointment of Duff Cooper as liaison between the British and French was an excellent decision. The French found him a man of great culture and a good buffer between Churchill and de Gaulle. If there was hard news he was a messenger with a soft tongue.

French liaison with the Allied commands was improved and a French National Commissioner for the liberated territories was appointed. Eventually General Eisenhower was given overall authority. His wise diplomacy, in so many areas, was crucial to the unification of the Allied cause. On the 30th December 1943 Eisenhower told de Gaulle that his earlier judgement of the Free French had been wrong and that he depended on the fullest support of French civil and military effort. De Gaulle praised this change of heart most forcibly. Churchill intervened to prevent any discord between Roosevelt and de Gaulle.

Diplomatic relations between de Gaulle and the Allies were improving at the start of 1944 and on January 1st a splendid diplomatic presentation and reception, with de Gaulle, promised a period of diplomatic calm. Only Roosevelt continued to deny de Gaulle recognition as the leader of Free France. This was to lead to difficulties in arranging the government of liberated French territory. The American view was that an occupation currency would be needed in the liberated zone and military control would be in force. De Gaulle knew that this would be fatal. The liberating army would become an army of occupation, however benign. France was not being liberated to be newly occupied. In this argument de Gaulle eventually won, and the local French support for the Allies in the newly liberated areas, as well as behind the German lines, was most valuable.

Early in January 1944 Duff Cooper approached de Gaulle with the news that Churchill had been taken ill while returning from the Teheran conference and was at Marrakech. He wished to see de Gaulle. The serious nature of Churchill's illness had been a tightly held secret. Lord Moran, his physician, had summoned senior medical help from far afield. Churchill had suffered from pneumonia, a series of small strokes, and several small heart attacks. During one night Moran had despaired of Churchill surviving the night. His bodyguard, Walter Thompson, kept watch through the night. In one passage in Thompson's memoirs it is recorded that he had difficulty detecting Churchill's breathing. There is an unusual vagueness in this small passage of the record and it may be that Thompson had needed to resuscitate Churchill.

Much has been made of what has been called a snub by de Gaulle in response to Churchill's request to see him, early in January 1944. The truth of the matter is that de Gaulle was very ready to go to see Churchill, but his duties made a small delay necessary. When the meeting was postponed de Gaulle sent a message of explanation:

'I have certainly received your message. I regret that our arrangement for last Friday could not be fulfilled. The work of the Consultative Assembly necessitates my being in Algiers next Monday and Tuesday, but I can come to see you on Wednesday the 12th, if that is convenient.' The difficulties of bringing together the disparate French factions necessitated de Gaulle's presence at the negotiations and the meetings. There is no evidence that he was in any way unwilling to meet Churchill.

On the 12th January de Gaulle went to dine with Churchill, and was delighted to find Churchill's convalescence well advanced. Churchill greeted de Gaulle warmly and they had a long conversation. Churchill tried to persuade de Gaulle to be less forceful in his treatment of Flandin, Peyrouton, and Boisson, whose actions for Vichy had been supported by Roosevelt, when he was trying to split Vichy from the Axis side. De Gaulle reminded Churchill that they would have to face a High Court trial over their actions for Vichy and that any easement of their position prior to this would be very incorrect.

De Gaulle did not wish to emphasise these points too severely and so he invited Churchill to review the troops the next day. This they did, taking the salute side-by-side, demonstrating Allied unity. There were still severe difficulties in the relations of the Free French with the United States. Churchill suggested that a meeting with Roosevelt would clear the air but de Gaulle was certain that until his authority was established on the true soil of France, the Americans would not recognise the validity of his leadership.

The spring of 1944 was a time of increasing preparation for the invasion. Everyone in Britain knew it was coming and everywhere preparations in the form of the assembly of men and equipment could be seen. It was a time when everyone knew and no one spoke. The secret was obvious, but still a secret. There were countless small items requiring attention. In the village of Whitchurch, in Buckinghamshire, a house called 'The Firs' stood at the southern end of the village street. Everyone knew it was a secret establishment for the development of special weapons. It was here that limpet mines and the PIAT mortar-Projector Infantry Anti-Tank-first saw the light of day.

In the middle of the village stood a very old fifteenth century house, 'Deerstalkers,' occupied on rental by a Frenchman and his wife and small son. In February 1944 P.M.G.Thorpe came on a visit from London. He was a representative of Johnson Matthey, the precious metal merchants. The question he put to the Frenchman, who was a very experienced fine jeweller, was about metal corrosion. The proposal was that silver should be used for the metal electrical connectors between the different concrete caissons of the Mulberry Harbour segments. The Frenchman was horrified. "If you do that, they will corrode in a week. They will be going into salt water." "What then?" asked the man from London. "Platinum" the Frenchman replied. "That is far too expensive" was the reply. "No it isn't," the Frenchman continued, "the amount you will use, just for the connectors, is tiny, and anyway it can be recovered later." And so it was that platinum was used. At the end of the war Thorpe bought the contract to salvage the metal from the Mulberry Harbours. Johnson Matthey came to hear of it and demanded that he should hand over the large amount of money raised by the melting down of this scrap. Thorpe refused, resigned his post, and used the capital to start a very successful caravan accessory business at Springfield Yeadon, in Yorkshire. It was one small item in the big war.

Churchill and de Gaulle met near Portsmouth to discuss the forthcoming invasion, with England the springboard and the Royal Navy the major protection for the invasion fleet. De Gaulle expressed his admiration of Churchill's personal courage. Churchill was determined that de Gaulle should play the leading part in the re-establishment of the true French State in the newly liberated France. Churchill wanted de Gaulle to go to the United States to persuade Roosevelt to accept this. De Gaulle asked why he should go and ask Roosevelt's permission and support to take power in France. The government of Free France already existed and was ready to take its proper place. De Gaulle had become aware that the invasion troops had been issued with so called

French money to be used in the newly liberated areas. It was a currency which the French Government would not, in any way, recognise. The United States had arranged to take control of the liberated areas and would become another army of occupation. Churchill explained, forcibly, that it was difficult keeping the Americans focussed on liberating Europe first when there was a world war demanding so much effort in the Pacific. Any difficulties in the details of liberating the whole of Europe could deflect the American effort from Europe to the Pacific. Great Britain had to go along with the United States to keep the European focus.

Churchill and de Gaulle then went to see Eisenhower at his nearby headquarters. Eisenhower showed them in great detail the plans for the invasion. The ships were ready to leave, the 'planes were loaded, the troops embarked. The coiled spring of liberation was about to be released onto the shores of Europe. The invasion would have to take place between the 3rd and 7th of June to fit in with the conditions of moon and tides.

Eisenhower asked de Gaulle's opinion of the plans. De Gaulle replied that the duty of the final decision of the day and hour was Eisenhower's and that it was in no way de Gaulle's place to intervene. De Gaulle's only comment was that his own views on the plans were identical to Eisenhower's. The risks of bad weather were less than the risks of delay. Delay would risk the secrecy of the operation and damage morale.

Eisenhower then showed de Gaulle the hand written text of a proclamation which he was going to broadcast to the French people. De Gaulle read it and disapproved. Eisenhower offered to change it. The message had been broadly put for the nations from Norway to Belgium. For the French, he invited them to obey military orders. They should then obey the civil authorities and later choose their government. So credibility was given to de Gaulle and the National Committee for Liberation, which had acted as the government of France. The Allied military would be acting as a government, a task for which they were totally unequipped. De Gaulle was told that there were difficulties in altering the text as it had already been printed.

De Gaulle saw Charles Peake, the Foreign Office official seconded to the Free French. The next day, the day of the Normandy invasion, the heads of the occupied countries, such as the King of Norway, would broadcast and this would be followed by Eisenhower's message. De Gaulle would then speak. De Gaulle would not speak in this order, but at another time. Early on the 6th June de Gaulle came from Churchill, who has furious. De Gaulle repeated that rather than following in the manner prescribed he would not speak at all. When the furore settled down it was agreed that de Gaulle would speak to France in the evening.

That evening de Gaulle made his broadcast. "The supreme battle has started. Mark well! The battle for France is France's battle! For the sons of France, wherever they are and whatever their duties, the clear and sacred task is to fight the enemy by all means in their power. All orders given by the French Government and French military must be obeyed exactly. At last the dark clouds of shame can be cleared and we will see again the sunshine of our greatness!"

In the next few days the news of the invasion was good. It was a success. The bridgehead had breached the walls of the fortress which the Germans had created on the coast of Europe. Bayeux was the first town to be liberated. French troops, ships, commandos and parachutists, had played their part. General Leclerc, with the French second armoured division, was nearly ready to cross the channel and join the Allied armies.

The French forces of the interior, under General Koenig, were in action destroying German communications and the ability to bring up reinforcements. At that moment the German V-1 flying bombs started to land on London, launched from sites in the Pas de Calais. The German ability to launch these weapons had been delayed by the RAF attacks on the German Rocket Experimental Station at Peenemunde in 1943. The launching sites, many of whose locations had been found by the Frenchman Michel Hollard, were attacked and many, but not all, destroyed. Their range was not sufficient to attack the invasion areas or the supply routes and they did not delay the progress of the invasion. Had they been used against the ports in England supplying the invasion they would have been much more damaging than against London. As soon as the attacks started, in 24 hours, the whole anti-aircraft defence of London was moved to form a belt of guns near the south coast of England, to bring down the flying bombs in open country. With attacks from fighter aircraft, with their throttle restrictions removed for added speed, many were brought down. The effect of the anti-aircraft fire was made more effective by the use of new proximity fuses.

If there was military progress, the diplomatic scene took longer to settle. On the 8th June Anthony Eden dined with de Gaulle. Eden pointed out that if Britain and France stood together the Americans would have to agree. Recalling the Franco-British agreement of 1943 would perform this useful function. They could then point out the absurdity of there being no proper organisation of authority in the newly liberated areas of France. De Gaulle pointed out that there was no place for any negotiation. Liberated France was France, and a liberated France was a sovereign power and the British had recognised him as its leader in 1940. Certainly the French people would be instructed to shun any occupation currency. There would be no French liaison officers attached to the American or British forces. They were not entering and occupying a foreign country. They were liberating an ally, and the local officials would be their contact, assisting the liberating forces in each department as they marched through France into Germany.

The American press became very hostile to de Gaulle's attitude. They did not understand that as the Allies marched through France it would be the French forces of the interior who would be added to the Allied ranks and would be keeping German troops from reinforcing the German defence against the Allied advance. This resistance would lead the SS Das Reich division, harassed in its drive north to oppose the Allied landings, to turn aside from its route to massacre the men, women and children of Oradour-sur Glane. The support for the Allied forces would bring great sacrifice and pain to the people of France. 30,000 civilians died in the battle for Normandy. Nor could de Gaulle allow the fruits of victory to be seized by the communists, who would be able to point out a resemblance of the Allied forces as an occupying army with some similarity to the German occupation.

There was growing disquiet amongst the other governments in exile in London about how the liberation might be seen in their own countries. After so much sacrifice were the fruits of victory to be snatched from them? By the 20th June all the governments in exile had given support to de Gaulle's position, with the exception of Holland. This was because of their difficulty with regard to the liberation of their colonies in the East Indies. There it would be American troops alone who were in a position to restore Dutch authority.

On the evening of the 13th June de Gaulle was dining with members of the British cabinet. He was intent on setting foot on French soil. Churchill sent him a letter forbidding the project, but in a discussion headed by Clement Attlee, Churchill's deputy, the arrangements were allowed to go ahead and the Free French destroyer *La Combattante* was allowed to continue her voyage to Portsmouth in preparation for the next day's voyage to France.

On the 14th June the ship anchored close to the coast of France at Courselles and de Gaulle's party stepped onto French soil, in the midst of a Canadian regiment that was landing at the same moment. General Montgomery provided transport for the group. A French officer was sent ahead to Bayeux to prepare the way. De Gaulle called on Montgomery in his caravan. He noted that Montgomery kept a portrait of Rommel, whom he had beaten at El-Alamein, in a prominent position. De Gaulle noted Montgomery's professionalism and wisdom, but also that it was coupled with a touch of humour. The military operations were going as planned.

As de Gaulle moved into Bayeux the officers of his government were taking control of the liberated areas. The Vichy official had not come from Rouen. When de Gaulle reached Bayeux his officer, de Courcel, was there, with the mayor and the municipal council.

They went on foot, from street to street. The inhabitants were astounded to see de Gaulle in their midst. They had heard his voice for years in his broadcasts, but few had any idea of his appearance. He received a tumultuous welcome. The news of his arrival spread and the citizens poured out of their houses. He was surrounded by children. The women were smiling and the men shook his hands. The multitude swept on together, full of pride and joy, national pride surging up from the depths of despair. The town had been liberated, but now, with de Gaulle's arrival, it was French again. Not just liberation from the Germans, but the pride of France had been renewed. In the Prefecture, where only an hour before had hung a picture of Marshal Petain, de Gaulle met the officials and the Bishop of Bayex and Lisieux.

The people gathered in the Place du Chateau and there de Gaulle addressed them. Maurice Schumann announced to the crowd, "Honour and Country. Here is General de Gaulle!" And there, after four terrible years away from France, they heard a French leader declare that the enemy is still the enemy and must be fought with all their might and that France must take a full part in that victory. A large stone plaque on the wall of the chateau marks the spot of this oration and in the adjacent street is a museum commemorating de Gaulle's first and later visits to Bayeux.

De Gaulle returned to England on the *La Combattante* next day. He presented the ship with the Croix de Guerre. Shortly afterwards she was sunk. Later that day Eden visited de Gaulle at Carlton Gardens. Roosevelt had heard of de Gaulle's welcome in Bayeux and had withdrawn the invitation for de Gaulle to visit Washington. Eden proposed that because of American anger at de Gaulle's refusal to accept the American method of ruling newly liberated France that Great Britain should act as intermediary in their relationships. De Gaulle wrote to Churchill apologising for the difficulties he had caused. Churchill replied deploring any difficulties in Franco-British relationships and emphasising their stout comradeship which had been formed in the darkest days. He hoped that it would soon be possible for France to re-establish her historic good relations with the United States. He offered his strongest support to that end.

If there was a conflict between de Gaulle and the Americans and British about the power of control of the areas of France as they were liberated there is no doubt about de Gaulle's friendship and regard for Churchill. On the 16th of June he wrote to

Churchill:

"Dear Prime Minister, in leaving the shores of Great Britain, where you were kind enough to invite me at a time which was decisive for the victorious outcome of the war, I wish to express to you my most sincere thanks for the welcome which was given to me by His Britannic Majesty's Government.

After the year which has passed since my last stay in your noble and valiant country, I have seen and felt that the courage and the power of the people of Great Britain has reached the highest level and that the feelings of friendship for the place of France is at the highest level ever. I am able to assure you, for my part, of the greatest confidence, and the unbreakable friendship, of France for Great Britain.

On my visit to France I was able to see the magnificent effort in progress of the British Navy, Army, and Air Force as part of the Allied force, together with France, now battling on the soil of France for our common victory. For your country, which played an exemplary part in this struggle, the last impregnable bastion of Europe of which you are a major liberator is about to fall. You have never ceased to direct and enthuse this immense effort. Allow me to say, you have gained immortal honour.

I earnestly hope you will accept, Mr. Prime Minister, the expression of my highest regard and very sincere devotion."

No political leader has ever received any expression of higher regard. The only equal could be President Kennedy's address on conferring Honorary Citizenship of the United States on Winston Churchill, but his was a formal honour, not an expression of such personal admiration.

On the 16th June de Gaulle flew to Algeria. When he met the other members of the provisional government he carried with him the aura of his reception in Bayeux. He had been greeted by the French people as their hero. As soon as Cherbourg was liberated the Place du Marche (Market Place) was renamed Place General de Gaulle.

If there was good news from France there were no less happy tidings from the war front in Italy. French troops, as part of the Allied advance, had broken through the German defences at the river Garigliano. This had opened the road to Rome and the Allied troops had entered the Eternal City on the 5th June. King Victor Emmanuel abdicated in favour of his son. A new Italian government was formed and on the 27th June de Gaulle paid a formal visit, landing at Naples. He established formal relations with the new Italian government and then went on to Rome, to meet the Allied military chiefs, including General Juin. In Rome he entered the Palais Farnese, taking over again this French property.

On the 30th June de Gaulle visited the Pope. The Vatican had shown great reserve in its relations with the Free French. The Papal Nuncio in Paris in 1940 had transferred his official functions to Vichy after the fall of France. During the war the Free French had continued contacts with the Vatican through the good offices of Cardinal Tisserant. The Free French had been made aware that the Pope wanted the end of Hitler's regime and so Pope Pius XIIth received de Gaulle. It was clear that some actions of the clergy in France would make things difficult in the future, especially in opposing the menace of Soviet influence. The Pope showed a special concern about the suffering of the German people. In Italy he expected confusion, with the Church being the bedrock of order. But above all the Pope was concerned about the effect of Soviet domination of Eastern Europe. He expected years of confrontation. In Galicia there was already persecution of the religious.

When de Gaulle returned to London he found that Roosevelt had renewed the invitation to visit Washington and sent General Bedell Smith to emphasise the importance of the invitation. De Gaulle was persuaded. The only object of the visit was to allow a frank exchange of views between the two men. There was nothing to discuss about policy or control. Once the news of de Gaulle's visit leaked out, Canada demanded that he should visit there also. De Gaulle arrived in Washington on the 6th July. His welcome by the President to the White House was most cordial. They had three meetings on their own. De Gaulle was lodged at Blair House, the special residence for honoured guests. Meetings were held with all the senior American officials, under Roosevelt's chairmanship.

The meetings established a cordiality which de Gaulle was able to report on at a press conference. Above all, it allowed Roosevelt to outline the objectives which the United States wished to see achieved as the outcome of the war. Moving from isolationism to a close involvement in European affairs was a major change of target and it somewhat alarmed de Gaulle. In Roosevelt's view the world would recognise four great powers, and France was not included. It was clear that the United States saw the price of its intervention on the side of democracy as the placement of American forces in every corner of the globe. In this Great Britain, gradually losing power over its dominions, would bend to the American will. All the futures of the minor states of Europe would depend on American control.

In all this Roosevelt's aims were benign. Twice in a century the United States had needed to come into Europe to sort out quarrels which were not of American origin. Its foundations as a country had started as an attempt by the Pilgrim Fathers to sever themselves from just such quarrels. De Gaulle understood Roosevelt's exasperation, that the United States had become embroiled in such a European conflict, when the supine indifference of some of Europe's greatest powers, at the time when their intervention could have been decisive, allowed tyranny to march unopposed into the Rhineland and then onwards to the conquest of the rest of Europe.

In all this de Gaulle found Roosevelt's arguments most persuasive, even seductive. However, there were dangers in such a policy. American control might seem sound from the western side of the Atlantic but it would not be tolerated from the eastern. Nor would the United States wish to be permanently committed to such a large and forceful presence away from its shores. Little did de Gaulle, at that time, realise how the Soviet threat would demand just such an American involvement in Europe for more than half a century. Perhaps the harsh lessons of appeasement had been learnt. De Gaulle tried to elevate France to the position of the United States' only true long-term ally.

This was a battle to try and place France in the position of the fifth great power in the world. De Gaulle knew how feeble was

France's claim to such a position at that time. It was a place which was finally secured for France at the Teheran conference, almost as an afterthought, slid through by Churchill when everyone else was tired and unfocussed on the real meaning of his efforts on France's behalf. It was like proposing a foal for the Derby even before the animal's maiden race. That was the confidence in the alliance between Churchill and de Gaulle and it fulfilled in every way Churchill's judgement of de Gaulle as the 'Man of Destiny.' Only de Gaulle could have inspired such confidence in Churchill and therein lay the destiny of France as a great power.

If this was France's destiny Roosevelt was not so sure. He questioned de Gaulle as to what would be de Gaulle's place in a liberated France. De Gaulle stated that France would recover her own position in world affairs. As to his own position, it awaited a decision by the people of France. Roosevelt smiled and was not convinced. He would wait and see. Before de Gaulle left, Roosevelt showed him the swimming pool where he exercised, to maintain his strength against the ravages of poliomyelitis. De Gaulle knew of this and before he left he presented Roosevelt with a clockwork model submarine which had been specially made in the arsenal at Bizerta. Roosevelt was touched by this act of kind consideration and sent de Gaulle a photograph on which he had written "To General de Gaulle, who is my friend."

If this gives the impression of harmony, it is mistaken. Shortly after their meeting Roosevelt wrote to a member of Congress that de Gaulle was concerned for France's position in the world after the war. Above all, Roosevelt considered that de Gaulle was an egoist. From Washington de Gaulle went to New York, where he received a tumultuous ovation from very large crowds. The French community, joined by many from across the country, gave him a rousing reception at the Waldorf-Astoria.

Onwards to Canada, where in Quebec de Gaulle inspired a surge of French pride followed by a wave of sadness at France's troubles. In Ottawa he was pleased to see again the Prime Minister, MacKenzie-King, whose steadfast support of the war effort had provided relatively the largest contribution to the Atlantic convoy escorts. Canada had provided one of the five major elements onto the Normandy beaches. They discussed the French contribution through the Canadian sites towards the development of the atomic bomb. MacKenzie-King promised special help for the reconstruction of France after the liberation.

During the visit de Gaulle stayed with the Earl of Athlone, the Governor General, and his wife, Countess Alice, who was the aunt of King George VIth. He received an unforgettable welcome and an introduction to many of the important personalities in Canadian life. He was able to inspect French airmen under training in Canada. In Montreal he was again received with great enthusiasm. The mayor asked the citizens to show de Gaulle that he was in the second greatest French city on earth, and they did, with a thunderous ovation.

He returned to Algeria on the 13th July. There he found a statement from the Americans recognising that the National Committee for the liberation was qualified to act for France. It was the end of any discord about who would be in charge of the liberated areas of France and by early August the agreement, so close to that which de Gaulle had proposed a year earlier, was agreed by all parties. De Gaulle was recognised as Master of France. If Roosevelt had thought him an egoist he was right, but he was also a firm patriot, a great ally, and a man devoted to the right of the French people to decide their destiny. He had made this very clear in many speeches, starting in Africa in 1940 and most recently in Canada. In his resolve that the people of France would be free to choose their future he was unswerving.

COMBAT

At the start of the battle for the liberation of France de Gaulle found himself at the head of the weakest French forces in the country's history. Military prowess had been France's core belief for fourteen centuries. If some battles had been lost there had always been compensating victories. To the British the conflict with Germany had occurred twice in the first half of the twentieth century. To the French the defeat of 1940 was the third time in 70 years that the Germans had been physically within, or with their guns in range of, Paris.

In the 1914-18 war France had been the leading military power on the Allied side. After the collapse in 1940 there seemed to be no possibility of the recovery of France's territory, position, or pride. There were enough forces available to be mobilised in Africa to form a very strong army. If the same call up regime which had been used in 1918 were applied to those of French origin in the African territories an army of more than 100,000 could be recruited. Even if this could be achieved and added to by young Frenchmen who joined by escaping from France via Spain, there would still be a critical shortage of specialists and an experienced administration. When the Americans supplied the equipment for the French forces they insisted on the troops adopting the American top-heavy administrative system, reducing the effective forces available.

General Giraud had seen the possibility of forming 14 French divisions. However by the time the American system had been measured to the available troops only isolated and fragmented units could be formed. The possibility of forming proper units was further reduced by the need to keep some troops in each African territory to maintain order and Free French sovereignty. All these difficulties would impede France's contribution to the Allied effort in the battle to liberate France.

On the 7th January 1944 de Gaulle had outlined plans for the formation of one complete army, 3 army corps, 6 infantry divisions and 4 armoured divisions. In addition there would be parachutists and commandos. Some commando detachments had been in the battle since 1941, and were fully battle hardened.

The Free French naval situation was rather better. The French navy had suffered severe losses on the 3rd July 1940 when, after Admiral Gensoul had refused the British demand that his ships should be put out of the reach of the Germans and Italians, the British attacked and sank the battleship *Bretagne* and damaged other ships, with the loss of life of nearly 1,300 sailors. To this loss of fine ships were added the shipping casualties, even worse, when the French fleet scuttled itself at Toulon in November 1942 as the Germans entered the harbour to take over the ships. If anything, the German attempt in 1942 to take over the French ships showed how necessary had been the tragic British attack of 1940.

Admiral Lemonnier had been appointed senior admiral for the Free French in 1943. He had gathered a fleet of 2 battleships, 9 cruisers, 4 light cruisers, 2 light aircraft carriers, 18 submarines, and nearly a hundred lesser ships. Damage to the arsenals at Bizerta and the facilities at Casablanca and Dakar lessened the opportunity to re-arm the fleet. However, by 1943 the battleship *Richelieu* was serving with the British Home Fleet at Scapa Floe. The British handed over 4 frigates and the Americans contributed 6 destroyers to the Free French navy.

The Free French Air Force had 4 fighter squadrons and 3 bomber squadrons in the United Kingdom. Another 21 squadrons were based in the Mediterranean theatre. Two squadrons had been sent to help the Russians. At the time of the North African invasion the Americans had destroyed all French aircraft which were then under Vichy control, leaving no French air power in North Africa. The Americans then started a programme of re-equipping the new Free French squadrons.

By the time this force had been built up it comprised 150,000 soldiers, 50,000 sailors, and an air force with 600 'planes and 30,000 men. Much of their equipment had been provided by the Allies in return for the use of French ports and facilities in Africa and the Caribbean. With these forces coming ready for action there was a renewal of French pride and a fiery determination of the troops to play a major part for France in the liberation of their country and the rest of Europe. De Gaulle inspected each ship, squadron and unit.

The Maquis were also gaining strength within France. Up until 1942 they had been a feeble and disorganised force, unable to make any significant contribution to the Allied cause. From that time the Germans had conscripted 500,000 French workers to make munitions or build defences, particularly along the Atlantic wall. The Germans called these Frenchmen 'The Army of the Armistice.' It was amongst these French that the Maquis was able to recruit. Initially they were small and isolated groups, without armament. Outside the main centres of population and communication the German presence was scattered and vulnerable. These isolated detachments could also be attacked by commandos coming from Britain, such as the raid by 13 commandos on the night of the 11th/12th November 1942 when they attacked the radio station at Plouezec, in Brittany, in an operation code named 'Operation Fahrenheit.' Churchill had authorised such raids to disorganise and frighten the Germans and give them no peace. "Set Europe ablaze" he had ordered. Either the Germans had to accept the losses caused by such attacks, increase the defensive garrisons, or abandon some positions. After the raid the Germans never returned to Plouezec.

Gradually these Maquis groups had been organised into larger detachments in the wild regions of the Massif Central, the Vosges, and other such isolated regions. Into these isolated areas the Allies had parachuted secret agents, to help with the organisation, and containers of arms. In these remote regions the Maquis had to assemble and train and, above all, be patient. Too early an action would allow the Germans to assemble mighty forces which could sweep through mountainous areas and, with air support, destroy the partisan groups before they could be of effective use. If a secret army were to be of use it had to be secret until its actions could be co-ordinated to strike a major and surprise blow which would aid the Allied invasion. What was later to become clear was that they were woefully short of any equipment to deal with armour. In retrospect it was easy to see that they needed to be given early supplies of the PIAT (Projector Infantry Anti-Tank) mortar. In the densely wooded countryside they could have come close enough to make very good use of such a weapon.

The main task of the Maquis was to attack isolated outposts, derailing trains carrying troops or preferably munitions and equipment, sabotaging vehicle parks and blowing up fuel dumps. Secretly the French peasants gave food and other support to these Maquis groups, until, with the invasion, they could come out of hiding and assume a much more important role in supporting the Allied advance. They were at great risk after each attack. It was a triumph to see German troops lying where they fell, with the lorries burning, but the retribution, particularly by the SS, was ruthless and merciless. So many died pierced by the bullets of firing parties, shouting "Vive la France!" In the subsequent peace, wherever such shootings took place, a monument was erected bearing the Cross of Lorraine and detailing exactly why and how those who had been killed had come to their fate. The traveller in France will be surprised by the number of these monuments and by the youth of so many who are remembered there, "Mort pours la Patrie."

In the more densely populated parts of France the Resistance remained in small groups, using false papers to remain undetected. Workers in government offices provided these false papers, often at great risk of detection and betrayal. The rate of sabotage gradually increased as more arms and supplies reached the groups. Gradually they were able to form guards to protect vital installations which the Allies would need after the invasion and which the Germans would be sure to try and demolish in their retreat. By early 1943 the Resistance forces totalled about 100,000. A year later, at the start of the invasion, their numbers had grown to 200,000. Such a rapid growth placed very great demands on the supply route and it was not possible to supply all the groups as effectively as was intended. Allied air control over France had made supply drops much easier, but as the volume and number of drops increased so did the German organisation to interfere with them and some fierce and unequal battles took place near the drop zones.

As well as difficulties with the supply of arms there was a need to provide money in a usable form. French francs were gathered from Britain and all the French overseas territories to supply the Resistance. As with any large organisation where funds are distributed without controls there were abuses, but when a final reckoning was taken these proved to be very small. With such a growth of the organisation it was essential to keep control. The greatest danger was that groups would become autonomous and act almost like bandits under the Resistance banner and that communist groups would seek an armed takeover of the State. To avoid this de Gaulle appointed inspectors and a commanding general.

Great plans were made for supporting the Allied invasion by taking control of the rail system, to block German re-enforcements by sabotage of track and locomotives and to prepare the way for the transport of Allied supplies from captured ports in the liberated areas, to support the advance. The details of many of these actions are shown in the film "La Bataille du Rail," made in 1946.

In March 1944, in preparation for the invasion, de Gaulle formed the French Forces of the Interior, the FFI. General Koenig was named as its commander in April. He was sent to Eisenhower's headquarters to co-ordinate the action of the French Resistance. The danger was that actions in France might give away the site of the invasion and that some vital structures or routes the Allies would need later would be uselessly destroyed.

The campaign in Italy was regarded by the Americans as an unnecessary diversion, but it gave French troops a chance to prove their worth in battle. The campaign also tied down many German divisions. The Americans had not understood that the wasting away of German units in Italy at a time when the growth of American strength for the invasion of France would give the invading Allied troops a necessary advantage.

The invasion would be a two pronged attack, first from the north and then from the south. The southern attack would allow Free French troops from North Africa to put into effect the plan which de Gaulle had envisaged and agreed with Churchill: it was the plan which they had hoped would keep France in the conflict all those years ago, and which was undone by all those defeatists who formed the Vichy government.

The Americans were doubtful that the two invasions could be managed: certainly not simultaneously. There would be a shortage of landing craft and the air support necessary could not be spared from the main invasion target of Normandy. The British had no new reserves to bring into the fight and advised against taking the Germans in a frontal assault at their strongest point. The Americans and French believed that any delay in taking on the Germans at full strength would give the Germans time to bring into action new weapons. Flying bombs, rockets and jet fighters were all due to enter German service and the Allies had no adequate counters to these weapons. The long range guns at Mimoyecques –the V3 weapon- would be able to fire shells to land on London at the rate of one every ten seconds. Speed of assault and victory were crucial to success. All realised that the war could still be lost.

It was certain that Russian advances in the east would allow them to be the liberators of Eastern Europe, but the British and their dominions had no further forces to send into the Balkans. Their efforts in the Far East had drained away too much of their vigour. The loss of so many troops, supinely captured at Singapore, was continuing to have its effect.

De Gaulle could not agree with Churchill's position that the attack should turn eastwards from the north of Italy. He could see the Allied forces wasting away in the spread of the Balkans. He could also see Churchill's long attachment to Greece still controlled his thoughts. At that stage Free French forces were becoming more important to the Allied cause. In the end it was Eisenhower's clear sighted view of priorities which ruled the action and the focus was back on liberating France as soon as possible. In any case, there was no way in which Free French troops were going to march into Austria and not into France! Through France and onward into Austria – yes; directly – no!

Russian pressure for a second front in the west increased and so, in December 1943, operation "Overlord" for the invasion of Normandy was finally and irretrievably set in train. The invasion through southern France remained doubtful. Churchill could not see how it could be managed and he feared that a small force landing in the south would be crushed. He was not reassured by the intelligence which indicated that the German divisions in the south were mainly static infantry divisions, unable to move swiftly to counter the invasion from the south. And yet Churchill still clung to the hope that a swift breakthrough in northern Italy would allow the Allied troops the opportunity to turn east to liberate the Balkans.

With General Giraud at Allied headquarters and taking part in all the discussion about the plan to attack it was possible for the Free French view to carry weight, especially when it agreed with the American ideas. It was hard for the French to accept that for the invasion of France that an American would command in the north and there would be a British commander in the south. De Gaulle felt very much as a second class Ally. He wanted to be included in the decision making, but this proved to be difficult. Eisenhower's strategy was focussed entirely on the military task of defeating the Germans. De Gaulle's need was to gain a victory that would not be thrown away politically to the communists.

When, in December 1943, Free French troops entered the Italian campaign, there was an opportunity to establish a sound French position. Three French divisions were in action, the most recent being the 4th Moroccan division. They were poorly provided with transport. It was suggested that it should be re-enforced by several battalions from the forces of General Juin. Instead General Giraud arranged that a further complete Free French division should also join the campaign. Eisenhower decided that the French 9th Colonial division should go to Italy instead. It gave de Gaulle the opportunity to notify Eisenhower that the disposition of French forces was under Free French control and the proper chain of command needed to be observed. The Allied High Command replied that there could not be divided control.

Conferences were arranged at which de Gaulle emphasised that, although the Free French forces were to be used for the execution of Allied plans, those plans needed to take account of French views. The French required to be consulted and the Free

French forces were essential to the Allied cause. For the invasion of France those forces would be necessary and might be removed from Italy for that purpose. At these meetings, in December 1943 and onwards, de Gaulle insisted that Free French troops in Italy and North Africa should take part in "Operation Anvil" in southern France and an armoured division should go from North Africa to England to take part in "Overlord" and the liberation of Paris. Once guarantees of this use of the forces had been given they would be fully at the Allies disposal. The required guarantees were given.

After that the Allied High Command kept the French informed of their plans and often took French advice. All the subsidiary commanders paid attention to French views. It was the first time since 1940 that France's military opinion had counted in the making of important decisions. It is not difficult to see why there was Allied reluctance to take account of the French position. The French troops were armed almost entirely by the Americans. Above all, American four star and three star generals were expected to take account of the views of a two star general who was acting on behalf of a country where he had not been elected or appointed to office. There was also the small matter of de Gaulle having been sentenced to death by France's "legal" government. But His Britannic Majesty's Government had recognised de Gaulle as the leader of the Free French within six weeks of his arrival in June 1940 and Churchill held fast to his decision and his word of support.

De Gaulle records his admiration of the Allied military leaders and in particular how free of intrigue were their actions. Straight talking, straight dealing, and then firm action were the hallmarks of Eisenhower's way of doing things.

In the naval sphere it was easy to combine the Free French fleet with the Allies. There were no major German surface fleet adventures to control. The main task was to counter submarine attacks on convoys and to defend against aircraft attacks. The French admirals had combined well, as in the old days, with their British and American counterparts. Gone were the dark days of 1940 when the British had attacked the French fleet at Oran and killed nearly 1,300 French sailors.

Of all the French generals, Juin and de Lattre de Tassigny made their mark in command of large detachments. Leclerc would further advance his reputation in the fight for the liberation of Paris and his onward thrust to Hitler's lair at Berchtesgarten. In early January French troops, attacking in the Allied line in Italy, pierced the German line and advanced 20 kilometres. Three French divisions, in line together, made the breakthrough, but on the left of the line Monte Cassino remained in German hands. The French had to delay their advance while their Allies on either side were still struggling to overcome stout German resistance. The French received generous congratulations from King George VIth and Generals Eisenhower, Clark, Wilson and Alexander.

De Gaulle met with General Alexander, who impressed him with his calm control and well formed plans for the Allied Italian campaign. In addition to the well known Allied nations there were troops from Poland, who would eventually take Monte Cassino, and a Brazilian division, to incorporate into the Allied force. Alexander explained his plan and pointed out that he was inclined to adopt General Juin's ideas for the campaign. This regard for a French general's plan greatly pleased de Gaulle. Here, for the first time, was a genuine and sensible recognition of the French contribution.

When de Gaulle visited General Mark Clark he was similarly impressed. This was in contrast to the very critical view of Mark Clark's plans which involved pressing forward to take Rome, which he achieved on June 5th, instead of cutting off German troops who were holding up progress from the Salerno landings. For future preparations the French 2nd armoured division left North Africa for England. The French 1st and 5th armoured divisions remained in North Africa, ready, as agreed, to take part in operation "Anvil" in the south of France. The 9th Colonial division was also part of this force. General Wilson wanted to use even more troops in Italy, but de Gaulle stopped this. The troops for operation "Anvil" would have to be reserved for that purpose. Already there were 120,000 French troops serving in Italy, making up more than a quarter of the Allied force.

On the 11th May the French forces launched an attack through the mountains and took the Germans in the rear. The use of small mountain passes which the Germans had not defended strongly enabled this penetration. To maintain the surprise there was no preparatory artillery barrage. The tiny mountain paths, going over the mountain crests, were in no way suited to artillery support as there were no entrenched German formations as targets. In this penetration the Moroccans of the 4th Division were particularly skilled in using the mountain paths.

After years of disaster and humiliation it was marvellous for de Gaulle and his generals to be able to celebrate a notable and valuable success in the Allied cause. Above all, it established fully the contribution of the French in Allied eyes, and gave them a firm claim for a major seat at the Allied counsel tables. The development of support services, including the medical and nursing services under the control of Madame Catroux, provided a fully adequate provision, French and German wounded being treated equally.

The French made further gains on the 20th May, while on their left the American 2nd Army was still delayed near the coast, fighting through the marshes. On the French right the British 8th Army, with the Poles, also broke through the German lines. By turning left the French were able to assist the American breakthrough and on the 5th June American, British, and French troops entered Rome. North of Rome the Allied advance continued, under the protection of nearly complete air superiority. General Juin's success in Italy led to his being named Chief of Staff of French National defence. He was to remain at de Gaulle's side until de Gaulle relinquished power.

Operation "Anvil" was finally fixed for the 15th August. By late July many French troops from Italy were taken on board ship ready for the landings in the south of France. Their ships needed escorting, but very many French ships were still needed to take part in convoy protection in the Atlantic, the Channel, and the Arctic. There was a squadron of French light cruisers available, with some other Allied ships, for the escort duty.

If, in Italy, French forces were winning their spurs in Allied eyes, in central France itself the battle had begun. From mid 1943 groups of resistance fighters, in growing numbers and with growing strength, had been attacking the Germans. So serious had the situation become that the Germans had to employ up to 7,000 men, artillery, and aerial support to deal with a single group of fighters. It took thirteen days of hard fighting for the Germans to win, and in the battle they lost 600 men. In one action the Resistance took 400 German prisoners, a large embarrassment to have to care for. In a train ambush 200 Germans were killed, while in a road convoy ambush 300 Germans died. The battle had moved from small, isolated attacks to repeated major battles. The German losses were robbing them of mobile troop re-enforcements, available in the centre of the country to counter an attack from any direction.

The German reaction was ruthless. They took 300 hostages. The Resistance replied by destroying munitions and blowing up the barracks at Bonne, killing 220 Germans and wounding 550. These attacks brought fear to German troops who had thought that a posting to central France was an easy billet compared to the Eastern Front. It was not only by open attacks that the Resistance were active. They gained information about troops dispositions, the location of ammunition and fuel dumps, and the assignment of aircraft to different landing grounds. All this involved the sending of large amounts of information to London for Allied use. In May 1944 700 telegraph reports and 3000 documents arrived in London from France. These included details of German command posts and photographs of defence structures.

The Resistance was warned on the 16th May that the invasion was coming, under the plan named "Caiman." When the invasion came on June 6th Eisenhower spoke on the radio to the Resistance to hold themselves ready but not yet to act. Later that day de Gaulle ordered them to act on the orders of their commanders.

The destruction of chosen rail routes was achieved by a combination of aerial attack and Resistance sabotage. In June and July the Resistance achieved 600 derailments, 1,800 locomotives were disabled, together with more than 6,000 wagons. Enemy communications were disrupted. All their telephone lines had been identified. In many areas of France the armed struggle was delayed to give the Allies the best advantage of the action without revealing the direction of attack. In Brittany there was no delay. The Resistance was joined by the 1st French parachute regiment, to prevent the retreat of the strong German garrisons towards the Seine, where their force would be a major obstacle for the Allied Expeditionary Force to overcome. In all, the Resistance mustered 30,000 fighters in Brittany. Fierce battles were fought. Although in places the Germans were successful their losses were severe. Amongst the French parachutists the losses were also severe. Of 45 officers 23 were killed. By the time Patton's armour broke through at Avranches, at the start of August, he found that the French had killed 1,800 Germans and taken 3,000 prisoners.

The Germans were able to resist only in tightly defended garrisons such as Brest, St. Malo, and Lorient. These would be overcome after very hard fighting. In the fighting in Brittany a total of four German divisions were destroyed. If the Germans had suffered heavy losses, in the Vercours they regained the initiative. Large supplies of arms were dropped to the 3,000 Resistance fighters on the high plain. They were supported by French, British, and American specialists parachuted in to give hurried training on the weapons. On the 14th July the Germans attacked. They used massive aerial attacks in an area where the Allies had no aircraft with an adequate range to intervene effectively, so far from their Normandy bases. The main German attack was made with gliders, swooping low and silently, so that they were upon the Resistance fighters before they were recognised as the enemy. The Resistance reaction was slow, but even with this setback it took the Germans ten days to gain control of the Vercours. It needed the equivalent of a whole German division to subdue 3,000 Resistance fighters. In retaliation the Germans massacred all the inhabitants of Vassieux. The final toll for the French was of half the men who had been sent in to help.

By the middle of July the Resistance was fighting hard in 40 Departments. All the Departments in the centre of France had come under the control of the Resistance and everywhere the Cross of Lorraine was appearing. German garrisons were cut off and attacked individually. Wherever the Germans remained in control they continued their massacres. To the infamous killing of the men and the burning of the women and children in the church at Oradour-sur-Glane were added the hanging of hostages, one to each of the ninety nine lamp posts, in the town of Tulle. There were other crimes of a similar nature committed in the towns of Asq, Cerdon, and other centres of resistance.

By the end of July 1944 the contribution of the French Army of the Interior was to contain the equivalent of 8 German divisions, preventing them form coming to re-enforce the German troops opposing the Allied Normandy landings. When two Panzer divisions were ordered urgently to Normandy with a 48 hour time schedule for their journey the obstructions imposed by the Resistance delayed them for 12 days. Another Panzer division was delayed for 23 days, after similar obstruction slowed their arrival at the French border from the Russian front by an additional 8 days.

In August the operation "Anvil" landings took place. The German opposition was much less than expected. The quick success of the landings prevented the Germans from destroying too much of the port facilities at Toulon and Marseille, making the supply and support of the Allied troops much quicker than had been foreseen. It had been expected that it would take the troops two months to reach Lyon, but the city was reached in 17 days.

As the Allies landed in the south of France the Allied forces in Normandy were breaking out of their bridgehead. The French 2nd Armoured Division, commanded by General Leclerc, had landed on the 6th August and by the 18th August was making good progress towards Paris. That would be a special battle.

Starting from very low levels of activity and support de Gaulle, recognised and supported by Churchill, had been able to bring considerable forces to the Allied cause. When de Gaulle had been under attack by the Government and the press of the United States Churchill had supported him. Churchill understood that de Gaulle carried the burden of the honour of France. Churchill's time in France in the First World War had given him a true understanding of its importance. They were true and faithful Allies.

THE LIBERATION OF PARIS

When General de Gaulle landed on the coast of France on the 14th June 1944 he had no troops and no major staff to support his arrival. It was into the town of Bayeux that he proceeded. In that town there is now a museum to his memory. It marks the place where he appointed the first elements of the government of a newly liberated France. His arrival was not announced beforehand and some of the population had to be told who this very tall visitor was. And then he was received with acclaim. The news of his arrival spread and his tour became almost a coronation.

On leaving Great Britain on the 16th June de Gaulle wrote to Churchill: "In leaving the territory of Great Britain, where you so kindly invited me at a moment which was decisive for the victorious outcome of this war, I send you my most sincere thanks for the way in which you greeted me on behalf of His Britannic Majesty's Government.

After the last year since my last stay in your noble and valiant country, I can see and feel the courage and the power of the people of Great Britain. It has brought about feelings of the highest regard and friendship for France and these feelings are stronger than ever. In can assure you, reciprocally, of the strong confidence and unbreakable friendship which France has for Great Britain.

On my recent visit I was able to see the magnificent effort which the British Navy, Army, and Air Force are making on French soil, with their Allies and with the French, and which will ensure our victory. For your country, which in this war was a shining example, the last and impenetrable fortress of Europe and which now is one of the principal liberators, and for you yourself, who have never ceased and now are still directing this immense effort, you will allow me to say, have earned immortal honour.

I am most keen that you should receive, Mr. Prime Minister, the expression of my highest regard, and my very sincere devotion."

There are those who have sneered at de Gaulle's contribution and made mountains out of hillocks of disagreement between these two men, but this letter, written when most of France was still occupied by the Germans and confidence in victory was great but victory was not assured, shows the true depth of comradeship between them. The cause of freedom, in all history, has never been better served.

The arrival of Allied troops in France did not originally include any major French units. It had been hoped that the French 2nd Armoured Division, under the command of General Leclerc, would be part of the initial invasion force. They were delayed because their vehicles could not be brought to England from North Africa in time and there were no spare vehicles with which they could be re-equipped, except by an assortment of vehicles which it would not be possible to maintain and supply with spare parts. The training of these troops had not gone well. Their experience in desert campaigns had been to use armour from hull down defensive positions in sand dune emplacements. From these positions they could ambush German armour, and did so successfully on several occasions. The war in Europe would be totally different. The use of air power would expose armour before it could be well camouflaged. Armour would be fighting armour on the move.

On the 5th April 1944 the French 2nd Armoured Division was ordered to embark from Africa to England. The first section comprised one thousand tracked armoured vehicles. It arrived in England on the 21st April. Arriving at Bristol these tracked vehicles crossed England on their own tracks to Dalton Hall, in the East Riding of Yorkshire, which was to be their base. Other parts of the division, which had come from Oran, were landed at Liverpool and Glasgow. General Leclerc came from discussions with General Koenig in London and took up command of the division on the 17th May.

The first task was to train the tank crews to fire and fight on the move. Their first results in test firings were mediocre in the extreme. In competition the British and Americans were achieving much higher scores. These deficiencies reached the ears of General Patton, commander of the American 3rd Army. On a tour of inspection he found that the guard of honour, made up of young recruits, was of a poor standard. It was made up of young Corsican volunteers, keen to join the liberation forces. All were volunteers and many had lied about their age to join. Some were only sixteen years old. Patton asked Leclerc if he intended to go to war using these "children." Putting these young recruits in the guard of honour had been a bad mistake.

On reaching the firing ranges Patton stated that the division needed much more training before it could be sent into the line. He himself assisted with some of the firing, showing how to correct the aim for moving targets. That evening the French held a conference. There had been insufficient preparation for the inspection and everyone was in despair, but they were resolute and even more eager to succeed.

The division's departure for France would have to be delayed. They could not be in the first wave of troops to land. Such a decision had a very severe effect on de Gaulle's purpose of speeding to the liberation of Paris, but the evidence of the division's faults could not be denied.

General Leclerc was furious. The next day he summoned all the officers in charge of the tank and artillery regiments. He told them that they would have to learn to shoot accurately on the move, not only from fixed positions. He sent many of his officers to nearby American tank units to learn their trade in war. The Americans were practising their gunnery from dawn to dusk and the French would have to become similarly committed. Every American officer had to take his turn to fire and the officers had to return the best scores. It was how they gained the respect of their men and the French had to learn the same lesson.

General Patton accepted an urgent invitation to revisit the division on the 28th June. As a result of his inspection on that visit he declared that the French 2nd Armoured Division were now champion shots. The worst unit had become the best. When Patton remarked that there were sailors amongst the troops he was told that that these were marines who provided much of the anti-tank artillery. Indeed, these troops had only had their weapons for a month. In the long tradition of Maitre Pointeurs (Master Gunners) they had scores better than that of the best British artillery that had fired on the same ranges a few months before.

General Patton told Leclerc that he would name the French 2nd Armoured Division as champion shots and their departure for France would be brought forward. On the 3rd July General Koenig presented the division, on behalf of the Provisional Government of the French Republic, with the new national and divisional standards, sewn in England by the Friends of the Free French. All the officers were given badges of the divisional insignia surmounted by the Cross of Lorraine. To the young cadets the ceremony showed the new French unity and pride.

On the 20th July came the order for the embarkation for France. The crossing to France went on well-oiled wheels to Utah Beach. At three o'clock in the morning of the 6th of August the first French armoured troops since 1940 were on French soil. General Leclerc, in an order of the day, reminded them that it was four years since French troops had been in control of French soil and that they would be greeting comrades who had suffered severely in their ruined country and who had, by their aid to the Allied cause, done so much to make victory possible.

The first French village reached was the hamlet of La Madeleine. There was a German counter attack to face, but this was warded off by General Bradley's divisions of the 3rd Army. Some of the division's supplies of fuel were lost in the German attack, but no serious damage was done. The division was separated into three main groups, with an additional reconnaissance unit. The American 3rd Army had broken through the German lines on the western side of the base of the Cherbourg peninsula, on the plain beneath the hill of Avranches.

The German 7th Army, under Hitler's orders, was trying to cut the American thrust in two, but the Americans swept round to the south, encircling German units and trapping them at Falaise.. Under Allied air attack the destruction of the German 7th Army began. The American encirclement from the direction of the Loire, first east and then north towards Alencon, suited General Leclerc's purpose.

On the nights of the 8th and 9th of August the French came under heavy German air attack. Some petrol tankers were destroyed and the tanks nearly ran out of fuel. Borrowing from other units, they kept going. On the 10th August the order came to advance. Strong opposition was met from the 9th and 116th Panzer divisions. General Leclerc found that progress was too slow. He ordered more use of the artillery against anti-tank guns and more diversions around strong points in villages. The objective was to press onwards, overcoming and bypassing the German units rather than fighting fixed static battles. To this end Captain de Laitre penetrated through the German lines with his light tanks and the advance was again on the move. Sadly, soon after Captain de Laitre was killed and his advance was repulsed.

General Leclerc was disappointed with the rate of progress. There was insufficient aggression by his troops. His officers told him that the men were exhausted, the ground was unknown, and the losses amongst the leading tanks were very severe. General Leclerc would not accept any excuses. Colonel Billotte, who knew Leclerc very well, sent him a message. "Put my unit into the battle and you will see what can be done."

Early next morning General Leclerc went forward to assess the situation. Reaching Clerance, where Captain de Laitre had been killed, he went by small lanes in a light vehicle, showing the men that main road fighting was not the way to break through. He was told that he was taking dangerous risks. He replied that they were calculated risks. In the afternoon of the 10th August General Leclerc led his troops from the turret of his tank 'Tailly', capturing the village of Bourg le Roi. At that moment his was the leading tank of the division.

Staying with the forward troops General Leclerc continued to lead the advance and by the next morning the leading units were in the outskirts of Alencon, where they refuelled. Using a civilian as a guide they pressed on and took the bridges, intact, in the centre of the town. Returning to order up reinforcements the general's jeep took a wrong turning at a roundabout and came face to face with a German army vehicle. At once his guard killed one German, one fled, and the third was taken prisoner. In the car they found a map and orders for a new German unit which was to take control of the Alencon area and protect the bridges.

Local Resistance leaders in Alencon informed Leclerc that German units were concentrating in the nearby Forest of Ecouves. This would be encircled and the mouth of the Falaise pocket closed, to complete the entrapment of the German 7th Army. The town of Sees was taken in combination with the 5th American Armoured Division. Then one group turned back to the west and entered the forest in a pincer movement, closing on the Germans as the other French detachments entered directly from the west. One medical unit of the French division was taken prisoner by the Germans for a short time, but managed to get away and rejoin their comrades.

General Leclerc's leadership in this battle gave confidence to all his troops. If they could cut through two Panzer divisions they could accomplish anything. He had led from the front and all would follow. On the 13th August they gained another 15 kilometres of ground, passing to the south of Argentan while the American 5th Armoured Division took the town. The river Orne was the 'Bomb Line' for the day. Allied aircraft attacked all armour on the Paris side of the river and on that day destroyed 50 German tanks and 400 other vehicles. There were still some isolated German tanks in Argentan and the French turned aside to silence them, to avoid being attacked from the flank.

There was a short period of further hard fighting between the armoured units of the two sides before the French won through, almost bringing the battle for Normandy to a successful conclusion. A few days later the British and Canadian troops finally closed the Falaise gap. Some 20,000 German troops had escaped but several German armies had been destroyed. The loss to the Germans in men and particularly in armour was very severe. Much of the German transport for the infantry was still horse drawn. The large numbers of horses killed in the battle made the countryside stink of decay for months afterwards.

In three days of heavy fighting Leclerc's 2nd Armoured Division had taken all its objectives and now the road was open to press onwards to Paris. The division's losses so far were 141 dead, 78 missing, 618 wounded. The Germans had lost 4,500 dead and had 8,500 taken prisoner. The French had lost 53 tanks to the

Germans' 113. Back in the Forest of Ecouves the American 79th and 90th infantry divisions were clearing the remaining German troops.

The Americans were not keen for the French to press on to Paris. General Eisenhower wanted to bypass Paris to avoid large numbers of his troops being swallowed up in months of hand to hand and street fighting. The French knew that it was essential to establish General de Gaulle's authority in the capital as quickly as possible to prevent a communist take over. A vacuum would be a disaster from which the recovery of democratic functions might become impossible.

The Paris police had gone on strike on the 19th August, occupying the Prefecture. They had opened fire on the Germans. Everywhere small groups of partisans were doing the same. Some of the buildings of the ministries were in the hands of the Resistance and they also occupied the town halls in the suburbs. Everywhere there was general insurrection. The liberation of Paris was urgent, to avoid the possibility of another Warsaw Uprising bloodbath.

The American liaison officers with the division were kept occupied while the plans for the rush for Paris were laid. In the hard fighting the French Sherman tanks had destroyed many of the heavier gunned German MarkV Panther tanks. The American officers were taken to see the results of the fighting. However successful the operation had been so far, the price of victory was painful. In the fighting near Argentan General Leclerc's cousin was killed.

By the time the Americans returned to General Leclerc's headquarters the first brigade had left for the attack on Paris. The rest of the division would set out on the 22nd August. Leclerc wrote to de Gaulle to get the American generals to issue the order for the taking of Paris, but he told his troops that they were going, with or without orders. On the evening of the 22nd August General Leclerc returned from General Bradley's headquarters with orders to move at full speed to take Paris. The race was on!

Strategically the Americans wanted the Paris bridges to be seized intact. The French 2nd Armoured Division would be accompanied by the American 4th Infantry Division. From Sees the line of attack would be through Mortagne, Chateauneuf, Rambuouillet and Versailles. The French were not to cross the line from Versailles to Palaiseau before mid-day on the 23rd August.

The real target of all their hopes was in reach. An officer of the 2nd company of 1st Infantry Regiment, from Chad, wrote in his diary, "We received the order to get our uniforms spotless. We would have the honour of entering Paris when the Germans had gone. We got our cleanest shirts out of our kit. We were so keen to see Paris and the Parisiens." In 1940 de Gaulle had given General Leclerc the order, under the hot sun of Chad, to liberate Paris and to go on to Strasbourg until all France was free of Germans. After fighting their way across Africa the first part of that task could now be completed. These troops from Africa had earned the right to take the glory.

But the Germans had no intention of giving up the ground. Lieutenant Colonel Guillebon's troops were unable to enter Paris on the 22nd August but they were in contact with the enemy and were able to assess their dispositions. The headquarters was able to detour along secondary roads and reach Rambouillet. From there one of the two columns would drive for the centre of Paris. The other would set out from Arpajon, thirty kilometres away and to the south of Paris. The group from Rambouillet was aiming for the Etoile, the Arc de Triomphe, while the group from Arpajon was targeted on the police headquarters. On the eastern flank the American 4th Infantry Division would approach from Vincennes.

The German defences of Paris contained large numbers of 88, 75, and 20 millimetre guns. Centres of defence would have to be overcome and the centre of Paris reached by infiltration along secondary roads. Strong defences could not be everywhere. Speed to reach and then to secure the Paris bridges before they could be demolished was essential. It would enable the Allies to move swiftly onwards to the battle for northern France.

Throughout the 23rd August General Leclerc was angered by the slow rate of progress. News of the battles in Paris between the Resistance and the German garrison reached the troops by direct telephone links. When they reached Longjumeau, to the south of

Paris and near the site of Orly airport, a gendarme came out onto the pavement and shouted that the Prefect of Paris wanted to speak to General Leclerc. The whole column broke out into uproarious laughter, but the Prefect was Charles Luizet and he demanded to speak to his old colleague from the Military Academy of St. Cyr, General Leclerc. They had occupied adjacent beds at the academy. Leclerc sent Colonel Crepin to speak on his behalf. The message was urgent and the 2nd Armoured Division should hurry. The police had taken over their headquarters and were engaged in fierce fighting but were running out of ammunition. To raise morale he wanted an artillery observation Piper Cub aeroplane to fly over the Prefecture and drop a message announcing the division's arrival.

Much has been written about what appears to be the slowness of the advance into Paris. In the American press, in particular, it was written that the French troops had been delayed by the ovation and greetings of the welcoming crowds. There was much hard fighting to be done against strong pockets of German resistance. By the evening of the 24th August the 2nd Armoured Division would lose 71 dead and 225 wounded. 35 armoured vehicles, 6 motorised artillery pieces and 111 other vehicles were destroyed in combat. These were very serious losses for any armoured division in so short a time.

Captain Caillet and Lieutenant Mantoux were given the perilous mission, to drop the message on the police headquarters. They would be in great danger from German anti-aircraft fire. To take an unarmed observation aircraft into such a cauldron would require great courage, but they did it, and their feat is recorded on a plaque on the wall of the Prefecture of the Paris Police.

Lieutenant Petit-Leroy reached General Leclerc's headquarters from Paris. There were about 20,000 Resistance fighters in Paris, but they were poorly armed to take on the German troops. The only method of dealing with tanks was by the use of Molotov cocktails, bottles of petrol with a lighted cloth in the neck, which would smother a vehicle in flames. These Molotov cocktails were being manufactured in the police headquarters. The police had been on strike against German orders since the 15th August. There were still two dangers to Paris: either destruction of the city ordered by a furious Hitler or a communist take-over by the communists with the intention of forming a "Commune of Paris," with a revolutionary government, toppling General de Gaulle from power.

General Leclerc dictated a letter to the German commander of Paris, General von Choltitz. He would be held responsible for the safeguarding of the treasures of the city. The difficulty was to get Lieutenant Petit-Leroy back into Paris. It was decided to use a captured German army car, but instead an armoured Jeep was chosen for the first part of this hazardous journey. When he reached the seminary of l'Hay-les-Roses he had intended to take to the bicycle, which he had left there, for the last 6 miles of his journey back into Paris. By using the Jeep through the back streets he would be able to get right into the centre of Paris, rather than the slower and riskier bicycle, back to the headquarters of General Chaban-Delmas in the centre of the city.

On the journey the Jeep was intercepted by an SS unit. The driver was killed and Lieutenant Petit-Leroy seriously wounded, and captured. The Germans found General Leclerc's letter to General von Choltitz and delivered it later that evening. Also that evening, at 7.0'clock, General Leclerc gave the order to advance in strength into Paris and sent the message that by the next morning the whole division would be in Paris.

At 20.00 hours the advance guard, 150 men, led by the tanks named Montmirail, Champaubert, and Romilly and led by volunteer guides went by the back streets, reached the Porte d'Italie and by 21.30 had arrived at the Place de l'Hotel de Ville - the Paris city hall. The 24th August saw French troops back in the city.

The headquarters of the division would advance to the Hotel de Ville. Other units would go to the Gare Montparnasse, at the telephone headquarters for the whole of the Paris region. As they advanced into the centre of Paris German firing came from the direction of the Palais du Luxembourg. It was thought that the firing was being controlled from an observation post in the Senate building. It was destroyed. There was no more firing directed from that point, but further firing came from the gardens of the Palais du Luxembourg and the School of Mines. The presence of this strong German detachment was confirmed by the Director of the School of Mines, who had escaped to bring news of the enemy. These enemy troops numbered between 500 and 600 men and they had with them a dozen tanks. They had orders to break out and attack General Leclerc's headquarters at the Gare Montparnasse, which were only lightly defended. The situation was serious.

An anti-aircraft gun detachment was sent to fire on the Germans. Other troops were sent to re-enforce General Leclerc's headquarters at 13.00 hours on the 25th August, to prepare for General de Gaulle's arrival.

French troops were entering Paris from several directions. Colonel Billotte's brigade entered through the Porte de Gentilly, got into a position above the Hotel de Ville, and were then able to attack General von Choltitz's headquarters at the Hotel Meurice, along the Rue de Rivoli. Colonel Dio's brigade came through the Champ de Mars at the Eiffel Tower and occupied the Ecole Militaire. They winkled out the German troops from the Chamber of Deputies and the Foreign Office headquarters on the Quai d'Orsay. Langlade's troops came up the Grandes Avenues to the Etoile, having to fight hard to overcome stiff resistance all the way. They were the first to reach the tomb of the Unknown Soldier at the Arc de Triomphe.

General von Chotitz was captured at his headquarters in the Hotel Meurice. He was taken to the Prefecture of Police and at 15.30 hours signed the order for a 'Cease Fire' The document was signed by General Leclerc in his capacity as Military Governor of the Paris region, fulfilling an appointment given him a long time before, in Africa, by General de Gaulle. Colonel Rol-Tanguy also insisted in signing the document, on behalf of the Resistance. De Gaulle was not pleased with Rol-Tanguy also having signed the document and he upbraided Leclerc for having risked dilution of military authority in the Paris region. The purpose was understood and the sole control of the French State put in place.

At the Gare Montparnasse General de Gaulle was met by a group of officers who were putting the cease fire in place. Among them was a sub-lieutenant of the navy, his son, Philippe de Gaulle. From there Philippe de Gaulle went to enforce the cease fire at the Palais Bourbon and the Hotel de Lassay. At the Palais Bourbon he was the only French officer amongst a stupefied collection of German officers, unable to comprehend that this young naval officer was there to take their surrender. They had de Gaulle's son at their mercy, but fortunately they chose to lay down their arms.

At the Latour-Maubourg barracks there was firing from the windows, which had to be suppressed. Some soldiers of the German army did not want to obey their general's order to cease fire. The French took over many other important buildings from the Germans and by the evening of that fine day Captain Girard, who had been with General Leclerc since Chad, was one of those invited to dine with the new Military Governor of the Paris Region, General Koenig, who had just arrived.

They went on foot that evening, and as they went to dine at the Invalides, General Leclerc remarked how marvellous it was that no major buildings had been destroyed and the bridges were intact. He remembered how, so long ago, General de Gaulle had given him the orders to liberate Paris. He always kept the letter with him and whenever he was subjected to de Gaulle's bad temper he reminded himself of the letter giving him his orders. How he treasured that document!

While they were at dinner they suddenly heard a furious galloping on the floor above. It was the Garde Republicaine evicting the last Germans, who had stayed behind to try to burn the documents of their occupation of Paris.

Attempts were being made to exchange German prisoners of war for imprisoned French Resistance fighters. Right up to seven days before the liberation of Paris French Resistance fighters were being taken from prison to be shot in Paris.

By taking over control so quickly from the military liberators of Paris it was possible to frustrate the attempts of the communists to set up a Commune in Paris. General Koenig summed it up by pointing out how the swift action to re-establish the French State had frustrated any attempt to provoke division and insurrection.

On the next day, the 26th August, all the troops gathered round the Arc de Triomphe to prepare to honour General de Gaulle. There was still a great danger of air attack and the crowds which had gathered were a very tempting target. Around the centre of Paris every available anti-aircraft gun was brought to readiness and they were all supplied with full stores of ammunition. General Leclerc organised the defence of the centre of the city.

The Spahis from Morocco had been one of the first regiments into Paris and they would have full honour by heading the parade. Like the waves of the sea the people of Paris poured forth to honour the one man who had refused to accept defeat and who, from the 18th June 1940, had been the head of the Free French and, as leader of the French fighting forces, had brought hope and now freedom to his beloved country.

. If the day belonged to the people of Paris it was only to gain strength to renew the push against the Nazi juggernaut: there was still so much of France to be liberated. From the prisons, from the slave labour camps, from the camps of the prisoners of war there were so many whose lives were hanging by the merest thread and whose need for liberation was urgent. The war would continue. Even at Notre Dame the rejoicing at the service of thanksgiving for the liberation of Paris was interrupted by shooting. De Gaulle did not flinch, though those around him were seen cowering from the shots. Who could do such a thing? When asked who it might be he replied "Find who would profit and there you will find the guilty." It was never proved, but the main suspects were those who had opposed the National Committee of the Resistance.

Later on the 26th August some of the troops fanned out to start the advance from Paris and to protect against any advance by the Germans from the north west of the city. The 47th German Infantry Division was approaching from the Pas de Calais. Their task was to mend the breach in the German lines which had allowed the liberation of Paris, to allow the German troops along the river Oise to escape, and if possible to recapture Paris. They reached the suburbs which had been liberated on the north western side of the city. The 4th American Infantry Division, with support from some British artillery, moved out to oppose the attack. German troops came to within eight miles of the centre of Paris.

General Leclerc joined this defence on the northern side of the city. A battle was fought on the edge of Le Bourget aerodrome. The Germans put up white flags on the hangars. Suddenly whole new groups of Resistance defenders appeared from the roadside drainage ditches to take the Germans from the rear. In the battle another cousin of General Leclerc was killed. The Germans tried another counter-attack but were driven off, leaving several hundred dead on the battlefield.

On the 30th August the French troops were relieved by the 28th U.S. Infantry Division, who thereby gained the honour of being able to parade formally through the centre of Paris. They marched straight through the city and off to war. The French 2nd Armoured Division had withdrawn to re-equip with men and material for the next part of the campaign. In the capture of Paris the division had lost 28 officers and 600 other ranks. Units of the Resistance forces joined the division for the march to the east. The other part of de Gaulle's original order to Leclerc, to raise again the French flag over the cathedral of Strasbourg, was yet to be obeyed.

The honour granted to the U.S. 28th Infantry Division in parading through Paris was not a piece of idle showmanship. De Gaulle had been very keen to show to the people of Paris that their liberation was an Allied undertaking and that he had Allied support for his position. On the reviewing stand were General Bradley and other senior Allied officers. This show of Allied unity prevented any possibility of a communist takeover. The 28th Infantry Division marched down the Champs Elysee, through Paris, and straight into the battle line. Never before or since has a parade gone marching straight into battle.

In the battle for Paris the various branches of the Resistance had lost 1,400 killed and 2,500 wounded. The Germans lost 2,700 killed and 4,900 wounded. Those who thought that Paris had been declared an open city which could be walked into without opposition were wrong. The city had been spared the massive aerial devastation and artillery bombardment which had laid waste most of the fine cities of Europe, but the wounds of the hand to hand fighting would take a long time to heal and the losses were not trivial. The demolition charges which had been set in place to destroy major buildings and fell the Eiffel tower across the Seine were not detonated.

The shortage of reconnaissance vehicles appeared to have been solved by acquiring some thirteen motorcycles and sidecars which had been intended to be supplied from the French factories to the Germans. Unfortunately their destination had been known and the French workers had sabotaged them so effectively that even the most skilled French army mechanics could not undo all the damage. Few of these vehicles, even after repair, reached Alsace, on the eastern frontier of France.

Just before the 2nd Armoured Division left Paris two young men presented themselves and demanded to joint the division. They were assigned to one of the peripheral units. They would not accept this and, with a malicious smile, said that their father had told them to attach themselves to the headquarters. The adjutant said that he would not accept any such orders from their father. "But our father is General Leclerc," they replied. These were Henri and Hubert Leclerc. They had been part of the Resistance near their home and were not novices in the use of arms and fighting skills.

It has often been said in England that the French force which contributed to the liberation of Paris was only a few armoured cars and not more than two hundred men. The French 2nd Armoured Division was more than 14,000 men, fully equipped with more than 4000 vehicles, and all volunteers. After years of defeat and disaster they were not going to be stopped on the road to Paris. 'The last time I saw Paris her heart was young and gay' went the song. The memory was treasured and the yearning for the best years had been irresistible.

LIBERATION

In the first six weeks after the Normandy landings the progress of the invading Allied force seemed very slow to those waiting anxiously in Britain. More and more men and armour were leaving for France, but there did not seem to be any great progress after the success of getting ashore and establishing the bridgeheads. Stories came back of severe fighting in the bocage countryside of Normandy. There were reports of Allied tanks trying to cut through the tall hedgerows and climbing nearly vertically up the deeply rooted hedges lining the roads. With their lightly armoured bellies exposed in this position the tanks were easy victims for the German army stick grenades. The problem was solved by welding sharpened prongs to the lower part of the front of the tanks. Instead of rising up the bushes forming the hedges the prongs bit deep into the root systems and the tanks could then break through.

After five weeks General Patton's 3rd Army broke through the German line at Avranches, at the base of the western side of the Cherbourg peninsula. Liberation came swiftly after the Allied landings in the south of France had taken place. These southern landings were unexpectedly successful. Instead of being opposed by a strong German defence the Allied troops brushed aside the German forces and quickly penetrated to Grenoble and into the Vosges mountains. So fast was the progress of this attack that after the initial delay in breaking out from Normandy that, by the end of September, apart from Alsace, some of the Alpine foothills and a few resisting outposts on the Atlantic coast, France was cleared of the invaders.

The German army, broken by the ill fortune of war, which had been thrust upon them by the strength of the Allied armour and air power, and assailed on every side by the French Resistance forces, was driven out of eastern France quicker than the speed of their advance in the 1940 invasion.

The speed of the liberation produced some serious problems. General Eisenhower had wished to introduce an occupation currency to take over from the old French currency, from which the

Germans, collaborators, and black marketers had profited. De Gaulle would have none of it. It would make the liberators seem like another set of invaders, He saw that it was vital to ensure that the country, emerging from the abyss of occupation, could breathe the heady air of liberation. Only in this way could the nation be reconciled and the bitter divisions healed. There were enough problems facing the new government - or whatever government - would have to deal with all the details of reconstruction of the country.

To aid the invasion the transport system of a large part of France had been systematically destroyed. It had not been possible to restrict this destruction to the area near the invasion beaches. Deception meant that much larger areas of damage had to be inflicted, beneficial perhaps in reducing the mobility and effectiveness of German forces deploying to counter the invasion, but sure to be an equal impediment to the Allied build up on the route into Germany. Those who lived near these targets paid a terrible price in suffering. In Normandy 30,000 civilians were killed in the course of the fighting, more than the number of soldiers killed on either side. Sabotage to prevent German troop reinforcements reaching their defending positions in time had done further damage. These actions had been met with ferocious retribution by some of the German troops. The worst was at Oradour sur Glane, where all the villagers were shot and then burned by a detachment of the Das Reich division of the SS. In Tulle, each of the 99 lampposts was the gallows for a Frenchman.

De Gaulle had to establish a central government quickly and ensure that it had a route to receive vital information and to disseminate orders: otherwise there would be chaos and even insurrection. The Resistance movement had been forged from disparate and previously mutually very hostile groups. It was essential to retain the patriotic welded unity that the urge for liberation had inspired.

At this time Paris had no reliable means of communication with the provinces. Almost all the telephone and telegraph lines had been destroyed. There were no civil communication aircraft. Of 12,000 locomotives only 2,800 remained serviceable and no train could leave Paris and reach any of the major southern cities. No train could cross most of the length of the river Loire and no train could cross the Seine for the majority of its course to the channel at Le Havre. 3,000 road bridges had been destroyed. Only a tenth of the road vehicles could be run. There were some vehicles driven by Gazogene, a fuel derived from wood or coke. Paris buses for some time after the war could be seen with their gas containers fixed to their roofs, while small vehicles towed their gas generators behind them.

Every element of normal life had been disrupted. There was no means of distributing food. No manufactured products could be produced and it was impossible to organise the normal transport of raw materials. To ease this situation, which had been foreseen, there was a special six months plan for the importation of American products. This had been agreed between the French provisional government in Algiers, and Washington. There was great difficulty in delivering these goods, because the major ports had been destroyed, either in Allied air attacks or in terminal destruction by the Germans just before they laid down their arms.

De Gaulle reports that the French received great help from the Allies in rebuilding the rail system and getting the airports into action. Many locomotives, delivered from the United States, were seen for several years after the war on French railways. The British War Department locomotives sent to France immediately after the liberation were soon returned to England, where they were also sorely needed. A petrol pipeline was laid from the Cotentin peninsula, near Cherbourg, across France, via Paris, to Lorraine. During this period, as French industry started up, its first production was to aid the Allied war effort.

The most important effect of the liberation was the end of silence. A nation which, for four years, had to be silent or speak very carefully in the quietest whispers, could again speak with a loud, clear, and free voice: and it all happened so suddenly – one day bondage, the next day free. There was, however, a sad delusion. Freedom did not automatically bring with it plenty. The warnings of hard times to come were but a faint and small voice in the clamour of the joys of liberation! It had been assumed that

Allies, who were so well equipped to effect their liberation, must have unlimited resources ready to assist the recovery of the people of France. They could not know that on the other side of the world the American Marines were engaged in a long and deadly war of total attrition against Japanese forces that would fight to the death for the glory of their Emperor and for every inch of every island in the long chain of Pacific islands leading back to their homeland. This struggle would consume the great American arsenal against whose productivity Admiral Yamamoto, the Japanese naval Commander in Chief for the attack on Pearl Harbour, had warned. "You have woken a sleeping tiger," he told both the Japanese Government and also his senior officers. He had warned that either Japan would win within six months, or a longer war would end in Japan's defeat. The demands of that longer war were already focussing America's main interest in the Pacific theatre.

De Gaulle was perplexed at the complications of the tasks which had to be undertaken. He doubted that he himself could make any great inroads into such a wide range of difficulties. He arrived in Paris to spend a miserable summer of insurmountable difficulties. The joy of liberation faded quickly against this background as Paris faced hunger close to famine; as winter came there was no heating, the street lights were out. He passed through the streets where the shops were empty, the factories silent, and at the stations no trains moved. He was certain that if something were not done quickly there would soon be dissention and even insurrection.

Having seen all this he was under no illusion that speedy improvements were needed. An end, or at least a great reduction, in the nation's suffering was necessary. His first task was to gather control of all the functions of government services and apply them evenly to the whole country. He had to weld the troops from the Empire, who had never surrendered, to those who had been taken out of the battle by the armistice and had remained in France. He could rely on the loyalty of those leaders who had remained free in the African territories and those who had joined the Free French cause early in the war. To these he had to add additional staff from those who had remained in Paris throughout the occupation. There would be serious differences between the two groups and a danger of a breakdown in the nation's unity. Pleven joined him in Paris to take control of economic affairs. Four ministers arriving from Algiers were sent to put in place the elements of government in the Midi region. Massigli was sent to London, as soon as Paris was liberated, to maintain foreign relations with the Allies. By the 9th September 1944, only two weeks after his arrival in Paris, he had formed the basis of the new government and founded the Fourth Republic.

He sought two ministers from the old government from before the armistice: the President, Jeanneney, was still in a department occupied by the enemy. His presence was vital to restore the legal authority of the state. General Catroux's presence was necessary to maintain authority over the army. Control of the economy was given to Pierre Mendes-France. In this short period of two weeks all the important ministerial and important foreign diplomatic positions were filled. A special ministry for dealing with those who had been imprisoned and deported was created. In all this he relied on the support of the Resistance and the Free French forces that had been loyal to him since the collapse of 1940.

On the 12th September he held a meeting at the Palais de Chaillot of 8,000 officials and other leaders of the New France. To them he explained his political ideas for the future. He drew on the wave of joy, of pride, and of hope. He saluted the efforts of the Resistance, the Allies, and the French army. He defined the need to separate the powers of government and of justice. The burning question was "What about the Milice?" the hated collaborationist police. He replied "We are still at war and we will have to take part in the occupation of Germany when victory comes. For this the whole nation must be united, to fight and to conquer. All French soldiers must become part of a united French army, and, like France, the army must remain whole and indivisible." And so de Gaulle set about restoring the unity of the French people simply by ordering it so. No one could oppose him, for his credentials were untouchable. He saw that there would be great difficulties in the new Europe about future relations with Germany. He declared that without France nothing could be decided for the new Europe that had any chance of providing a lasting peace. A hundred million lived under the French flag and no advance in human terms could proceed without the contribution of France.

He made it clear that liberation would not bring an end to France's difficulties. Special regulations were necessary to speed reconstruction and the interests of individuals would have to be subjugated to the general welfare. He had a special message for the members of the Resistance. "Those of you who followed the symbol of the Cross of Lorraine! Those of you who were steadfast in support of the nation's honour and the cause of liberty, must now join the effort to regain our greatness. This is how you will gain the great victory for France!" De Gaulle would not express any thoughts for the long term future, because the immediate needs of the country would take all their energies. While in London and Algiers it had been a question of what might one day be possible, now, in Paris, it was time for action. The mystique which had surrounded the Free French had now to be used as a force for that action to be immediate. Politics could not be allowed to divide the leadership of the nation. As de Gaulle left the Palais de Chaillot he was full of worrying doubts. The acclamation which had followed his speech and that of Georges Bidault did not have the fervour which had followed his speeches at the Albert Hall in London, or in the heat of Brazzaville. The sweat of the labour of reconstruction was not as attractive as the fervour of lighting the torch of liberty. It might be easier to rouse the people than the political functionaries. He had some political capital to spend because of his position, but it could soon be exhausted. The first urgent task was to unify the whole country by establishing the control of the government in every part of France.

Messages coming from every department spoke of confusion but not of disorder. The senior officials nominated before the liberation were now at their posts, but they had great difficulty in exercising their authority. Four years of pent up hatreds against those who had collaborated were now exploding. Armed groups of Resistance fighters were starting to take their revenge, without the niceties of justice intervening. In many places public anger was brutal. Personal vendettas could be pursued under this cover. The communists, with their organisation in place, were starting to take over control in some areas. In two months de Gaulle managed to regain and enforce the central control of government.

In France the situation was so different from that in Great Britain. Only the Channel Islands had been occupied, and many of the residents had been evacuated before the Germans arrived. There was no general splitting of the population into those who collaborated with the occupier and those who were part of an underground resistance movement. You will not find in England the same memorial as that which stands in the square outside the town hall in Cherbourg. That monument is dedicated to those who had been shot, those who had been deported, those who had been resistance fighters – the Maquisards -, and those who had been taken hostage.

On the 14th September 1944 de Gaulle went to Lyon. Ten days before the city had been liberated by the French 1st Army and by the Americans. He found the airport was covered in debris and the hangars had been demolished. All the bridges across the rivers were down, bar one. All the railways in the area were out of action. The destruction was terrible, but the spirit of the people was in total contrast to the ruins. Everywhere there was boundless enthusiasm to get on with the work of reconstruction. Yves Farge, the local Resistance chief, was busily at work organising volunteers to their tasks. The enthusiasm had to be kept under control while government functions were restored.

The next day de Gaulle took the salute at a parade of the local Resistance forces. It was a moving experience to greet, and be greeted by, these irregular soldiers who had fought so long and so hard for their freedom. It was good to see the mutual respect and regard between the Resistance fighters and the regular troops. But in Marseille the atmosphere was sombre. The severe destruction of the town and of the port by the Germans in 1943, added to by the recent Allied bombing and the battles of August 1944, had completely flattened large areas of the city. The port was heavily mined. Nevertheless, the local inhabitants, aided by the Americans, who wanted to get the port into action quickly, were setting about removing the debris. For the local population the conditions were miserable. There communists were exploiting the situation and had even started summary executions. It took considerable effort to re-establish the control of the state and the rule of law.

At Bordeaux, on the 17th September, de Gaulle found that access to the port was prevented by German troops who were holding out near the mouth of the river Gironde, at the Pointe de Grave. The FFI forces were in contact with German troops on both banks of the river Gironde. The German Admiral Meyer had delayed making any approaches about surrender until de Gaulle's arrival. The mayor of Bordeaux had been a collaborator and many local groups were seeking revenge. These armed groups were refusing to obey the official authorities, who needed de Gaulle's backing to regain control. All the local functionaries were in attendance when de Gaulle addressed the crowd from the same balcony from which Gambetta had addressed the crowds in 1870. He tolerated no dissention from the local officials; either comply with his requirements to do their duties, or they would be off to prison. He felt that by the time he left Bordeaux all was in order.

German troops were still present in strength in the La Rochelle region and a large force had to be gathered, with armoured and air support, to dislodge them by force. The German troops, lacking supplies, were becoming disorganised and undisciplined, and thereby more dangerous. De Gaulle was able to gather a motley collection of irregular armed forces to confront the Germans. After he had spoken to them they formed into an effective force to, at least, contain the Germans.

When, on the 25th September, de Gaulle made another trip from Paris, it was to Lorraine, which Patton's 3rd Army had just liberated. In this region there had been no Vichy influence. The enemy invader had always been the enemy. There was no discord amongst the Resistance leaders and this unity prevented any political difficulties. It emphasised the sharp contrast between what had happened in the occupied and the unoccupied zones of France. The corrosive influence of the Vichy government on French society was becoming clear.

And so de Gaulle continued to make short trips to many of the regional centres. Wherever he went he was acclaimed. He took little account of this but speedily put in place the authority of the state, to re-establish legal control. What was certain was that from his position at the time of surrender in 1940 he had acquired the status of the saviour of French honour and become the focus of the foundation of the new, the Fourth Republic. In Dijon General Giraud told him "How things have changed!" De Gaulle thought to himself "It is true for us, but not so much has changed for the French people." And so he saw the need for urgent action to bring the fruits of victory to the tables, and the lives, of the people.

Early in November he toured the alpine region, ending with a triumphant reception in Grenoble. Here he took pleasure in reviewing the 27th Alpine Division, which had frustrated Italian attempts to seize part of south-eastern France. In these short trips he had been seen by about 10 million citizens and he had restored some measure of unified control from the central government. Despite the rejoicing and the flag waving, de Gaulle was depressed by the state of the infrastructure and the condition of the people. He was also furious that political dissention and the ambition of the communists were threatening the united effort of recovery. But he could also see that the people were desperate to avoid anarchy and were turning to him as the unifying leader. It is clear that he felt this weight of the mantle of responsibility: he understood only that the duty had fallen on him. It was now to become fully true: the words which Churchill had spoken as they passed after the meeting at Tours in 1940, "L'home du destin!" The man of destiny.

At this time there was no voice raised against him and his authority was unchallenged. He used it only to rebuild his shattered country. Petain and the residue of the Vichy government had taken refuge in Germany. The last President of the Republic, Albert Lebrun, sent him a message of agreement, supporting all his actions. Lebrun also expressed regret for having accepted Paul Reynaud's resignation as Prime Minister on the 16th June 1940, and his terrible error in having asked Marshal Petain to form the next government. It had been General Weygand's firm opinion that there was nothing else to do than seek an armistice, which had been the crucial advice. "What can you do," wrote Lebrun, "if you have generals who will not fight?"

At the end of August 1944 General Eisenhower had given orders to the armies on the Allied left flank, under General Montgomery to push forward hard through Belgium and Holland to the river Rhine and to enter Germany and finish the war. On the right flank of the advance the French 1st Army and the American 7th Army were to advance to the Rhine through Alsace. De Gaulle was especially keen to drive all German troops out of France. On the 6th September 1944 de Gaulle had written to Eisenhower urging all speed in the use of the French 1st Army and offering the 2nd Armoured Division as an addition to the force. He expressed his wish that the French troops should enter Germany at the same time as the American and British armies. However the Allied advance had been stopped before reaching the German border. Hitler had taken control of the organisation of German resistance following the failed plot against his life in July 1944. By bringing into use V1 and V2 rockets, rocket and jet propelled fighters, and new types of tanks, the Germans had halted the Allied advance. Allied supply lines, lengthened by the movement forward of the advancing troops, had reduced the ability of the front line to break through into Germany.

The French 1st Army had fought hard to break out from the Mediterranean shores and on the march north the need to maintain defences against an attack from Italy had caused some delays. The German 19th and 1st Armies, comprising 10 divisions, were strung out across the centre of France to the foothills of the Alps. Their resistance delayed the deployment of additional Allied forces. This resistance increased the Allied shortage of fuel and ammunition, but did not prevent some major Allied successes. In the Toulon and Marseille regions they had taken 40,000 prisoners. French troops of the 2nd Corps trapped the German 1st Army and, with help from the Resistance forces, in a desperate four day battle, forced the major part of this German army to surrender. Other French divisions had helped close the trap. General Elster, the German commander, avoided surrendering to the French but on the 11th September surrendered 22,000 German troops to the Americans.

With French troops, many from North Africa, guarding their right flank in the Alps, the French and American forces had advanced 700 kilometres in three weeks. The advance could have been even faster if the petrol supplies, unloaded at ports on the south coast of France, could have been brought forward faster. In the whole campaign the progress had been aided by the actions of local Resistance fighters. Based in the areas of the fighting they had less need for special supplies brought in over long distances. By the 12th September 120,000 German troops had been taken prisoner on this front. It was a third of all the German prisoners taken in the western front campaign. On the 13th September Eisenhower wrote to de Gaulle. He would combine the 1st French Army and the American 7th Army as the Army Group South. The Americans would be on the left flank and strike north towards Strasbourg. The French, on the right, would force their way along the Swiss border, from Vesoul, through Besancon, reaching the German border at Colmar. De Gaulle agreed, with the exception of keeping back the 1st French Division for duties in Paris, if necessary. He also asked Eisenhower to release French divisions from the Atlantic coast region to join the thrust towards Strasbourg. He was keen that as much as possible of France should be liberated by French forces. For this, Leclerc's 2nd Armoured Division would continue to fight in the American sector, as it had done in the liberation of Paris. All this would take time. In the west Montgomery had been checked; in Lorraine Bradley had also been halted. Although the Russians had advanced through many of the eastern European countries they had not yet penetrated into Germany. These delays were grievous to the French people but it did give a better chance for French troops to make a major contribution to the victory. The greater part French troops could play in the victory the greater would be the recovery of French honour after the disaster of the armistice. It would fulfil what de Gaulle had told Churchill, so many years before. "We have lost a battle, but we have not lost the war." It would unify Metropolitan France with the Empire. Already, by the 20th September, the troops coming in from the Empire had been joined by 50,000 men of the Forces of the Interior to aid the operations of General de

Lattre de Tassigny.

There were severe shortages of equipment, too great to enable the large number of Resistance fighters who wanted to join the regular armed forces to be incorporated into units, but by special decree on the 23rd September all members of the irregular forces were officially called up into the army. So many were available that 40,000 were able to be divided between the navy and the air force. This left 300,000 soldiers for the army. Seven new divisions were formed immediately. There were no factories capable of producing the heavy weapons necessary to face the Germans, so these had to be provided by the goodwill of the United States. President Roosevelt was reluctant to provide these heavy weapons. After the war considerable quantities of arms would be in the hands of the 'revolutionary forces.' By the end of the winter at the end of 1944 the French army would be able to play a major role in the final battles and France would demand a say in the conditions of victory.

In part the problem was solved by replacing North African troops, who had seen two years hard fighting, with recruits from the Maquis. For heavy equipment the French salvaged any discarded American equipment they could find and rebuilt and repaired it, and brought it into action. This was the advantage of local facilities and skills, which the Americans did not have.

Three French generals led the attack in the east, de Lattre, Monsabert, and Bethouart showed skill and determination that brought admiration from de Gaulle. Here were generals who were skilled in their craft and with unlimited enthusiasm to rid their country of the invader. It was all so different from 1940. When de Gaulle went on to visit the 2nd Armoured Division he found that it had acquired large amounts of arms and supplies and now lacked for nothing. They had repulsed a counter attack by many German tanks near Dompaire, but this slowing down of their advance was not to their liking. General Leclerc had started out by capturing Koufra in 1940. When de Gaulle had congratulated him Leclerc had replied that it might be the capital of Chad, but it was only a small triumph in the whole French scene. They had agreed that Leclerc's task was to go on from liberating Koufra to liberating

Strasbourg, and finally evicting the Germans from France. He had achieved success but had not yet completed the task assigned to him by de Gaulle all those years ago. He was not a man to be thwarted.

There were political difficulties. On the 16th July 1944, in Algiers, the Government had declared that the liberation would bring a large and immediate increase in salaries. On the liberation of Paris the Government had introduced a 40% increase in salaries. On the 17th October family allowances were increased by 50%. Although these seemed like massive increases the prices index had risen from 100 in 1938 to 300 in 1944. De Gaulle realised that although these rises were needed, the payment of such large increases would reduce the money available for reconstruction. It was an unhappy dilemma, particularly for a country where industrial production and economic activity were down to 40% of that of 1938. To get control of the nation's finances would require hard disciplines, and a special liberation tax. In a radio broadcast on the 19th November de Gaulle told the French people "It is a triumph which I demand!" This measure prevented runaway inflation. It was also urgent to set up special courts to deal with collaborators before reprisals and summary executions could get out of hand. There was a danger that some of the paramilitary forces could run amok, so they had to be firmly controlled. To this end all arms not in the hands of the official armed forces would have to be handed in. This command was regarded as an insult by the Resistance, but it had to be done to prevent the possibility of a civil war between the opposing factions who had been held together in the common cause of liberation.

The first parliament would comprise 248 members, of whom 173 represented Resistance organisations. Felix Gouin was elected President of the Assembly, as he had been in Algiers. It had taken only ten weeks since Paris had been liberated. The French army, side by side with its allies, had joined the battle at the Atlantic coast, at the gates of Alsace, and in the Alps. Public order had been restored, the justice system was in place, and reconstruction had started. De Gaulle was ready to relinquish power because his main task had been completed, but France's place in the new international order was not yet secure.

To the newly liberated France many nations sent their greetings. De Gaulle was the internationally recognised leader of France and no other politician had any equal stature on the international stage which would have allowed France's cause to prosper. His authority, alone, was recognised. Gone were the days when President Roosevelt could contemplate installing others, such as Darlan or Giraud, as head or chief representatives of the French nation. But for how long could de Gaulle continue to exercise such authority? For how long would the people be prepared to follow his lead? Whatever doubts de Gaulle himself may have had, the people of France had none. Those who had rallied to the cause of French freedom after hearing his speeches at the Albert Hall, in London, in France's darkest hour would never forget how he had raised the proud face of France from the dust of defeat. French men and women in occupied France had heard him on the radio from London. They knew the voice and now they could see its owner, one of the main purposes of the trips he made from Paris to all the newly liberated Departments of France. They would be loyal forever to the spirit he engendered and to the man himself. To those who may doubt those emotions try finding even the smallest French town without a Rue or a Place de Gaulle. His authority with the Allies and the neutrals, by the very speedy resurrection of the State, demanded respect.

On the 23rd October 1944 Great Britain, the United States, and the Soviet Union recognised the new provisional French Government. This allowed General Eisenhower to transfer authority in the land of France to the government of de Gaulle. After this leadership, other governments hastened to bestow the same recognition. When asked by the press his attitude to this recognition de Gaulle replied, "The French Government is happy to be called by its proper name." In Paris those embassies which had been closed during the occupation threw open wide their doors. Not all those who had established relations with the Vichy government were welcomed. The Vatican's representative to Vichy could not be accepted by de Gaulle: Mgr. Valeri was replaced by Mgr. Roncalli. The first French ambassadorial appointments were

Massigli to London and Bonnet to Washington.

There would be serious problems with Germany after the war. In a single lifetime there had been three Franco-German wars. In the first, French territory was seized. In the second, in 1918, Alsace and Lorraine were returned to France. The cost of this conflict had been ruinous. Recovery had been made harder by the refusal of the British and Americans to enforce the reparations agreement on Germany. The most recent war had seen the French army vanquished and 2 million Frenchmen seized, as prisoners or forced labourers. By some miracle a remnant of independence and sovereignty had been preserved in the furthest parts of the French Empire. Would a full renaissance of France's power, prosperity, and influence be possible?

German aggression would have to be permanently halted, not for a year, a decade, or a century, but forever. The French could never live with a possibility of a new threat. Would the leaders of Europe choose wisdom and peace? A centralised Germany was not acceptable, so that the new state would have to be a federal one, with separated focuses of power. The military manufacturing capabilities of the Ruhr would have to be kept under international control. The Saar, with its German character, would have to become economically joined to the adjacent industrial regions of France. The Rhine could become an international highway for the peaceful development of trade, perhaps rekindling the old trading partnerships of the towns and cities of the Hanseatic League. No additional territory would be taken by France and this would leave open the door for reconciliation. It would be an environment in which the peoples of Europe could express their democratic freedoms and resist the tide of Bolshevism from the east.

The Dumbarton Oaks conference, which set up the United Nations, did not include France. The idea had been that the United States, Great Britain, Russia, and China had been the powers that had poured out their blood as the price of freedom. Discord between these allies had necessitated a conference in Quebec and a visit by Churchill and Eden to Moscow in the autumn of 1944

It was clear to de Gaulle that after the war France would be the only power with a major army in the west of Europe. As he put it, the United States would have withdrawn to its own hemisphere and Great Britain to its own island. He therefore invited the western leaders to Paris on the 30th October. The Americans declined, but Churchill and Eden arrived on the 10th November. It was a wonderful opportunity and Churchill was the focus of a marvellous reception. De Gaulle, with all his ministers, met them at Orly airport. Churchill's wife and daughter were at the Quai d'Orsay to meet him and they were entertained in great state. The Germans had occupied the building and Churchill was to sleep in the same bed and use the same bathroom as had Hermann Goering. It made the nightmare of the meetings, in the same building, with Reynaud and Gamelin in 1940, drift into the dark cave of unwanted memories. The French, understanding well that taking over the luxurious quarters of the vanquished proves the conquest, had made sure that this triumph of the liberator was accorded to Churchill.

On the 11th November, the next day, de Gaulle accompanied Churchill on the celebration of victory. They stood side by side at the Tomb of the Unknown Soldier, under the Arc de Triomphe, and laid enormous wreaths: the two leaders who had known at closest hand the trials, tribulations, and sacrifices of two World Wars. There was a march past, after which they then walked together, side by side, down the whole length of the Champs Elysees. The acclaim for them was stupendous and de Gaulle let Churchill take the prior place to respond, Churchill waving his cap in the air to the crowds. They went next together to Clemenceau's statue, where Churchill placed a tribute of flowers. On de Gaulle's orders the band was playing 'Father of Victory,' "For You," as de Gaulle told him. To de Gaulle this was full justice and reward. It brought back to de Gaulle an evening of a sad day at Chequers when Churchill had sung to de Gaulle an ancient song of Paulus, without missing a word.

At the Invalides the two men bowed at the statue of Marshal Foch, after which, the illustrious Englishman bent forward over the tomb of Napoleon. He told de Gaulle "There is nothing more grand!" There followed a State luncheon at the Ministry of War. Churchill recalls how de Gaulle made a very flattering speech.

After the meal Churchill told de Gaulle how touched he had been by all he had seen and heard. There were several other official functions, grand dinners and receptions; all were to cement their friendship. De Gaulle asked what had caused the greatest difficulty. "Getting unanimity. After such momentous events, for you and I, and after so many offensive words both spoken and written, that I have retained an unbounded enthusiasm for our cause. It is in the depths of the soul of the French people that they have been completely with you, who have served them, and with me, who has aided you" Churchill was greatly impressed by the efficiency of the ceremonial. The British cabinet had opposed his visit, fearing disorder in Paris. Churchill told de Gaulle that seeing the good order of the crowds and the discipline of the troops was like being at a resurrection.

They held a conference to examine Franco-British co-operation in world affairs. The question of France's occupation zone in Germany was raised, but Churchill was evasive on the detail. There was no clear decision on the exact geography of the French zone of occupation and there was no certainty over the future shape of German institutions. There was also great doubt about Russian intentions and the future frontiers of Poland, whose delineation was certain to cause trouble. The 'Naughty Paper' of the Moscow conference was referred to. Only for Greece had Britain been able to retain an agreed dominant position. This agreement for Greece was subsequently broken, with the communists fighting a civil war which was to end only in 1949.

It was clear that the British no longer had a strong hand to play in eastern Europe and the French had not even been admitted to the game. The Russians, by force of arms and conquest were, and would remain, dominant. The British were not in control and had become minor players compared with Russia and the United States. This was evident at the Teheran conference and re-enforced at Yalta in early 1945. What Churchill did bring was an invitation for France to join in the formation of the European Commission in London, but this might not be full membership, only in association with Great Britain. It was a good first step, but not good enough. Churchill certainly expressed the view that the French people deserved to be masters of their own affairs in the European field, without their affairs being decided by others. On the next day, the 12th November, Churchill was received at the Paris town hall, by the Municipal Council, the Conseil de la Resistance, and many other Resistance fighters who had taken part in the liberation. "I am going there" Churchill told de Gaulle, "To meet these revolting men!" On his return Churchill told de Gaulle of his surprise. He had expected to find a revolutionary fever amongst the many disparate groups represented. Instead he had been met by a throng of parliamentarians, and saluted by the Republican guard. He had expected to find a crowd who bore some resentment and who might harangue him, but there had been none of this. "It is better for public order, but it is much less picturesque!"

On the 13th November de Gaulle took Churchill to Besancon to review the French 1st Army. It was a day of continuous snowfall. The army was brand new, with new equipment and all ranks showing a renewed discipline and pride. Churchill told de Gaulle that he had renewed and justifiable confidence in France.

De Gaulle wanted this new confidence converted into political recognition. He told Churchill "You British will end this war covered in glory. We French will recover, but we will never regain our former power. Your power will tend to move out to the Commonwealth, but above all the power of the United States and Russia, and later China, will dominate the world. We will face a new world. We older powers will be weaker. But if we French and you British act together nothing can be decided without our agreement. Should we therefore not sign an agreement on this?" He continued, "The balance of power in Europe and the need to keep peace in the states of eastern Europe depends on keeping the United States and Russia from quarrelling. If we can agree to act together it will be a great thing for the world. I am ready to put my signature to such an agreement. England and France will organise the peace, just as twice in thirty years we have had to organise for war."

Churchill replied "I never thought that France and England could be separated. I agree that we should, today, conclude an alliance in principle. It would be best if we could persuade the strongest nations to march forward at our side. The Americans have tremendous resources with which they have helped us. Russia is like a large animal which has been hungry for a long time and with which you could not now interfere, any more than you could stop a hungry animal in a flock of prey. But this hungry animal must not be allowed to eat everything. I will try and slow Stalin down, for although he has a great appetite he also knows how to face reality. After a big meal there is digestion. It would be as if Saint Nicholas could bring back to life the children eaten by the ogre."

"As for France," said Churchill, "Thanks to you she will recover. Do not be too impatient. Already the doors are half open. Later they will be fully open. You will see that quite naturally you will take a seat at the council table of great affairs. Nothing can impede us if we work together. Just let me get on and do it."

On the 14th November Churchill left to inspect the British sector of the front. Eden had already returned to London. And so it was made clear that England was in favour of the restoration of France's position in world politics. France's help would be necessary to strengthen the European position with the two greatest powers. However de Gaulle was not yet entirely satisfied that Churchill was yet ready to play a joint role with France in European affairs. He really doubted that the British would be able to resist the pressures of the Russians and Americans.

Following Churchill's reception and acclamation in Paris and on his tour with de Gaulle Churchill sent a most warm message of thanks to de Gaulle:

"Now that I am back home, let me express to Your Excellency and to your colleagues of the French Government my profound appreciation of the splendid hospitality and innumerable kindnesses and courtesies shown me and my friends during the memorable days which I have just spent in France. I shall always recall as one of the proudest and most moving occasions of my life the wonderful reception which the people of Paris gave to their British guests on this our first visit to your capital after its liberation. I was also most grateful for the opportunity of seeing for myself something of the ardour and high quality of French troops, which are completing the liberation of their native soil under the skilful leadership of General de Lattre de Tassigny. The welcome extended to us was indeed a happy augury for that continued friendship between our two countries essential to the safety and to the future peace of Europe."

De Gaulle replied:

"In the name of the Government I thank you for your message. France, its capital, and its army are happy to acclaim in your person not only the Prime Minister of a country which is most dear to them, but also the most glorious fighter who maintained the Alliance through the darkest days until the deserved victory was won.

Let me say how happy I was, personally, to see you again."

As soon as Churchill and Eden had left Paris the Russian ambassador brought an invitation for de Gaulle to go to Moscow. De Gaulle accepted, for he was keen to meet Stalin and his ministers. It would be an opportunity to discuss the arrangements for peace. It would also be an opportunity to discuss methods to prevent both any further danger from Germany and an Anglo-Saxon hegemony.

De Gaulle reported to the National Assembly that relations with Great Britain were good and that France would take her place at the European Assembly in London. Germany would be forced to remain at peace and there would be three centres of European power, London, Moscow and Paris.

De Gaulle left for Moscow on the 24th November. On the way he visited King Farouk, in Cairo. He found the king very sensitive to the international situation. Egypt had not taken part directly in the world conflict. King Farouk applauded the end of Fascism, but the victory of the western powers might unbalance the delicate equilibrium in the Arab states. Some Egyptian army officers, such as Neguib and Nasser, had hoped for a German victory and had actually plotted and acted in support of the Germans, hoping that this would rid them of the British presence and bring freedom from British domination. They had not understood Hitler's utter contempt and hatred for anything other than the blue-eyed Aryan and that his victory would have brought the Arabs only permanent enslavement.

At that time Allied troops were occupying Iran and when de Gaulle met the Shah he encouraged him to take every possible step to maintain his sovereignty and promised France's support. Passing on from Teheran de Gaulle arrived in Baku, there entering Soviet territory. At Baku he was received with full military ceremony. His onward journey was delayed. The Russians said that his French aircraft did not conform to Russian standards and in any case poor weather made flying dangerous.

De Gaulle and his party would travel to Moscow by the use of the Czar's Imperial train, dating from before the First World War. While this was being arranged de Gaulle was treated with great ceremony. Because of the state of the track the journey was extremely slow, taking four days.

At de Gaulle's request they visited Stalingrad, so that he could pay tribute to the defenders. They found that the city was almost totally demolished. The tank and tractor factory, which had been the seat of the last ditch stand by the German army, had been completely rebuilt and re-equipped. De Gaulle presented a Sword of Honour to the city, as a tribute from the people of France. De Gaulle was well received in Moscow and the French delegations spent eight days in discussions with the Russians.

These discussions were greatly facilitated because some senior members of the French delegation spoke excellent Russian. The Russian parade of troops and armaments greatly impressed de Gaulle, as had been the intention. De Gaulle did not find Stalin other than devious and obstructive and indeed, ruthless. Stalin had expansionist dreams targeted in every direction. Stalin had emerged from the internal struggles at the foundation of the communist party to become a distrustful, determined, and difficult personality. During their discussions, whether he was speaking or not, Stalin's eyes were lowered to where he was continually writing. Both Russia and France had suffered German invasion, so that between them there was a special bond of suffering. They would deal severely with Germany, but any measures they proposed would have to be discussed with the United States and Great Britain.

Russia needed to modernise its industry and war had achieved this. 18,000 factories had been moved eastwards, beyond the range of German bombers. The output of Russian tanks became more than five times that of the Germans. In all, de Gaulle had fifteen hours of discussion with Stalin. It was also clear that the Molotov-von Ribbentrop non-aggression treaty had given Germany the opportunity and the impetus to use all its troops on Germany's western frontiers, mainly against France.

Stalin wanted to know what guarantees France demanded in the west. He would not discuss the questions of the Rhine, Saarland or the Ruhr except as discussions with all four nations. Surprisingly, in the east, Stalin outlined that all the old territories of Silesia, Pomerania and eastern Prussia should be returned to Poland. But as far as the Oder-Neisse line was concerned Stalin favoured the cause of Czechoslovakia. Whereas the question of the Rhine boundary was not yet an urgent matter, the Oder river had already been reached by the Russian troops. Stalin suggested a pact between France and Russia. De Gaulle reminded Stalin that there was already a pact between Russia and France, dating from 1935. Stalin and Molotov declared that the pact of 1935, signed with Laval, had never been implemented. De Gaulle reminded them that there had also been a pact of 1892 because of the threat from Germany.

Eventually a new agreement was reached, and Stalin raised his glass in celebration. "This treaty will be a real one, not like that concluded with Laval!" When de Gaulle congratulated Stalin on the Russian successes in Hungary Stalin replied, "These are only small towns. It is Berlin and Vienna where we must go!" Stalin sympathised with de Gaulle in his difficulties in restoring order in France. De Gaulle tactfully replied that he could not follow Stalin's example, for Stalin was inimitable.

Stalin then went on to mention Thorez, the communist leader in France. The French Government had allowed him to return to Paris. De Gaulle was sullenly silent "Do not be upset at my indiscretions," Stalin told him. "He is a good Frenchman; I would not put him in prison." Then Stalin smiled; "At least, not at once," he concluded. De Gaulle replied, "The French Government treats

Frenchmen according to the service they have given."

In Moscow the Free French party were received with great honour and dignity. They met many intellectuals, such as Victor Fink and Ilya Ehrenburg. In their turn, the French gave grand receptions for many of the Russian leaders. Always Molotov was in attendance. Then there arose difficulties, over the ratification of the treaty. If the French Government was only provisional, how could the treaty be ratified? De Gaulle pointed out that the Russians had already signed such a treaty with Benes, who represented the provisional Czech government. Furthermore, the Czech provisional government was still in London: they had still not regained their homeland.

There was certain to be a row over Poland. After the First World War French troops had gone to the Poles' assistance, helping to recover their eastern territories from the Russians. De Gaulle had been one of those French officers who had been part of the French support for the Poles, and had been decorated by the Poles, as well as being wounded. The Polish Government, in exile in London, had never ceased to fight the Germans. In the Battle of Britain pilots of a Polish squadron had scored the greatest number of German aircraft which had been shot down.

Stalin declared that for centuries the Poles had been Russia's enemies, but now things would be different and he wanted Poland as a friendly ally. Poland had always been the corridor through which Russia had been invaded, whether it was by Napoleon or Hitler. If Poland's eastern frontier was moved westwards to the Oder-Neisse line it would be a stronger barrier against any future German aggression. To be a strong bulwark against any such future German aggression, Stalin declared that Poland would have to be democratic. Stalin stated that the Warsaw uprising had taken place at a time when the Soviet army was not yet ready to intervene. In the liberated territories the Polish Committee for the Liberation had started distributing land to the peasants and the lands of the reactionary émigrés had been given to the peasants, who had been very grateful. Stalin said that Poland would gain great strength from these reforms, just as the French had done from the Revolution.

De Gaulle pointed out that the future of Poland should be the affair of the Polish people. If Stalin thought that the British and Americans were not prepared to make progress on this issue he was wrong, for they had not spoken their last word on this matter. Stalin was sure that those countries which had sided with the Germans would pay the price "according to their merits."

While de Gaulle was in Moscow Churchill sent a message indicating that he expected Stalin to sign a pact with de Gaulle on the same terms as the one which he had concluded with Great Britain in 1942. Churchill suggested that they should sign a tripartite pact. The Russians tended to be favourable to the idea, but de Gaulle was not. Churchill had dealt directly with the Russians and had not kept de Gaulle informed. France and Russia were the nations which were most at risk if there were to be any further German rise of militarism, so that their problems and concerns were shared, and quite different from those of Great Britain. France and Russia had been invaded and occupied, Great Britain had not. In France and Russia some elements of the population had supported the German invaders, whereas Great Britain had been spared this division of loyalties.

De Gaulle was also very keen to renew the very special relationship between France and Great Britain. If there were a tripartite pact in place, including Russia, it could allow Russia to have a right to a say in the special relationship. Britain and France had world empires and their need for co-operation would be essential for the avoidance of international chaos. The Russians could not offer to France the same agreement over the future of Germany which they had offered to Great Britain and the United States. De Gaulle saw the future as being served best by a series of bipartite treaties, with the United Nations serving as the place for broader international agreements.

Stalin eventually agreed to de Gaulle's suggestion of a bipartite treaty. Above all, Stalin was firm on the matter of the future of Poland. He insisted on a free, democratic, and anti-German Poland and he would not tolerate the government in exile in London, which was so anti-Russian. No mention was made that the old hatred of the Poles for the Russians had been further inflamed by the massacre of 10,000 Polish Officers by the Russians in the forests of Katyn. Stalin urged de Gaulle to recognise the Committee of Lublin, containing his own protégés. De Gaulle replied that France was not ready, on those terms, to sign a security pact with Russia. France would only recognise a Polish government, free and democratic, chosen by the Polish people themselves after their liberation.

The next day, the 9th December 1944, de Gaulle came under further pressure to recognise the Committee of Lublin, but his refusal was uncompromising. So Stalin's wish, to be able to announce to the world that the communist inspired government of Poland had been recognised by France, was frustrated. De Gaulle had to meet some members of the Lublin Committee before he left Moscow. He expressed France's sympathy for their country and France's wish to see a free and independent Poland. France did not wish to meddle in Poland's affairs.

Mr. Bierut, of the Committee, did not speak at all of the war, only of agrarian reform. Others wanted de Gaulle to recognise the Committee as the Government of Poland. They said that they had 10 divisions fighting with the Russians. They would not recognise the efforts and the successes of the Free Polish forces that had fought in Poland in 1940 and had then continued the battle in France, Africa, and Italy. De Gaulle offered a liaison officer to be appointed to them, to deal particularly with French prisoners of war liberated on Polish Territory. He would also receive in Paris a member of their organisation of equivalent rank, for liaison purposes. Recognition as a Polish Government he would not bestow. He told them bluntly that France recognised the Polish government in exile, in London.

De Gaulle saw the British and American ambassadors in Moscow and brought them up to date with his negotiations with the Russians and the position he had taken in repudiating the claims for recognition of the Committee of Lublin. He warned the ambassadors of the overtures in that direction which the Russians had made, and would pursue.

De Gaulle wanted to inspect the regiment "Normandie-Niemen," which had been fighting alongside the Russians. When his trip to Russia by air, and also his visit to the squadron, had been prevented by bad weather and the train journey into Russia had become necessary, the visit to the squadron had been cut from the programme. When Stalin heard of de Gaulle's disappointment he arranged for the whole squadron to be brought to Moscow by train. There it was possible for the formal inspection to take place: armed forces from the west fighting alongside the Russians in the continuing struggle against the Germans. De Gaulle was able to personally decorate many of the regiment for their valour.

At a magnificent farewell banquet Stalin and de Gaulle sat side by side. Stalin asked de Gaulle's opinion of the Committee of Lublin. The reply was not to Stalin's liking and the matter was dropped. After toasting the United States, Great Britain, and France, Stalin then toasted each of his senior generals and officials. Each had to come and clink glasses with the Marshal. In introducing each toast Stalin described the duties of the official and then made some special comment. Some he praised: the official in charge of supplies of men and material was exhorted to do his duty well, or he would be hung. Stalin's dominant control was evident and it made de Gaulle even less likely to agree to Stalin having France's support for the domination of Poland.

The time for toasts had arrived. Pleasantries and compliments were exchanged about and between Russia and France. Appropriate flatteries were danced delicately on the air. Stalin proposed toasts to the United States and Roosevelt, and Great Britain and Churchill. Other Allied personalities were toasted and then he came to the Russians. There were thirty individual toasts, with the personality stepping forward to receive the acclamation. Each toast was accompanied by a comment. "Ah, Voronov, it is you who have provided our battlefield armaments which have destroyed the enemy!" "Admiral Kouznetzov, you must be patient, but one day you will control the seas!" To Yakovlev, "Your 'planes sweep the sky." To others the toasts were accompanied by menaces. This was a genuine Russian bear, able to strike in any direction at will.

The Russians still wanted the Franco-Russian pact signing to be accompanied by French recognition of the Committee of

Lublin. Georges Bidault, the foreign affairs minister, told de Gaulle that there was a complete impasse on this matter; there was no point in continuing the discussions. De Gaulle rose and thanked Stalin for the welcome that he had received "in your valiant country. We are agreed that France and Russia will fight together until the final victory." He then took Stalin's hand and bade him farewell. Stalin was stunned. As de Gaulle waved farewell to the assembled guests Molotov ran after him, furious. At his car de Gaulle thanked Molotov for the great welcome he had received. Molotov was totally in disarray, seeing his carefully prepared entrapment of the French sidestepped. If the French could not be persuaded to the Russian view on the Polish question the failure to get the Franco-Russian pact signed would be a great setback for the Soviets, and de Gaulle was due to leave in a few hours.

At two o'clock in the morning a message was received at the French embassy that Molotov wanted the signing to go ahead. The French would announce that a representative would be sent to the Committee of Lublin and the pact would be signed. De Gaulle would tolerate no mention of the Committee of Lublin. All de Gaulle would agree to was a later announcement that Commandant Fouchet had arrived in Lublin, which would be true. The Russians wanted the announcement on the date of the pact, the 10th December, but de Gaulle insisted on the 28th December for the announcement, when Fouchet would actually be in place. The two announcements would not be simultaneous. The final details of the pact were agreed and at four in the morning the treaty was signed. The foreign ministers signed, while Stalin and de Gaulle stood behind them and then shook hands. "We must celebrate this!" Stalin exclaimed. Suddenly the room was transformed and a whole new meal was brought in.

When they were seated Stalin turned to de Gaulle and said in a soft voice "You have held your ground well. It was good timing. I like to do business with someone who knows his mind, even if he does not agree with me!" The atmosphere was much more pleasant than a few hours earlier. In their discussions Stalin expressed pity for Hitler, who had no future. When de Gaulle invited Stalin to Paris the reply was that Stalin was old and would soon die. Death was the only victory.

Surprisingly, Stalin expressed the opinion that the Czars had been wrong to try to enslave the Slavic peoples; they should be free and independent. He expressed the same wish for the Poles. When Stalin asked for de Gaulle's views on this de Gaulle agreed with Stalin's expressed views, and then emphasised his agreement with what had been said, making it clear that the words were not matched by the deeds.

De Gaulle resisted further pressure to sign an agreement recognising the Committee of Lublin. When Stalin assessed that the diplomats' pressure on de Gaulle had failed he feigned displeasure at the diplomats' efforts. "Ah, they should all be shot!" he said, "send for the machine gunner." They then adjourned to watch a film about the way in which the Germans had treacherously invaded Russia. The Russians had responded by fighting valiantly and eventually defeating the Germans in the heart of Berlin. Their methods then produced peace and prosperity. "The end of the story does not please you?" Stalin enquired. "It is your victory which pleased me," de Gaulle responded. And with that the meeting concluded and de Gaulle left Moscow.

Back in Paris on the 16th December de Gaulle found that the Franco-Russian pact was welcomed. It was not so much the pact itself, but the recognition it gave to France's re-establishment as an important power in the world. If this was de Gaulle's belief, he was quickly disabused of the position. Early in 1945 the Anglo-Saxon press announced a meeting between Roosevelt, Stalin, and Churchill. They would decide the future of Germany after the victory. They would also decide the fate of the peoples of Europe and the method for setting up the United Nations.

De Gaulle was upset, but not surprised, at his exclusion. If he were to be excluded from the discussions it was not entirely bad news, for the "Big Three" would have to get his approval to put any of the measures into effect. France was now a power to be recognised and to be taken account of, with a substantial military presence in the European theatre of operations. He would be in the position of an examiner marking their work. It was also clear from where France's exclusion had emanated. Churchill and Stalin had kept him informed, while Roosevelt had not, and clearly still distrusted de Gaulle's motives. Some explanation was due, and Roosevelt sent Harry Hopkins, his special representative, to Paris on the 27th January 1945, just before the start of the Yalta conference.

Hopkins spoke frankly with de Gaulle, noting that there was severe coolness in the relationship between France and the United States. He pointed out that the United States felt badly deceived by France's actions in 1940 in seeking an armistice. Everything that had been declared about continuing to resist the Germans had been overturned in an instant. The great men of France had suddenly thrown in the towel and capitulated, leaving the United States with the opinion that no French leader could be trusted.

Hopkins went on to note that around de Gaulle a strong force of Resistance had grown up, and that these troops had returned to the battle against Germany. The United States had recognised de Gaulle as the leader of this movement and that all the French people also recognised him as their leader. For the United States to have written France off completely had been an error, and now recognition of France's resurgence was overdue. There were still concerns about de Gaulle's long-term position. Could he be overthrown, with resulting disorder, violence, and destruction of France's effort in the war? This was the reason for their reserve.

This was a repeat of Roosevelt's comments of six months earlier. At that time France had not been liberated and the provisional government was still in Algiers. Since then Paris had been liberated and the government had returned to its rightful place, the French people had acclaimed de Gaulle and taken pride in the resurrection of their army and the part it was playing in the war effort.

De Gaulle's response was to point out the great destruction of France which had taken place in the First World War. The United States had only joined the Allies after three years of warfare, and then only when its trade had been severely damaged by the U-boat attacks. There had been no help in getting back France's territories of Alsace and Lorraine, which had been seized by Germany after the Franco-Prussian war of 1870. Nor had the United States been prepared to give any support or guarantees of France's security, as had been promised. The reparations which it had been agreed would be paid by Germany had not been forthcoming, so that the destruction of France's industries was slow to be repaired. This shortage of industrial capacity and development meant that the build up of French armaments in the 1930's had been slower than was necessary to oppose Germany. Then the United States had given Germany help in rebuilding its industry. The result was Hitler, and Hitler with real power.

The United States had distanced itself from France and this lack of support had been most damaging in 1940. President Roosevelt's hesitant response to French appeals for assistance, both military and civilian, had discouraged the French Government and given support to those who sought respite from the destruction of war by means of the armistice. It was true that after the Japanese attack on Pearl Harbour the United States had put the might of all its power into the Allied cause, and that without America's might the war could not be won. Even when the Allied cause had needed its greatest support, the Free French had been denied the essential arms which they had needed.

Hopkins was somewhat stunned by this attack. He expressed the hope that their future hopes and their future as two great allies would move smoothly forward together. De Gaulle asked how the United States could hope to consider the future of Europe with its other allies without France's contribution. Hopkins replied that the American Government placed the greatest importance on France taking part in the European Commission, to be held in London, and on an equal footing with the United States, Great Britain, and Russia. De Gaulle pointed out that some of the important questions could not be settled by the Allies, but only by agreement between France and Germany. One of these issues was the status of the river Rhine as the border between them. For centuries it had been the cause of conflict: the future must be better.

De Gaulle finished by telling the Americans that if there was a cold wind blowing on their relationship it was for the Americans to add warmth; the French wish was for a warm friendship.

While the leaders of the three great Allies were meeting at

Yalta de Gaulle drew France to their attention. On the 5th February 1945 he spoke on the radio. He laid out the terms for a European settlement from the French position. The war would end with French troops in position from one end of the Rhine to the other. The independence of countries, such as Poland and Czechoslovakia, would have to be assured. France had 100 million men available and would need to be satisfied. It was a strong and challenging set of demands. If France were not within the 'Big Three' discussions she would certainly have her say.

From Yalta a joint communiqué emerged on the 12th February 1945 German unconditional surrender was required. Each of the three great powers would occupy a region of Germany and the control would be exercised by a joint commission. And then came the reward. France was invited to join the other three powers in occupying a zone of Germany and take part in the government of Germany. It was Churchill who had insisted on this, pointing out that without France's inclusion there could be no possibility of reconstructing a secure and stable basis for peace in Europe. All German troops were to be disarmed and the German High Command dissolved forever: war criminals would be tried and Germany would pay reparations.

To set the stage for world peace a meeting, called by the 'Big Three,' would be held in San Francisco on 25th April, 1945. At this conference France would take her place with a seat on the Security Council. Hungary, Romania, and Bulgaria – countries which had ended the war on the German side – would allow their peoples to make a democratic choice of government. The exact terms of how the Russian occupation of these countries might end were left vague, because agreement had not been reached with the Russians on any timetable for their withdrawal. Poland's eastern boundary would move westward to the Curzon line and in return she would receive substantial territories in the north and west, including Danzig in her territory without the need for any corridor of connexion through a foreign land.

On the day the Yalta communiqué was issued de Gaulle received the formal invitation for France to join as one of the occupying powers of Germany. The second invitation he received was for France to take her place as one of the five great powers initiating the formation of the United Nations, with a permanent seat on the Security Council. France could never have achieved this from her position as a vanquished nation in 1940 without de Gaulle's firm resolution to uphold the honour of France and to bring her back into the fight on the Allied side. The other essential to the restoration of France's restoration was Churchill's support against Roosevelt's ideas and in the councils of the 'Big Three.' Freedom's champions had scored so well – together.

If the real outcome was reasonably satisfactory there was a further row with Roosevelt in store. Roosevelt suggested meeting de Gaulle in Algeria, in the same way as the leaders of minor states had been received in Roosevelt's progress from the eastern Mediterranean. De Gaulle could see no reason why Roosevelt could not come to Paris. De Gaulle was not aware of how ill Roosevelt was and took the invitation as a personal and national insult. His refusal was described in the American press as the act of a 'prima donna.' De Gaulle's response to Roosevelt was very different from his reply when, a year earlier, a very ill Churchill had wanted de Gaulle to visit him while he was recuperating at Marrakech. De Gaulle feared for the life of his old friend and went quickly to the meeting. Their discussions were amiable and fruitful. Photographs of that meeting show de Gaulle regarding Churchill with an affectionate concern, which was deeply felt.

ORDER

Circumstances brought a wind of change in favour of the Free French, for they had the authority and the drive to motivate and direct the nation. The suffering and destruction of the country and the overturning of law and institutions produced every chance of general disorder. The joy of liberation could not hide the disastrous state of the nation's affairs. The diet had been reduced to 1,200 calories a day and the only additional sources of food were to be found on the black market, ruinously expensive and totally demoralising. The shortage of material for clothing reduced the people to making clothes out of wood. Coal was reserved for the army, the railways, and hospitals. It was one of the coldest winters of the century and in homes, workshops, offices and schools, everyone froze. Gas supplies were available only for an occasional hour and electricity was mostly cut off. Trains were rare and the scarce joy of a bicycle was the main method of transport.

Recovery was slowed by the absence of 4 million young men, removed to Germany either as prisoners of war or as forced labourers. In one prison camp prisoners were invited to work for the Reich. After several failed attempts one French prisoner stepped forward. Asked if he would be prepared to work for the Reich he confirmed his willingness. Asked his occupation the replied, "Undertaker." For this insult he spent many days in solitary confinement.

The national crisis fully engaged de Gaulle's efforts. Some of the problems were insoluble for the time being, but a sound basis for the future had to be established. Above all, law and order had to be maintained, for any lawlessness would have disrupted the transport of supplied across France to the battlefront as it approached, and crossed into, Germany. The Resistance had suffered terribly at the hands of collaborators and informers. Retribution had to be according to law, and not to the whims of those with the guns in their hands. Great political changes were possible, but these had to be accomplished by the democratic will of the people, expressed through an elected parliament. There was great fear that disorder would break out under the force of political intrigue, destroying the hopes of the honest citizens for the future of their children.

After the First World War France had no great reserves of coal or petrol to help in reconstruction. In the 1930's much of the available industrial production had been devoted to building fixed fortifications, in the Maginot Line, to defend the country against renewed German aggression, in a manner which would avoid the ghastly losses of troops in trench warfare. At the time France went to war again there was a major social and political division amongst the French people and it was this that was blamed for the disaster of 1940. At that time most of the French people were struggling in poverty, while a few flaunted their wealth. Only the unity imposed by the common struggle against Hitler bound the nation. Would the arrival of peace break that unity asunder? It was clear that a definite path of national reconstruction, fair, demanding of universal effort, would be the only way of maintaining the national unity forged in war.

There was danger that communism would seem attractive to those consumed by anger and without other hope. It was a wonderful opportunity for the communists to emerge as the salvation of France. On one of the first stamps issued after the liberation the symbol was that of the Victoire de Samothrace, a magnificent statue in the Louvre. Whoever could appear as this shining example of victory could capture the imagination of the nation.

De Gaulle saw the danger and was quick to call the Consultative Assembly into session. All the good intentions had to be translated into action. Under de Gaulle's leadership all the necessary laws to establish fully the mechanism of action for public order and progress were passed. Social and economic progress, which had been delayed for half a century, was quickly set in train. The collieries in the north of France were nationalised and an agency for controlling petrol supplies was put in place in 1945, to ensure proper availability of the necessary fuel and lubricants for industry. A plan for atomic energy was started, for without indigenous gas or oil France would be at a great disadvantage economically in the years to come. Such major tasks, particularly the forward development of atomic energy for electricity generation, could only be achieved in a nationalised industry. This has led to 75% of France's electric power being generated from the atomic programme.

The Bank of France was also nationalised. Those French financial institutions in the empire overseas which had been used by the Free French were united in an overseas banking system. It could be used by the government as a method of providing the investment necessary for the development of the overseas territories. The motor industry started to rebuild, with the leadership of a nationalised Renault car factory. The shortage of transport demanded some quick solutions. The nationalisation of Renault was done out of urgent necessity and not dogmatic principle. To protect workers in the future the foundation of a social security system for all was laid. Everyone would contribute, everyone would be covered, and the anxiety and distress of illness, accident, age, and unemployment would be lifted from the brow of the people.

The importance of agriculture to the economy was so great that special measures to ensure the continuing rights of farmers to their land had to be enacted. There could be no hint of the seizure of land taking place in eastern Europe happening in France. Otherwise any loss of confidence in the long term future of French agriculture would have led to a massive desertion of the fields for the factories.

To avoid any major disruption in the battle over wages workers' councils were started in large organisations, to try and achieve an equitable but sustainable reward for the workers without prolonged industrial strife. De Gaulle wanted workers to benefit from success in the same way as shareholders. It was not because he was a socialist, but he had seen that the people had suffered as a whole and the progress of a united nation demanded some significant equality of rewards. This policy partially disarmed the communists. If the 'Egalite' of the national motto could be achieved by agreement and not by revolution, so much the better. It was a method of re-enforcing the authority and power of the state, rather than allowing a political party to march as the vanguard of the people's progress.

If the state were to lead the development of France after the war it would need civil servants of the greatest ability. In August 1945 de Gaulle founded the Ecole Nationale d'Administration. Admission was strictly by open competition on the basis of examination and promotion on graduation was equally and strictly fought for. It was a creation which was to give France a quality civil service ahead of the rest of the world. If this would benefit the future of France, in the mean time one had to live. The starting up of factories and the rebuilding of bridges, ports, and railways was urgent. There was a danger that the communists would use their already large following to seize power. Only de Gaulle had the authority and the support to prevent them, for in political terms they formed the largest single party and the other political parties were in a rudimentary state of development, with so many of their members tainted by collaboration, and no cohesion of ideas about any policy which could attract widespread support. The suggestion of forming coalitions, which would be a popular front against communism, was rudely rejected.

The communist leader, Maurice Thorez, who had been condemned five years earlier, for desertion, was pardoned by an amnesty. Relieved of this danger, he made few demands. By accepting the pardon his previous conviction was both officially recognised anew and also brought back to the public attention. In advancing the communist cause he was effective in keeping the miners at work when their efforts were vital to the economy.

It was clear that with the formation of the political parties under a rainbow of banners that de Gaulle's place at the centre of power would not be an indefinite tenure: nor did he want it to be. George Bidault's slogan was "Revolution under the law!" The disappointment was that there were the same disagreements and discord between political leaders as had been present before the war. These were to continue in the early post-war years, resulting in the leadership of the French government becoming one of the fastest revolving merry-go-rounds. This turn of events made de Gaulle apprehensive for the future.

He considered that for the future of French democracy major changes to the constitution would have to be approved by the people in a referendum. The pre-war dithering which had emasculated decision making in the time of the greatest crisis could not be allowed to continue into the post-war era, or violent revolution might be the outcome. He knew, expected, and wanted his practical supreme authority to be temporary. This was not appreciated by the Americans, who were scared of the possibility of a new Napoleon emerging. Churchill understood the frailty of the French political system only too well – he had faced its weaknesses in 1940. For Churchill there had always been the essential Chamber of Parliament to address. Throughout the war he had faced some opposition from a vocal minority of about 25 members. He had spoken in the House to give an account of the war, often in the most sombre terms, concealing little of the depths of the disasters that seemed to come as an avalanche at times.

Churchill had the supreme confidence that Parliament was secure in its long and durable traditions. He did not realise how the hopes of the people after all their suffering, and the expectations of the soldiers, would soon combine to deliver one of the most severe political rebuffs that any leader of Britain has received. Even before the war had ended he would be turned out of office, not because of criticism of the conduct of the war or any ingratitude for the force of his leadership during the war, but because the social revolution which his loyal deputy, Clement Attlee, offered to the people seemed to offer a genuine Utopia. It was only later that the people realised that it was a real Utopia in the fullest terms of an accurate translation from the Greek – nowhere to be found. After the economic collapse resulting from the faulty economic strategies of Keynes and Dalton, Churchill was called back as Prime Minister in 1951. De Gaulle was also needed back at the helm, in France, when political collapse threatened the whole integrity of the French State.

If, in the war's last months, some formality attended de Gaulle's attendance at the Consultative Assembly, it did not prevent him taking part in the proceedings. He was not prepared to be a figurehead. The debates were often furious and full of expressed anger, but it was surely better to ventilate this volcano than to allow it to erupt in protests on the streets. After the debates de Gaulle's summing up pulled together the various strands and expressed the common ideals. He had become, at least for the time being, in all but the process of formal election, the President of France. The mood among the people wished it so. Arguments about how to finance the restoration of the status of those who had been imprisoned or enslaved in Germany or by the Vichy government caused furious disagreements in the Consultative Assembly, so that in March 1945 the members came to de Gaulle asking that the government should take more account of the decisions of the Assembly.

The delegates of the Resistance made up most of the membership of the Assembly and they considered that they had earned the right to speak for the people, and that those who had sided with Vichy had no such right. De Gaulle reminded them that the Resistance movement had been much greater than the movement in France and that France was greater than all the Resistance movements. He emphasised that until elections could be held no one had a sole right to speak for France or the French people. The most important task was to re-establish on a firm footing the rights of free speech and the freedom of the press.

Dealing with the effects of collaboration with the Germans would be a major task. 60,000 French had served their masters, 200,000 French had been deported, of whom only 50,000 survived. 35,000 had been condemned to death by Vichy tribunals and 70,000 interned. The anger that this provoked after the liberation required the Government to keep a cool head. The courts set up to deal with collaborators had difficulty keeping clear of the influence of the crowd in the audience. 2,071 death sentences were pronounced. These were then submitted to de Gaulle, who acted with the advice of a Mercy Commission. He found nothing in the world so sad as the list of their crimes against their fellow countrymen. 768 of the sentences were carried out. 39,000 were sentenced to terms of imprisonment, while in Belgium the equivalent number was 55,000 and in Holland 50,000.

Of those senior officers who supported the Vichy government,

271

a special court sentenced Admiral Esteva to a term in prison, General Dentz was sentenced to death but de Gaulle commuted it, and Marshal Petain, in view of his age, was also spared from the firing squad. The Marshal was eighty nine years old at that time. He had taken refuge in Switzerland but had returned to France voluntarily.

France and Britain both ended the war with severe destruction of their economic base and their monetary reserves almost totally depleted. The same had not been true of Belgium. Not only had the effects of the occupation been much less severe, but throughout the war Belgium had amassed great monetary reserves in the United States by the sale of minerals, particularly uranium. In France the only wealth which could be quickly taxed was from the ill gotten gains of collaboration, and these were seized.

The reconstitution of government took much effort but the general attitude towards the difficult tasks ahead drew to de Gaulle's side many of goodwill. He often took counsel from the former President of the Senate, Jules Jeanenney, who had been a minister of Clemenceau. Not only were there the difficulties of reconstruction of a ravaged country, the prisoners of war and others displaced in the overturning of civilisation had to be welcomed and welded back into French society. There was bitterness and there were hostilities. De Gaulle took great trouble to foster the re-unification of his country. Many could not understand his comparatively forgiving attitude to those who had not swum strongly against the tide of disaster. He had, all the time, the long term good of his country in mind. Wounds can heal, amputations cannot. Quickly the French people saw and understood his purpose. They also understood that he had no long-term political ambition. Trained as a military man he had seen the failures in the political life of his country. He hoped that new and patriotic vigour would give unity to the national purpose.

The damage to the transport infrastructure was so severe that in December 1944 de Gaulle created a special Ministry of Reconstruction. The damage in some areas prevented any possibility of rebuilding what had been there before. Even in 1947, a visitor to Caen, scene of the heaviest fighting in the Normandy campaign, could find no organised semblance of the layout of the town. It shocked even the visitor used to the devastation of the worst areas of central London.

The Council of State met at the Hotel Matignon. The debates were well ordered, each minister presenting the tasks and the proposals of his portfolio. Questions and objections were heard in a thoughtful and ordered manner. If the aims were clear, the methods were not, and there was some quite heated discussion, which foretold the future of the heated and divisive political debates that were to emasculate political incisiveness for fifteen to twenty years to come, and lead to the move from the Fourth to the Fifth Republic.

In the six months prior to victory de Gaulle addressed the Assembly on some thirty occasions and spoke frequently on the radio. It was important to make the people understand that the great convoys of supplies passing thorough their country, and whose goods were denied to them, were essential for victory. Although France was becoming totally liberated the battle still raged eastwards into Germany. He decided not to occupy the Elysee Palace. That honour would be reserved for an elected President.

Through the autumn of 1944 and the spring of 1945 de Gaulle visited numerous cities and towns throughout France. He formally, on behalf of the provisional government, installed the mayors and governors. Everywhere he received a tumultuous welcome. In Paris, on the 2nd April 1945, he formally returned standards to 134 regiments that had been reconstituted, and 60,000 French troops marched past.

THE FINAL VICTORY

In the autumn of 1944 the Allied advance from Normandy had reached the borders of Germany. There were still some German troops holding out in isolated pockets in France, mainly around the mouth of the river Gironde, preventing the use of the port of Bordeaux. But the decisive battles for the final destruction of German forces would take place on German territory. De Gaulle hoped that the contribution made by the French forces would renew a sense of pride in the French nation before the end of the war.

Eisenhower's abilities as a diplomat had kept the different vanities of some of his commanders under control and focussed on the joint task, sometimes with difficulty. De Gaulle wanted French troops to be a fully integrated part of the Allied armies, but now they were fighting on French, and soon German, soil France's interests were his special concern. As the campaign developed French troops made up a quarter of Eisenhower's forces. The demands for the supplies for the armies meant that nearly the whole of the French transport system was taken over and controlled for this purpose. The demands and trials of combat meant that there was no special consideration for the French position by SHAEF - the Supreme Headquarters of the Allied Expeditionary Force – indeed it was realised that the war could still be lost.

General Juin, the French Commander-in-Chief of National Defence, did much to smooth over the conflicts which arose from this situation. Eisenhower's plan in the autumn of 1944 was to reach the Rhine, and take the fight onto German soil. In the south of the Allied front General de Lattre de Tassigny had 8 French divisions in the battle. In Alsace, General Leclerc's 2nd Armoured Division was attached to the American 7th Army, with the task of liberating Strasbourg. There were still 90,000 German troops fighting in the west of France. General Larminat had 3 divisions with which to defeat them. The French air force, spreading out from England, across France and the Mediterranean, and with 2 squadrons in Russia, could put 1,000 aircraft into action.

In fierce fighting, in fifteen days, the 1st French Army killed 10,000 Germans and took 18,000 prisoners. The American 7th Army broke through the German lines and allowed Leclerc's 2nd Armoured Division to press on to liberate Strasbourg. General Patch gave Leclerc his head to press on and he captured Strasbourg on the 23rd November, taking prisoner 12,000 German soldiers and 20,000 German civilians. The German general, holed up in Fort Ney, finally surrendered on the 25th November. De Gaulle announced the joyous news to the Consultative Assembly – France's last major town had been liberated. For Leclerc it was the completion of the mission de Gaulle had given him four years before, in the depths of Africa.

If the determined French attacks had liberated Strasbourg the Germans were not going to give up the whole of Alsace without a severe struggle. Fighting was intense in many other areas. The seven German divisions already fighting there were re-enforced by a further division, brought back from Norway, and a Panzer division, fully equipped with 'Panther' tanks, which quite outclassed the Shermans of the French and American divisions. It was particularly difficult to dig the Germans out of their positions because of the major waterways of the river Rhine and the Rhone canal. The German troops were supported by artillery hidden in the hills of the Black Forest, just across the Rhine.

There was a severe deterioration in the weather in early December 1944. The winter of 1944-5 was to prove to be the most severe for ten years and it made any coherent advance impossible because of the difficulties in bringing up sufficient supplies, as many of the roads quickly became so muddy that even tanks and jeeps became bogged down. Under the cloak of the winter fog and snow the Germans had quietly assembled a major new army, fully equipped with the latest tanks and supported by mechanised infantry. Their attack was through the Ardennes region, where the line was thinly held by inexperienced troops. The thrust, Hitler's last great gamble, was aimed to split the British forces in the north from the Americans to the south, and thrust through to take the port of Antwerp. This would deny a major supply route to the

Allies and might cause such dissention that the Allied unity would be ripped asunder. Hitler's view was that splitting the Allied forces would cause furious arguments between the commanders and produce the same disarray that had lead to the fall of France in 1940.

The circumstances of 1944 were quite different. North of the German attack Eisenhower attached the American forces to Montgomery's command, where they worked well with the British. He brought elements of Patton's Third Army in a sweep round to the south of the bulge through the Allied line, then north with the target of Bastogne, in Luxembourg. In Bastogne the U.S. 101st Airborne Division was to fight one of the great heroic battles of the whole war. With the Americans surrounded the Germans offered the Americans terms for surrender The American commander, General McAuliffe's, one word reply was "Nuts!" and had the double virtue of brevity, and by reason of its rough colloquialism, the effect of confusing the Germans for some hours while they tried to comprehend the meaning of the American general's reply.

These pressures caused Eisenhower to start moving troops away from the region of Strasbourg. De Gaulle heard of this and rushed to see Eisenhower. Around Colmar the French troops were finding great difficulty in overcoming the Germans. Most of the fighting since the landings in the south of France in August had been done by colonial troops, with French officers. These were now becoming tired out and disillusioned. They felt that they were detached from the sympathy and understanding of the people of France. To prevent a serious drop in morale de Gaulle ordered these units to be strengthened by 10,000 young French soldiers from the training depots. The 1st French Division disengaged itself from the fighting to open the river to Bordeaux, and rushed to Alsace. The newly formed 10th Division, drawn from young men who had fought for the liberation of Paris, had quickly improved its abilities and de Gaulle ordered it forward into the line.

On Christmas Eve de Gaulle went to Strasbourg, where he was acclaimed, despite the city being virtually under siege. He celebrated Christmas Midnight Mass, at Erstein, with General

Leclerc. The next day he received a warm welcome from General o'Daniell, when he inspected the American 3rd Division, which had taken over from the 36th. In further inspections along the line, the French generals pointed out to de Gaulle that they had insufficient troops, armour and artillery to make further advances. At Mulhouse, inspecting the Magnan Division, de Gaulle was made aware that there did not seem to be any way of dislodging the Germans from the north of the town.

In this tour of inspection de Gaulle was received and acknowledged as the leader. His appointment had only been officially as a two star general and there was no government authority to promote him further. Indeed, the Vichy government had deprived him of his citizenship and sentenced him to death. But all accepted his right to the leadership, by this time even the Americans. From the civilian population of Alsace the Germans had conscripted many young men into the German army. Sent to the eastern front, many had been killed fighting against the Russians. It was clear that Alsace was loyal, but unsettled. If there were military setbacks there could be serious trouble, which de Gaulle would have to deal with promptly.

The German attack in the Ardennes, with 24 divisions, 10 of them Panzer, had made deep inroads into the Allied lines. The most forward German units were approaching the river Meuse by the 25th December, producing the "Bulge" by which the battle became known. There was a clear and serious danger that if the Germans could cross the Meuse they could break out into the flat lands beyond the river and split the Allied armies in two. Eisenhower judged that every focus of strength had to be put in the way of such a disaster. The German breakthrough had already covered 50 miles.

With Montgomery attacking from the north and Patton from the south the Germans were held, but this left Patch's army weakly equipped to hold against any German attack in his sector. By moving the French 2nd Armoured Division to support Patch that sector could be held, but it would further weaken the sector around Colmar and Strasbourg. If the loss of Strasbourg back to the Germans might be strategically necessary, it would be politically disastrous in France. The return of the Germans, followed by the Gestapo, wreaking revenge, would be an intolerable wound to a nation which had suffered so much. Blaming the Allied High Command for any such failure would not do, because de Gaulle had placed the French troops under the orders of that command. To save Alsace de Gaulle would have to withdraw the 2nd Armoured Division from Allied control. If they lost Alsace fighting on their own it could be accepted, not otherwise.

De Gaulle had received no word from Eisenhower about any such movement of French forces away from Strasbourg. He had received some degree of warning when, on the 19th December, de Lattre had been refused any re-enforcements for the attack on Colmar because so many troops were being sent to support the southern attack on the German penetration through the Ardennes. General Devers moved his headquarters 80 miles to the rear and de Lattre was given orders to prepare defensive positions in depth. French signallers intercepted German radio traffic which made the threat of a German attack in that sector not only likely, but imminent. French liaison officers at Allied Headquarters reported to de Gaulle that there was some confusion and disarray. Alarm notes were being sounded as far back as the routes to Paris because of the danger of paratrooper assaults. Hitler had promised to be in Strasbourg for New Year.

De Gaulle gave orders that Strasbourg was to be defended. He also sent a further division to the front and ordered that the crossings of the Meuse were to be defended to allow a sudden American withdrawal if necessary. 50,000 men of the army of the interior were sent to aid the defence of the Meuse river crossings. The Allied position was made worse by the appearance over the front lines of several dozen German jet fighters, the first in the world to enter combat. They were only thwarted by massive American bombing attacks on their bases.

In a letter to Eisenhower on the 1st January 1945 de Gaulle emphasised the importance of defending Strasbourg. He offered to send all the troops in training directly to the front, starting with the 10th Division, under General Billotte. The French would send the troops needed to defend Strasbourg On the 2nd January de

Lattre told de Gaulle that he had received orders to retreat and that the Americans had already started to do so. General Devers was told to tell Eisenhower that France would defend Strasbourg with whatever troops she had available and that de Gaulle would visit Eisenhower on the next day.

De Gaulle knew that his strategy carried great risks. He also knew that his determination to save Strasbourg undermined Allied unity, with his giving of countermanding strategic orders. But if you are French, and it is your country, and you have only just got rid of the cruel invader, and you are de Gaulle, and you know so well Churchill's determination to defend his country 'on the beaches, in the streets, and in the hills, and never surrender,' could you do less? General Devers sent a message to de Gaulle that the American 7th Army would defend Strasbourg to the end. But de Lattre had received orders from Devers to retreat into the Vosges by the 5th January. De Lattre sent a message to de Gaulle that he would send the experienced 3rd North African Division to Strasbourg and use the inexperienced 10th Division in the Vosges.

On the afternoon of the 3rd January de Gaulle, accompanied by Juin, went to Eisenhower's headquarters in Paris, where the seriousness of the situation was explained. The use of the jet fighters and the new Panther tanks by the Germans had broken Allied morale in some places, In Alsace the Germans, in their pocket around Colmar, were a great danger. It was for this reason that Eisenhower had wanted to shorten the Allied line.

De Gaulle replied that for the French Alsace was sacred. The Germans had always claimed the territory and from 1871 to 1918 had occupied it. If it were lost the Germans would wreak a terrible vengeance on the civil population. That was why de Gaulle had given the French 1st Army the order to defend the city, by whatever means. De Gaulle did not want to break the central army control and he urged Eisenhower to give Devers the orders to join in the defence of Strasbourg by holding firm in Alsace, and not withdrawing.

Eisenhower told de Gaulle that his reasons, however excellent, were political and not military. De Gaulle replied that armies were to serve the political needs of their States. Churchill had come to the meeting, warned by de Gaulle about the serious state of the campaign. Churchill stated "All my life I have understood the special place of Alsace in the feelings of the French people. I agree with general de Gaulle that it should be considered."

Eisenhower explained to de Gaulle that if the French 1st Army and other forces operated independently of the Allied High Command they would not be supplied with food, petrol, or ammunition. De Gaulle replied that without supplies the French forces could be overrun by the Germans and produce a wide breach in the Allied line. Such a withdrawal of support from the French troops would, in any case, result in the French people blocking roads and railways and taking supplies for their forces, producing complete chaos. This would be unthinkable and de Gaulle asked Eisenhower to reconsider the whole strategic situation.

Eisenhower expressed agreement with de Gaulle's point of view. He did it after full consideration and frank discussion, which de Gaulle considered typical of his sympathetic character. At this part of the meeting Churchill was a silent witness. Orders were given to General Devers to halt his retreat. Eisenhower explained to de Gaulle how his task was complicated by the political considerations of the Allied nations and the demands of the competing elements of the armed forces. He complained about Montgomery's conduct, a general of great value, but an acerbic critic and a deviant subordinate. De Gaulle reassured him that he would still come out the victor. At the entrance to the Hotel Trianon they parted on good terms. It was the outcome produced by a great diplomat. It showed how sound his appointment had been and when de Gaulle had left Churchill congratulated him. He told Eisenhower "I think you've done the wise and proper thing."

In the following fortnight the Germans fought severe battles around Strasbourg. The American line bent, but did not break. French forces also had to give some ground. By the 20th January the German offensive around Strasbourg had been blunted and broken. Hitler did not spend any part of the New Year in Strasbourg. The same repulse of the German attack had eventually been achieved in the Ardennes. The American resistance at

Bastogne had delayed the Germans and used up so much of their fuel that they were not able either to bring up supplies or capture any American fuel dumps. The weather cleared and the German armour came under merciless attack by the rocket firing Allied aircraft. It had been a bold and desperate German gamble, and in the end it had failed.

The battle to save Strasbourg had been savage, but the French success raised the morale of the troops, who had started to doubt their ability to beat the Germans in a long and hard campaign. By early February a combined American and French force broke through the German lines north of Colmar. By the end of this stage of the campaign a further 22,000 German prisoners had been taken. It had been a desperate struggle to save Alsace from recapture, but it had succeeded. At Saverne de Gaulle decorated Devers, Patch, and Bradley – three American generals who had fought so hard alongside the French.

The next target was to enter Germany. The French wanted to play a full part in the campaign and re-establish their position as a major European power. For the future, France and Germany would have to establish arrangements which would prevent forever further conflicts which had put them at each other's throats three times in seventy years. To the British and Americans it was the second major conflict, but neither country had been invaded and suffered the damage that the European battlefields had seen. Nor had the civilian populations of Britain and the United States been subjected to the personal brutalised terror of the Gestapo. As Churchill had put it, "Every human bond between man and man had been broken."

In early March Montgomery's and Bradley's Army Groups had reached the Rhine. It might have been expected that for the thrust across the Rhine the French 1st Army would be left on the French side of the Rhine, but it would have deprived the French of being full partners in the battle and the conquest. De Gaulle saw the importance of full French participation, to take France's own zone of occupation of Germany. Eisenhower originally assigned to the French 1st Army a purely defensive role. The French learned that the Allies intended to use the bridging equipment of the

French armoured divisions to cross the Rhine, but American troops would be crossing over it. Any advance through the sector facing the French would have to penetrate the defences of the Siegfried line. Because of the Allied view that the French would only take a defensive role in the next stage of the advance they had been kept short of ammunition.

The valleys of the Black Forest were considered to be easy territory to defend, but they were not guarded by the best German troops. If these defences could be penetrated the Allied advance could turn north towards Stuttgart. The whole strategy was altered in the Allies' favour by the Americans in Bradley's sector being able to seize the bridge at Remagen intact, rapidly cross the river to form a bridgehead which was quickly re-enforced, and speed onwards into central Germany. German disorganisation made the French sector a minor area of interest by comparison once, in a hard battle, the Americans had destroyed the remaining German units on the west bank of the Rhine.

By the 24th March French units were on the east bank of the Rhine. Allied air forces had destroyed German communications to divide German army units from each other and deprive them of supplies. The French units had become much more effective now that they had fully established bases in central and northern France, much closer to the front line and with greatly shortened lines of delivery for supplies. The destruction of German air bases had almost completely freed the skies above the battlefield of the Luftwaffe.

Montgomery in the north and Bradley in the centre were pushing forward strongly into Germany. In the French sector, by the 4th April, 130,000 French troops with 20,000 vehicles were on the east bank of the Rhine. The breakout into the centre of Germany was pressed forward, using 80 divisions - American, British, French, Canadian, and Polish, with 12,000 aircraft. Hitler's Reich was doomed and prolonging the war only added mightily to the destruction of Germany and the misery of her people. And yet, on the radio, Goebbels was still claiming that Germany would win the war.

On the 25th April de Gaulle broadcast that the battle needed to be pressed forwards as speedily as possible, to bring an end to the suffering of the German people. There was still the possibility that ardent Nazis would withdraw into a southern redoubt near Hitler's eyrie at Berchtesgarten. There was also the possibility that the privations of the peoples of Europe would lead to massive revolution if the hopeless state of so many was not addressed quickly. Above all, food was needed. The taking of so many men from the land and the removal of farm horses for use by the German army for transport destroyed agriculture across the continent. All this was Hitler's vengeance.

There were still some German forces holding out on the west coast of France, and these had to be dealt with. They had been left in place when French troops had been drawn to the east in the desperate defence of Strasbourg. It was clear that the German Government would soon fall to the Allied conquest and the signing of an act of surrender by the Germans would be the least damaging end to the conflict in those areas. It would certainly reduce the chances of severe slaughter.

However, de Gaulle was riding a tiger. 70,000 long serving members of the Maquis, with many of the units from the French Empire, did not wish to lay down their arms without earning their own laurels on the battlefield. From the 14th October 1944 they had organised themselves in a sort of fashion into an army. They had assembled three divisions, with artillery and air support. They had no armour with which to take on the German forces in their western French fortresses. The 1st Free French Division was assigned to support them as soon as it could be spared by the Allied High Command, but in the end it was Leclerc's 2nd Armoured Division that was assigned to the task. The Americans helped with an artillery brigade in support.

15,000 German troops with 300 guns were in position at the mouth of the river Gironde. Between the 14th and the 18th April 1945 the Germans were overcome. On the 30th April French troops landed on the Ile d'Oleron and by the next day the isle was free. 18,000 German prisoners were taken further up the west coast. At St. Nazaire and Lorient American troops took into custody 90,000 Germans when they laid down their arms. On the eastern border of France, in the Alps, French troops liberated the isolated towns and villages. American troops had been on their way to do this, but had been diverted to oppose the German breakthrough in the Ardennes.

In the Far East there was co-operation between the Free French and the British over the defence of Indo-China against a Japanese invasion. With Vichy supporters in control there should have been no danger of a Japanese invasion because of the Axis pact, but the danger was great. De Gaulle appointed General Mordant to take command of the troops if Indo-China were invaded. The British provided a base for Free French Special Forces near Calcutta. The total French forces in Indo-China were some 50,000 men, of whom 12,000 were Europeans. They were virtually without aircraft or armour. If attacked, de Gaulle's orders were to resist as long as possible. The forces in Tonkin could retreat towards the Chinese border, being supplied from the air by the Americans.

On the 9th March 1945 the Japanese ordered the French admiral and general to place their forces immediately under Japanese control. Despite their hopeless position most of the French troops defended their positions stoutly. By this means the Japanese were delayed in completing their conquest until the 1st April. One column and several small groups of men escaped into China. It had been hoped to re-enforce Indo China with troops from Madagascar and Africa, but there was no American transport available.

If there were reverses in the Far East the focus of France's future would be decided at and beyond the German border. France's influence after victory would be entirely proportional to the amount of territory over which she had gained control. It was necessary to show how quickly the French army was being rebuilt. On the 2nd April de Gaulle presented regimental banners to the colonels of all the new regiments which had been raised. The ceremony was held on the Place de la Concorde. It was a very public statement that the preponderance of American troops in the closing stages of the European campaign was by no means total. The British were advancing into Germany along the North Sea coast, liberating Belgium and Holland on their route.

In the Ruhr basin General Bradley's forces encircled General Model's army group and took their surrender. Some American troops were moving to the south of Germany and unless the French advanced quickly their path towards the river Danube would be blocked. It was clear from the political view that the race to control Europe was well under way. Any advance towards the Danube was impeded by the presence of the German 19th Army in the Black Forest. This delay allowed American troops to take Stuttgart and to go south to Schaffhausen, at the Swiss border. The French troops accelerated their attacks and the German troops in the Black Forest were surrounded. After crossing the Rhine the French troops had taken 110,000 German prisoners.

The roses of victory were not without their thorns. On the 24th March the French were ordered by the Americans to withdraw their advance units from Stuttgart as it was not planned that it should be in their zone of occupation. De Gaulle ordered de Lattre to stay put and to form immediately a military government When the Americans protested de Lattre showed his orders from de Gaulle, citing the fact that the individual nations' zones of occupation had not yet been agreed. The disagreement went to a higher level. Eisenhower wrote to de Gaulle that the French action broke the agreements concerning the re-armament of the French forces. However he would accept the situation and would not in any way cut off the arms and supplies to the French because of their action. He did not want to do anything to harm the exemplary spirit of co-operation between the French and American forces in the battle.

De Gaulle could do nothing but reply in mellifluous terms, promising to settle the matter by political agreement. On the 2nd May Eisenhower wrote that he was happy to leave matters as they were, as they each understood the other's position. There the matter rested, and so did the French, still in Stuttgart. De Gaulle had gained control of a significant part of Germany and Eisenhower had off-loaded that responsibility. The two military men had shown the political skill which was to be recognised and rewarded later by the political command of their respective countries.

The German state was collapsing in disorder. The people regarded occupation from the west as a sort of deliverance, from the east by the Russians as something to be greatly feared. It was in Russia that German destructive brutality had been at its worst. Having recovered the Russian territories that the Germans had occupied, and seeing what had been done to their homeland, the Russians were in no mood to be merciful.

At the end of April Bradley's forces reached the river Elbe, near Torgau, and there met the Russians. In the north Montgomery's troops captured Hamburg, Kiel, and Lubeck. By these advances German troops in Denmark and Holland were cut off from Germany. The Russians took Vienna and Patton got into Czechoslovakia. Patch went into Austria, as far as Innsbruck. The French also advanced into Austria, and their flag flew from the top of the Vorarlberg. Leclerc and his armoured column reached Berchtesgarten: he had come from the sands of Africa to Hitler's lair. It was one of the longest campaign trails of the Second World War. Hitler's death was announced by the German radio on May 1st. Mussolini had died a few days earlier, his death at the hands of his own countrymen.

In Europe the guilty had been tracked to their lairs, stripped of their power, and totally vanquished. They had set out with the most grandiose ambitions of conquest and glory, but their cause was rotted from the inside by their inhumanity. To defeat them had required the greatest efforts and the greatest sacrifices. Almost the whole world's abilities had needed to be mobilised, and the greatest Alliance of all time forged, to assemble the necessary power and force to grasp victory from the tyrants. At the start, in the darkest days, the most resolute and determined fighters for freedom were Churchill and de Gaulle. Together they had achieved the near impossible – apart either might have faltered or failed. If either of their countries had not been victorious the future of Europe could not have achieved a stable peace in which reconstruction could resurrect the hopes of its people. Perhaps their enduring memorial is the years of tranquillity that have spared so many children of Europe from the horrors of war, to, at least, their middle years. No earlier generation, in the whole history of

Europe, has enjoyed such a long period of peace. There is good reason for thankfulness.

ALLIES AND FRIENDS

The meeting between Roosevelt, Churchill and Stalin at Yalta, in the Crimea was designed and indeed destined to settle the shape of continental Europe for the next fifty years.

It was the time when Churchill became aware that the last vestige of Britain's power on the world stage was passing. No more would Britain be the country to dominate the outline of world events. The sacrifices of the war effort had beggared the country and unlocked its hold at the centre of the Empire and Commonwealth.

Not only had power shifted, but so had influence. Roosevelt was certain that he could develop a special relationship with Stalin which would solve the differences about post-war spheres of influence. Roosevelt's view was becoming increasingly taken up with events in the Pacific. He had agreed that the war in Europe should be the first priority for victory with some reluctance. The United States had not been attacked and humiliated in Europe. It was at Pearl Harbour, in the Pacific, that the infamy of an attack without a prior declaration of war had so damaged and outraged the United States. Whatever the feelings of the American people about the injustice and the dangers arising from Hitler's adventures in Europe and Russia, it was only Pearl Harbour that had really hurt. And so Roosevelt was keen to make common cause with Stalin. His intention was to persuade Russia to come into the war against Japan.

American losses in the battles to take island after island in the slow battle up the island chain towards the Japanese homeland had proved an almost intolerable burden. Only resolution and the skill of the United States Navy in repulsing the Japanese attack on the island of Midway had turned the tide. Japan lost four aircraft carriers in the battle, to the loss of a single American carrier, the *Yorktown*. And the *Yorktown* had not been in first class condition for the battle. Severely damaged in the Battle of the Coral Sea she had returned to Pearl Harbour in order to be made seaworthy to return to the United States for a full refit. Admiral Chester Nimitz, the American Commander, would have none of it. *Yorktown* would sail for battle in forty eight hours. Although the *Yorktown* was lost the Japanese losses were particularly severe as a large number of their most experienced navy fliers were lost and could not be replaced.

This was the background against which President Roosevelt's intentions should be measured. He was also trying to gain more active support from China. General Chang Kai Shek was invited to Yalta and part of President Roosevelt's time was spent in conference with him. All these tasks were a further strain on the President's health. He was seen to be extremely tired. Churchill sensed that he was very ill, but did not know that the American President had only six weeks more to live.

In the conference sessions Churchill was very keen to focus on re-establishing the old countries of eastern Europe. He felt a particular duty towards Poland. The original pact between the Russians and the Germans in 1939, had effectively divided Poland between them. When Hitler invaded Poland, on the 1st September 1939, neither of Poland's guarantors, France or Britain, had sent any troops to Poland's defence. When Russia joined Germany in the invasion of Poland it took only six weeks for the Polish defenders to be crushed and Poland dismembered. Many Poles fled Poland and after great difficulty many reached first France and later England. They formed squadrons in the Royal Air Force and these were amongst the most successful in the Battle of Britain.

Churchill, ever the man of history and honour, tried to recover for Poland all the territories to the east which Russia had seized, but Stalin was adamant and Roosevelt would not press the matter. And so Poland lost half her land. If Poland was in part a lost cause, what of France? France had no place at the negotiating table. It was Churchill who put the French case. If Stalin was obdurate about his hold on eastern Europe he was surprisingly tolerant about the future place of France. It was agreed that France would be one of the four occupying powers of a conquered Germany. And so France was recognised as one of the Great Powers of the post war period and obtained a permanent seat on the Security Council when the United Nations was formed. This was a great victory of the alliance between Churchill and de Gaulle. Churchill could have given de Gaulle no greater lift for the future status and standing of France. But perhaps the secret of Stalin's support for France lay in de Gaulle's strong stance at their meetings in December 1944 in Moscow. If de Gaulle could stand up to Stalin his recent history showed that he was also prepared to stand up to any Anglo-Saxon hegemony.

When the day of victory came, on the 8th May 1945, de Gaulle sent a telegram to Churchill:

> At the moment when the gunfire ceases in Europe
> I send to you my dearest thoughts of friendship and
> admiration. None of this would have been possible
> without you. I will always remember your sincere
> hope and most ardent wish that our two ancient and
> great people will go forward together to a prosperous
> peace and glory.

Both Churchill and de Gaulle left office as heads of the governments of their respective countries within a year. Churchill did not even survive as Prime Minister until the end of the war. After the defeat of Germany a General Election was held in Britain. Churchill's election platform was backward looking. The socialist utopia offered by Clement Attlee captured the imagination of the servicemen's vote, following the bad memories of the way ex-servicemen had been treated after the First World War. The cruel unemployment leading into the 1920's and 1930's was a real fear, and Churchill had no policy to prevent a repetition. Churchill had been a great war leader, but he was old, tired, and ill, and needed rest. Socialist failures would lead to his recall to the Premiership in 1951.

De Gaulle had never wanted a political career. The conversion of the Consultative Assembly into an elected chamber required political groupings and he was not willing to become embroiled in the manoeuvrings into which the formation of the political parties would become embroiled. His time in service as the head of his country was done, and so in January 1946 he relinquished office. He left with the grateful thanks of his nation, unsullied by the intrigues which were to make France's political life so unstable that the average duration of any government remained below one year for nearly a quarter of a century. Three political groupings emerged, the Christian Democrats, the Socialists, and the Communists. Their share of the vote required a coalition of any two of them to form a government. The personalities involved were not adequately malleable to the needs of their country and France's progress of recovery from the destruction of war was slower than it should have been. The saving grace of the situation was the high quality of the French civil service, which de Gaulle had done so much to establish.

Churchill's and de Gaulle's relationship continued after the war, free of the pressures and turmoil which had sometimes proved vexatious. In 1950, on the 22nd August, Churchill wrote from Chartwell:

My dear de Gaulle,
I had the pleasure of receiving the Comte d'Harcourt at luncheon down here last week on my return from Strasbourg.
I must indeed most cordially thank you for the very generous tribute you have paid me in your memoirs.
It is remarkable that in spite of all the hard contretemps of war through which we lived we should both have gained so much understanding of each other's position, and preserved everything that matters in fundamental goodwill. I often look with pleasure on the gallic cock which you presented to my wife and am reminded of the historic events in which we were comrades through trying to serve our own countries and the common cause of freedom and tradition which united us and stands above all.
How terrible it is to feel that all that we were able to achieve is now plunged in the greatest peril I have ever known, and that is saying a good deal.

With the kindest regards
believe me,
Yours sincerely,
(Signed)   Winston S.Churchill

In 1958 General de Gaulle, as Head of the French Government, invested Churchill with the Cross of the Liberation. It was the highest honour available to those who had contributed to the restoration of the freedom of France. It showed the certain high and enduring regard in which Churchill was held. There was no need and no advantage in bestowing the honour. The honour showed continuing and mature gratitude for Churchill's support. Winston and Clementine were greatly moved by the honour and the occasion.

Clementine's enduring faith in the General was financially rewarded. She won a £50 bet that he would one day be called back to lead France.

In 1960 the Churchill's attended de Gaulle's Sate Visit to London. The General and Madame de Gaulle paid a private visit to Winston and Clementine at Hyde Park Gate – a gesture which touched them greatly.

Both great men faded with the years. Churchill died in January 1965, de Gaulle in 1970. Churchill's funeral was a great State occasion, exceptional for a commoner. In the January cold thousands queued silently in a long snaking line at times over a mile long. It was a gesture of affection and tribute, silent as memories of his leadership in the nation's greatest hour of danger came flooding back, particularly to the many ex-servicemen, who wore their medals in proud remembrance.

As Churchill's funeral procession passed the Cenotaph his family, in their carriage, noticed the large group of the French Resistance, deeply affected by emotion. They had been given hope and strength by Churchill's voice alone.

In St. Paul's Cathedral the Churchill family noted General Gaulle particularly. They were struck by his gaunt pallor. This is clearly seen in the photographs. The dockside cranes along the

Thames dipped in tribute as the launch carrying Churchill's body passed. As the train carrying his body passed through the countryside people stood bareheaded in the fields and on the station platforms. He was laid to rest at Bladon, by Blenheim. He had safely returned home.

Lady Churchill presented Churchill College, Cambridge, with copies of General de Gaulle's speeches, which had been personally inscribed.

A year after Winston's death Lady Churchill received a letter from General de Gaulle, then President of France:

'We have now arrived at a sad and moving anniversary. I wish you to know, that in sending you my thoughts on the great memories which I have of Sir Winston Churchill, I understand, better than ever the grandeur of his personality, the vast scope of his work, and above all the strength and the quality which united me to him and above all, which has united England and France.

I also want you to know, both my wife and I myself, how deeply we feel your loss, and especially the loss of so dear and glorious a husband.'

She was deeply moved by this letter.

In rekindling the flame of the honour of France, which he did at the end of the war by relighting the eternal flame to the unknown warrior at the Arc de Triomphe, de Gaulle earned the undying and eternal gratitude of the French people, which is recorded in the countless named roads, squares, avenues and other public works to his honour.

Churchill is remembered by the naming of a Cambridge college, a statue in the most prominent place in Parliament Square outside the House of Commons, a rehabilitation centre for war disabled named in his honour at the Royal British Legion Village at Maidstone in Kent, and numerous other buildings and roads. By vote of the people he was named 'The Greatest Briton of All Time.'

These two men combined together in the cause of freedom in freedom's darkest hour. Wherever freedom is threatened the story of their alliance can bring hope.

CHURCHILL AND DE GAULLE

THE GREATEST ALLIES

EPILOGUE

On a bright spring morning early in 1946 a little boy, with his parents, boarded one of the first Golden Arrow train trips to France after the war at Victoria station. He was so excited that he completely lost his voice. The train was made up of shiny Pullman coaches in their traditional umber and cream livery. The Pullman car attendants were resplendent in the smartest uniforms. Their white jackets with their blue facings had Pullman company badges in fine enamel at the top of each lapel.

The train left smartly on time and coffee was served on the journey to Dover. After a smooth crossing on the special cross channel ferry the berthing was made quickly. Porters transferred the luggage to the waiting train. And what a train! The large blue coaches were adorned with large amounts of gold lettering and decoration. Inside the polished wood and engraved and cut glass panels gleamed. At the head of the train a large brown engine with the Nord insignia snorted steam impatiently.

Soon the train was underway. Dinner was served. Every table had the crispest and most dazzlingly white linen. The cutlery, crockery and glasses shone. And what a number of glasses. What could so many at each place be for?

Soon the meal was served. So many courses! And what food and wine. What a contrast to the rationing in Britain. A different wine came with each course. But look out the window. Through each town the train passed very slowly. On each side the station buildings were in ruins. Everywhere there were wrecked engines, wagons and coaches. The devastation was terrible. The tracks going off in every direction were mainly torn up after a few yards, with the twisted rails bent upwards. And through this scene of almost total wreckage the gleaming Fleche D'Or train passed, slowly through the damaged towns and much faster through the countryside.

At the end of the meal the man, who spoke perfect French, for he had served in the French army although he had spent the war in England, called the senior conductor and the waiters over. He complimented them on the meal and on the wines and then he asked how it was that in a scene of such destruction it was possible to run such a train, with everything to the highest standards of quality, at least equalling the best which had been achieved before the war.

'Monsieur,' the conductor replied, 'you see the terrible destruction of our country. But this train is the standard of the new France. It will be the best. Nothing can be better!' And with that tears were rolling down everyone's cheeks.

The train drew into the Gare du Nord. The little boy followed his parents down the steps from the train onto the platform. The author had arrived for his first trip to Paris.

APPENDIX

MANY LATER TRANSCRIPTS OF CHURCHILL'S AND ATTLEE'S SPEECHES HAVE HAD THE ORIGINAL REFERENCES TO DE GAULLE CUT OUT. THE SEVERED REFERENCES ARE QUOTED HERE.

CHURCHILL TO HOUSE OF COMMONS, JUNE 25TH 1940

"We shall certainly aid, to the best of our ability and resources, any movement or any action by Frenchmen outside the power of the enemy, to work for the defeat of Nazi German barbarism and for the freedom and restoration of France."

CHURCHILL TO HOUSE OF COMMONS JULY 4TH 1940

"We are also repatriating all French troops who are in this country, excepting those who, of their own free will, have volunteered to follow General de Gaulle in the French Forces of Liberation, of whom he is the chief."

CHURCHILL TO HOUSE OF COMMONS 20TH AUGUST 1940

"That France should lie prostrate at this moment, is the crime, not of a great and noble nation, but of what are called 'The men of Vichy.' We have profound sympathy with the French people. Our old comradeship with France is not dead. In General de Gaulle and his gallant band, that comradeship takes an effective form. These Free Frenchmen have been condemned to death by Vichy, but the day will come, as surely as the sun will rise tomorrow, when their names will be held in honour, and their names will be graven in stone in the streets of a France restored in a liberated Europe to its full freedom and its ancient fame."

CHURCHILL TO PARLIAMENT OCTOBER 8TH 1940

"I do not propose to give the House a detailed account of the episode at Dakar. I could easily do so in private, but it would be out of proportion to the scale of events. Moreover, I do not relish laying bare to the enemy all our internal processes. This operation was primarily French, and, although we were ready to give it a measure of support which in certain circumstances might have been decisive, were no more anxious than was General de Gaulle to get involved in a lengthy or sanguinary conflict with the Vichy French. That General de Gaulle was right in believing that the

majority of Frenchmen in Dakar was favourable to the Free French movement, I have no doubt; indeed, I think his judgement has been found extremely surefooted, and our opinion of him has been enhanced by everything we have seen of his conduct in circumstances of peculiar and perplexing difficulty. His Majesty's Government have no intention whatever of abandoning the cause of General de Gaulle until it is merged, as merged it will be, in the larger cause of France."
RT. HON.C.R.ATTLEE, DEPUTY PRIME MINISTER, HOUSE OF COMMONS, JANUARY 1943

"We are all under a great debt to General de Gaulle for his bold and uncompromising reassertion of French resistance; and for ourselves we look forward to the day, and we will do our best to hasten it, when the whole French Empire and those steadfast and heroic forces of resistance in France itself, gathered round a single authority on French soil, can join with us in a common effort with the United Nations to break down the power of the enemy and achieve the liberation of France.

RELEVANT QUOTATIONS

CROSS OF LORRAINE – IN SEARCH OF CHURCHILL – MARTIN GILBERT –PAGE 232 – 'One often repeated story is that in 1940, after a dispute with General de Gaulle, Churchill remarked 'The greatest cross I have to bear is the Cross of Loraine.' I published this in the first edition of my one-volume Churchill: A Life. Within a week of publication several readers had written to me to point out that the phrase was not Churchill's at all, but that of his liaison officer with de Gaulle, General Spears. They were right; hanging my head in shame, I amended my version for subsequent editions.'

PATTON – THREE YEARS WITH EISENHOWER – HARRY C.BUTCHER PAGE 647. 'Steve told the Supreme Commander a story about Patton, which, he said, was being widely repeated at home. It seems that the War Department had found that Patton's colourful and profane phrases made his daily situation reports too florid. Consequently, the War Department had instructed General Patton to write his reports in less colourful and more official language. Patton complied. His firs report was a model of such military literature, but below the signature was a postscript: "I peed in the Rhine today."

BIBLIOGRAPHY

ENGLISH TITLES

A MAN CALLED INTREPID WILLIAM STEVENSON   MaCMILLAN LONDON LTD 1976

ASSIGNMENT TO CATASTROPHE   MAJOR-GENERAL SIR EDWARD L. SPEARS   WILLIAM HENEMANN LTD. 1954 AND THE REPRINT SOCIETY 1956

DE GAULLE   JULIAN JACKSON   HAUS PUBLISHING, LONDON 2003

GREEN BEACH   JAMES LEASOR   WILLIAM HENEMANN 1975   CORGI BOOKS 1976

MECCANO MAGAZINE   JULY 1941 GREAT WAR LEADERS NO. 20

THE BATTLE OF THE BULGE CHARLES B. MacDONALD   BOOK CLUB ASSOCIATES 1984, WITH WEIDENFELD AND NICHOLSON

THE FALL OF FRANCE   JULIAN JACKSON OXFORD UNIVERSITY PRESS 2003

THE LAST GREAT FRENCHMAN CHARLES WILLIAMS   LITTLE BROWN AND COMPANY 1993 ABACUS 1995

WINSTON CHURCHILL'S TOYSHOP STUART MACRAE THE ROUNDWOOD PRESS 1971

WINSTON CHURCHILL EIGHT VOLUMES VOLUMES 1 & 2 RANDOLPH CHURCHILL VOLUMES 3 TO 8 SIR MARTIN GILBERT HENEMANN 1966-1988

ENGLISH AUTHORS

CHURCHILL, RANDOLPH WINSTON CHURCHILL VOLUMES 1 AND 2 HEINEMANN 1966

GILBERT, SIR MARTIN, WITH RANDOLPH CHURCHILL FOR FIRST TWO VOLUMES WINSTON CHURCHILL   EIGHT VOLUMES HEINEMANN 1966-1988

JACKSON, JULIAN DE GAULLE HAUS PUBLISHING, LONDON 2003

JACKSON, JULIAN THE FALL OF FRANCE OXFORD UNIVERSITY PRESS 2003

LEASOR, JAMES GREEN BEACH WILLIAM HEINEMANN 1975 CORGI BOOKS 1976

MACRAE, STUART WINSTON CHURCHILL'S TOYSHOP THE ROUNDWOOD PRESS 1971

SPEARS, MAJOR-GENERAL SIR EDWARD L., ASSIGNMENT TO CATASTROPHE WILLIAM HENEMANN LTD. 1954 AND THE REPRINT SOCIETY 1956

STEVENSON, WILLIAM A MAN CALLED INTREPID MaCMILLAN LONDON LTD. 1976

WILLIAMS, CHARLES THE LAST GREAT FRENCHMAN LITTLE, BROWN AND COMPANY 1993 ABACUS 1995

FRENCH TITLES

APPEL DE GAULLE, CHARLES   MEMOIRES DE GUERRE VOL 1 LIBRAIRIE PLON   1954

DE GAULLE ET CHURCHILL   FRANÇOIS KERSAUDY PERRIN 2001 TEMPUS 2003

DE GAULLE ET ROOSEVELT   FRANÇOIS KERSAUDY PERRIN 2004

DE GAULLE L'APPEL DU DESTIN MAX GALLO EDITIONS ROBERT LAFFONT 1998

DE GAULLE LA SOLITUDE DU COMBATTANT MAX GALLO EDITIONS ROBERT LAFFONT 1998

HISTOIRE DE LA RESISTANCE   FRANÇOIS –GEORGES DREYFUS EDITIONS DE FALLOIS 1996

L'ARMÉE DE VICHY ROBERT O. PAXTON TALLANDIER 2004

L'UNITÉ DE GAULLE, CHARLES MEMOIRES DE GUERRE VOL 2

LA DISCORDE CHEZ L'ENNEMI DE GAULLE CHARLES LIBRAIRIE PLON 1972

LA FRANCE ET SON ARM E DE GAULLE CHARLES LIBRAIRIE PLON 1938 AND 1971

LE FIL DE L'EPEE DE GAULLE. CHARLES LIBRAIRIE PLON 1971

LE SALUT DE GAULLE, CHARLES MEMOIRES DE GUERRE VOL 3 PLON 1959

NOUS, LES FRANÇAIS COMBATTANTS DE 39-45 PIERRE MESSMER AVEC PELLISSIER ET TAURIAC
TALLANDIER 2005

POUR COMBATTRE AVEC DE GAULLE 1940-1946 GENERAL DE BOISSIEU PLON 1981

SOIXANTE JOURS QUI ÉBRANLÈRENT L'OCCIDENT BENOIST-MECHIN ABIN MICHEL 1956

FRENCH AUTHORS

BENOIST-M CHIN SOIXANTE JOURS QUI BRANLÉRENT L'OCCIDENT ALBIN MICHEL 1956

DE BOISSIEU, GENERAL POUR COMBATTRE AVEC DE GAULLE 1940-1946
LIBRAIRIE PLON 1981

DE GAULLE, CHARLES APPEL MEMOIRES DE GUERRE VOL 1 LIBRAIRIE PLON 1954

DE GAULLE, CHARLES L'UNITÉ MEMOIRES DE GUERRE VOL 2 PLON 1956

DE GAULLE, CHARLES LE SALUT MEMOIRES DE GUERRE VOL 3 PLON 1959

DREYFUS, FRANÇOIS-GEORGES HISTOIRE DE LA RESISTANCE EDITIONS DE FALLOIS 1996

GALLO, MAX DE GAULLE L'APPEL DU DESTIN EDITIONS ROBERT LAFFONT 1998

GALLO, MAX DE GAULLE LA SOLITUDE DU COMBATTANT EDITIONS ROBERT LAFFONT 1998

KERSAUDY, FRANÇOIS DE GAULLE ET CHURCHILL PERRIN 2001 TEMPUS 2003

MESSMER, PIERRE WITH PELLISSIER AND TURIAC, NOUS, LES FRANÇAIS COMBATTANTS DE
39-45

AMERICAN TITLES

CRUSADE IN EUROPE DWIGHT D. EISENHOWER HEINEMANN 1948

D-DAY STEPHEN AMBROSE SIMON AND SCHUSTER 1995

THE BITTER WOODS JOHN S.D.EISENHOWER PUTNAM 1969

THE FRENCH OFFICER CORPS UNDER MARSHAL PÉTAIN PAXTON, ROBERT O. PRINCETON
UNIVERSITY PRESS 1966

AMERICAN AUTHORS

AMBROSE, STEPHEN D-DAY SIMON AND SCHUSTER 1995

EISENHOWER, DWIGHT D. CRUSADE IN EUROPE HEINEMANN 1948 BIRLINN LTD. EDINBURGH
2001

EISENHOWER, JOHN S.D. THE BITTER WOODS G.P.PUTNAM 1969
BIRLINN LTD. EDINBURGH 2001

MacDONALD CHARLES B. THE BATTLE OF THE BULGE BOOK CLUB ASSOCIATES 1984, WITH
WEIDENFELD AND NICHOLSON

PAXTON, ROBERT O. L'ARMÉE DE VICHY TALLANDIER 2004 AND THE FRENCH OFFICER CORPS
UNDER MARSHAL PÉTAIN PRINCETON UNIVERSITY PRESS 1966